MERLEAU-PONTY'S *PHENOMENOLOGY OF PERCEPTION*

This is an advanced introduction to and original interpretation of Merleau-Ponty's greatest work, *Phenomenology of Perception*. Timothy Mooney provides a clear and compelling exposition of the theory of our projective being in the world, and demonstrates as never before the centrality of the body schema in the theory. Thanks to the schema's motor intentionality, our bodies inhabit and appropriate space: our postures and perceptual fields are organised schematically when we move to realise our projects. Thus our lived bodies are ineliminably expressive in being both animated and outcome oriented through-and-through. Mooney also analyses the place of the work in the modern philosophical world, showing what Merleau-Ponty takes up from the Kantian and Phenomenological traditions and what he contributes to each. Casting a fresh light on his magnum opus, this book is essential reading for all those interested in the philosophy and phenomenology of the body.

TIMOTHY D. MOONEY is Associate Professor of Philosophy at University College Dublin. He is the author of numerous articles and book chapters on Merleau-Ponty and Husserl, and the co-editor (with Dermot Moran) of *The Phenomenology Reader* (2002).

MODERN EUROPEAN PHILOSOPHY

Titles published in the series

MERLEAU-PONTY'S
PHENOMENOLOGY
OF PERCEPTION
On the Body Informed

TIMOTHY D. MOONEY

University College Dublin

CAMBRIDGE
UNIVERSITY PRESS

CAMBRIDGE
UNIVERSITY PRESS

Shaftesbury Road, Cambridge CB2 8EA, United Kingdom

One Liberty Plaza, 20th Floor, New York, NY 10006, USA

477 Williamstown Road, Port Melbourne, VIC 3207, Australia

314–321, 3rd Floor, Plot 3, Splendor Forum, Jasola District Centre, New Delhi – 110025, India

103 Penang Road, #05–06/07, Visioncrest Commercial, Singapore 238467

Cambridge University Press is part of Cambridge University Press & Assessment,
a department of the University of Cambridge.

We share the University's mission to contribute to society through the pursuit of
education, learning and research at the highest international levels of excellence.

www.cambridge.org
Information on this title: www.cambridge.org/9781009223393

DOI: 10.1017/9781009223416

© Timothy D. Mooney 2023

First published 2023
First paperback edition 2024

A catalogue record for this publication is available from the British Library

Library of Congress Cataloging-in-Publication data
NAMES: Mooney, Timothy, 1962– author.
TITLE: Merleau-Ponty's *phenomenology of perception* : on the body informed /
Timothy D. Mooney, University College Dublin.
DESCRIPTION: Cambridge, United Kingdom ; New York, NY, USA : Cambridge University
Press, 2022. | Series:Modern European philosophy | Includes bibliographical references and index.
IDENTIFIERS: LCCN 2022023319 (print) | LCCN 2022023320 (ebook) | ISBN 9781009223430
(hardback) | ISBN 9781009223416 (epub)
SUBJECTS: LCSH: Merleau-Ponty, Maurice, 1908–1961. Phénoménologie de la perception. |
Perception (Philosophy) | Phenomenology. | BISAC: PHILOSOPHY / History & Surveys /
Modern
CLASSIFICATION: LCC B2430.M3763 P47348 2022 (print) | LCC B2430.M3763 (ebook) |
DDC 142/.7–dc23/eng/20220708
LC record available at https://lccn.loc.gov/2022023319
LC ebook record available at https://lccn.loc.gov/2022023320

ISBN   978-1-009-22343-0   Hardback
ISBN   978-1-009-22339-3   Paperback

Contents

Acknowledgements

Though I am indebted to more people than I can name, my hope is that I have remembered most. In University College Dublin (UCD) I have benefited for many years from the close friendship and sage advice of Tom Garvin, Steven Loyal and Brian O'Connor. I also owe much to Ger Casey, Gerald Mills, Jeanne Riou and Peter White, and outside UCD to Eileen Brennan, Eoin Cassidy, Walter Hopp, Noel Kavanagh and Tanja Staehler. Thanks too to Joe Brady, Joseph Cohen, Desmond Earley, Bryan Fanning, Andreas Hess, Séamas Kelly, Wolfgang Marx, Fran O'Rourke and Rowland Stout. I am grateful to Maria Baghramian for facilitating the writing of this book in her time as head of the School of Philosophy at UCD. In earlier times there I received much help and encouragement from John Chisholm, Richard Kearney, Dermot Moran and Liberato Santoro, and at the University of Essex from Simon Critchley and Onora O'Neill. Further afield and more recently, I am indebted to Sylvain Camilleri, Rasmus Jensen and Felix O'Murchadha. Other friends and colleagues from home and beyond have read chapters and done much to improve them. My thanks to Rubén Flores, Lisa Foran, Niall Keane, Don Landes, Elisa Magri, Conor McMullin, Katherine Morris and Declan Sheerin. Many fine students attended my course on *Phenomenology of Perception* and helped me refine my views, among them Luna Dolezal, Thomas Finegan, Roderick Howlett, Sheena Hyland, Patrick Levy, Jonathan Mitchell, Michael O'Hara, Joe Roy, Cinzia Ruggeri and Mary Shanahan. Outside academia, I am grateful to Brenda and Manuel Doyle, Catherine Fitzpatrick, Paddy and Catherine Hoare, Lia O'Hegarty, Maggie Overend, Caroline and Paul Quigley and Robert Shouldice. My thanks to the National University of Ireland for the generous Grant towards Scholarly Publications. Springer AG has given permission to quote from my journal article and book chapter (copyright 2011 and 2017) and Taylor and Francis Ltd to quote extensively from the new translation of

Phenomenology of Perception (copyright 2012). I would also like to thank Hilary Gaskin of Cambridge University Press for all her help and professionalism. My greatest debts are to my mother and father and Simone Guéret for her love, support and humour. This book is dedicated to Simone, our parents and our family.

Abbreviations

The following abbreviations will be used to provide references for primary sources in English translation. The latter will be placed in parentheses in the main text and are also employed in the footnotes. Wherever they are made, emendations to the translations will be indicated in the footnotes.

Works by Merleau-Ponty

PP	*Phenomenology of Perception*
PrP	*The Primacy of Perception and Other Essays*
SB	*The Structure of Behaviour*
Sns	*Signs*
VI	*The Visible and the Invisible*

Works by Kant and Heidegger

A/B	*Critique of Pure Reason,* A ed./B ed.
BT	*Being and Time*

Works by Husserl

APS	*Analyses Concerning Active and Passive Synthesis*
CES	*The Crisis of European Sciences*
CM	*Cartesian Meditations*
EJ	*Experience and Judgement*
Ids1/ Ids2	*Ideas,* bk 1/bk 2
LI 1/LI 2	*Logical Investigations,* vol. 1/vol. 2
PCIT	*On the Phenomenology of the Consciousness of Internal Time*
TS	*Thing and Space*

Preface

Never quite eclipsed by other and more fashionable approaches, the account of engaged awareness set out in *Phenomenology of Perception* has come back into its own in recent years. The new movements of embodied and situated cognition owe much to it, and their leading proponents have been careful to acknowledge its importance.[1] In his magnum opus, Maurice Merleau-Ponty exploits both physiology and psychology in the service of his project. He also draws on the diverse expressions of human existence in speech, sport, fine art and dance, and the book itself has an expressive power that exceeds its explicit statements.[2] For many a newcomer to his thought, it still appears as exciting and forbidding as when it was first published in 1945, and these were my experiences when I began to turn its pages. Exciting because it promises to cast new light on our embodied and perceptual life and on our lived world, and forbidding because Merleau-Ponty's exposition is extremely dense in places and frequently elliptical, for all of his elegant style that has been largely reflected in the new English translation. He often returns to a point much later in the book to clarify and expand on it, and on many occasions it takes much effort to find out whether he is setting out his own position or one that he will come to reject.[3] In this study of his great work, I give sustained attention to his account of our projectively perceptual lives. Once his theory of projection and of its expression is brought to the fore, his lines of critique are easier to discern.

In the most general of terms, Merleau-Ponty seeks to show that perception is not so much an event *in* the world as our opening up and progressive revelation *of* the world. We might say that each of us as an actively embodied perceiver is 'the "flaw" in this "great diamond"' (*PP*, 215). His

---

[1] Gallagher 2017, 5, 10–11, 78–9; Varela et al. 2017, xv–xvii, 3–4.   [2] *Sns*, 10–11;Morris 2012, xii.
[3] In his new translation, Donald Landes preserves the elegance of the original without compromising its accuracy in philosophical terms. See Mooney 2012, 592–3. Landes gives the pagination of the second French edition (Merleau-Ponty 2005) in the margins.

chief target is 'objective thought', originally the thesis that the world is made up of fully accessible objects, and in modernity the allied thesis that only natural science can comprehend them properly. Since the sixteenth century, objective thought has taken two distinctive forms. For 'empiricism', the conscious perceiver can be reduced to the world of causal and physical processes without remainder. For 'intellectualism', consciousness cannot be reduced to this world either in fact or in principle, though everything outside mind and within the world – including our bodies – can only be genuinely known through the scientific concepts and theories that we formulate and impose as rational beings. On the first and bottom-up account, consciousness is absorbed into the scientific universe that is the only genuine reality. On the second and top-down one, it is granted a strange autonomy outside the world-picture they otherwise share. Both are in agreement in dismissing body and world as actually experienced.

Through our bodies as we live and use them and develop through them, according to Merleau-Ponty, we open up the inexhaustible world of possibilities, one of which is scientific research itself. The fundamental philosophical act is 'to return to the lived world beneath the objective world ... to give back to the thing its concrete physiognomy, to the organisms their proper manner of dealing with the world, and to subjectivity its historical inherence' (*PP*, 57). Only then will we bring to explicit awareness our being in the world, with the aim of grasping 'the project of the world that we are' (*PP*, 427). It is to be emphasised that Merleau-Ponty's concern is not with our bodies alone. To give an anyway adequate view of our existence he must bring out the unity of the human perceiver in all of its attributes, from the affective and imaginative through to the cognitive and volitional. He only foregrounds *le corps propre* because it furnishes our first articulations of the world prior to language, reason and reflection. In a posthumously published prospectus of his thought, he gives his best summation of how it is characterised in his big book:

> [T]he body is no longer merely an object in the world, under the purview of a separated spirit. It is on the side of the subject; it is our point of view on the world, the place where the spirit takes on a certain physical and historical situation. As Descartes once said profoundly, the soul is not merely in the body like a pilot in his ship; it is wholly intermingled with the body. The body in turn is wholly animated ... A "body or postural schema" gives us at every moment a global, practical, and implicit notion of the relation between our body and things, of our hold on them. A system of possible

movements or "motor projections" radiates from us to our environment. Our body is not in space like things; it inhabits or haunts space ... For us the body is much more than an instrument or a means; it is our expression in the world, the visible form of our intentions. Even our most secret affective movements, those most deeply tied to the humoral infrastructure, help to shape our perception of things.[4] (*PrP*, 5)

It is by way of the phenomenological method as recast in an existential mould that Merleau-Ponty supplies the evidence to back up these claims. In this monograph, my concern above all is with the *phenomenology of perception*. While I concur with Ian Hacking that *Phemenology of Perception* is essential reading for any school as a classical work of Western philosophy, I cannot agree that it is not to be read as a contribution to that school called phenomenology.[5] Without a grasp of earlier moves in phenomenology, much of its contributions will be missed, and I situate it within that school and the wider philosophical tradition. It is an exercise in 'transcendental' or 'a priori' philosophy in which the conceptions of constitutive syntheses and of the productive imagination can be traced back to Immanuel Kant.[6] Much of the working terminology and transcendental analyses point for all that to the pervasive influence of Edmund Husserl, the founder of the phenomenological movement whose contribution is increasingly recognised in contemporary scholarship.[7] Having been introduced to Husserl's work by Aron Gurwitsch in Paris, Merleau-Ponty went on to study the former's unpublished manuscripts in the newly established archive in Leuven. He adopts and adapts Husserl's method of *epoché* and reduction and many of his central ideas. These include perceptual fulfilment and horizons, genetic constitution, passive and transition syntheses and operative intentionalities, the founding and founded, the lived body and our somatically founded agency awareness. The method and all these other ideas will be explicated in the coming chapters.

Merleau-Ponty is generous to a fault in acknowledging Husserl's influence, and he builds on a claim that is defended throughout the latter's work, namely, that things have significance before we can articulate them

[4] Translation emended.
[5] Back cover endorsement of 2014 paperback edition of Landes' translation.
[6] Gardner 2013, 130–1; 2015, 312–21; Matherne 2014, 130–46; 2016, 194–226.
[7] Heinämaa 2002, 127–46; Moran 2010, 175–95; Smith 2007, 1–22.

intellectually.[8] From the outset Husserl models his act, content and object schema of conscious perception on the expressive and indicative functions of language, though he holds that the 'content' of an object in our early experience – this content being the significance or sense that it has for us – is pre-expressive and hence pre-linguistic and pre-conceptual.[9] He shows that this sense is constituted through the lived body and its skills. In studying the deep structures of somatic and temporal experience, more-over, he appreciates that not everything in perception is conscious and act intentional with a content and an object, even when it is fully developed (*PCIT*, 7). All this being said, Husserl does not provide an account of the unthematic way we relate to things in what Hubert Dreyfus calls our skilled coping.[10] Martin Heidegger provides one of the first such accounts, drawing on Jakob von Uexküll's theory of ethology in which organisms in their environments do not encounter things as discrete or self-standing, but as opportunities to be taken up towards certain outcomes.

Gurwitsch also introduced Merleau-Ponty to Heidegger's work, and indeed to gestalt psychology and the case studies of pathological motility

---

[8] Merleau-Ponty is most sympathetic to Husserl's later work. This is because it moves away in his view from an obsessive 'logicism' (or prioritisation of the absolute validity of logical laws), because it develops the notion of an historical constitution of significance and because it recognises the parallels between 'transcendental psychology' and 'transcendental phenomenology' without col-lapsing the one into the other (*PP*, 509–10). He is critical of Husserl's middle period because of the emphasis on the sense-giving or centrifugal acts of the conscious subject. A model of an interpreting sense that informs a 'hyletic layer' of otherwise bare sensations has not yet been abandoned definitively. See *PP*, 253, 539 and *Ids1*, 203–5, 238–9.

[9] On an interpretation popularised by Hubert Dreyfus, Merleau-Ponty advances far beyond Husserl because he jettisons the latter's theory that all perception and action is mediated by conceptual meaning contents (Dreyfus 2002, 372–3). Taylor Carman notes that these are not ideas or images interposed between perceptual awareness and things, while agreeing that Merleau-Ponty rejects the 'semantic paradigm' of conscious acts that require linguistic and propositional contents to pick out and engage with the things. It is rather that a thing's sense in early childhood is something like its minimally intuitive coherence and perceptual significance as constituted with our bodily skills and dispositions (Carman 2020, 22–5, 37). Carman cites Husserl's remark that the meaning of the word 'meaning' (*Bedeutung*) is extended to all acts beyond the linguistic sphere of expression, whether or not they are interwoven with expressive acts (Carman 2020, 24; *Ids1*, 294). But Husserl immediately qualifies this, adding that he still speaks of 'sense' (*Sinn*) as different to meaning, since the latter only comes into play in the linguistic sphere of logical or conceptual signification in developed awareness. Only then can a meaning colour a sense. In the simplest perceptual act the 'noematic sense' of its object pertains to the 'noematic core', to the enduring thing as determined by the sense and as genuinely reached in the perception. It is made clear that 'expression' is distinctive in *adapting* meaning to every sense and to its core, raising these 'to the realm of "Logos", of the *conceptual* and, on that account, the "universal"' (*Ids1*, 295). Husserl consistently holds that 'we must liberate the concept of sense from its relation to expressions … every intentional lived experience possesses as such its intentional sense; the latter becomes precisely a specifically *meant* sense when the ego becomes a subject who carries out acts thematically and becomes the subject of thematic interest'. *APS*, 33, my italics.

[10] Dreyfus 2002, 378–81.

and cognition that he draws on so extensively.[11] Yet Merleau-Ponty almost always underplays Heidegger's importance, though he reads Husserl through invariably Heideggerian and therefore existential spectacles (without any of the latter's philosophical antipathy to the former). Heidegger's influence is notable in his account of our habitually employed implements that are 'ready-to-hand' for our practical projects, and so too in his interlinked conceptions of existential temporality and of the 'intentional arc' or 'fundamental function' of projection through which our existence is futural and self-transcending. Merleau-Ponty maintains that most of the moves made by Husserl and Heidegger are reconcilable, and when we look at his philosophy of embodied existence in the round we find a sustained exercise of reconciliation. Ideas taken up from his phenomenological predecessors and from Kant are deftly aligned with each other and with discoveries in physiology and psychology. The foremost of these is of the aforementioned body schema, the sub-reflective organisation of posture behind one's pre-reflective postural awareness. The ideas and discoveries are shown to be complementary, their implications being drawn out in the service of a wider and deeper understanding of our being in the world. My core contention is that in Merleau-Ponty's theory our body schemas organise both our postures and milieus projectively. Their motor intentional predelineations gear us into the world towards the fulfilment of our tasks. This is fully compatible with his view that, as agents, we are at one with the bodies expressing our agency. With great acuity he foregrounds the ways that consciousness shines through the lived body, which in repose as well as movement is most closely comparable to a work of art.

Merleau-Ponty states over and again that transcendental phenomenology has to be existential. Transcendental and somatic conditions of having self and world are inseparable from our specifically human existence, which on occasion he will simply call 'existence' (*PP*, 169, 173, 481). Tom Baldwin has added that he sees our bodies as ambiguous in being both transcendental and empirical. They constitute the basic structures of the perceived world, yet their perceptual and motor capacities (and the capacities for language, reason and reflection that they found) are evolved capacities of our species that are never free from all natural constraints.[12] Ambiguity is a recurring theme in the book, and for Merleau-Ponty the term has manifold meanings that have been teased out adeptly by Tanja Staehler.[13] Our existence is ambiguous in

---

[11] For an account of Gurwitsch's influence on Merleau-Ponty, of his critique of *Phenomenology of Perception* and of Merleau-Ponty's response, see Toadvine 2001, 195-205.
[12] Baldwin 2019, 20–1.   [13] Lewis & Staehler 2010, 188–97.

that it is natural and conventional, somatic and spiritual, conditioned and free. We live the unity of our body, milieu, historical situation and mind, but we cannot finally split it through analysis because these are not discrete elements. All its diverse features are interdependent and intercoloured. We only know ourselves in ambiguity, not as an imperfection of existence but as its definition. Everything we live, perceive and think is a nexus with several senses and an ineliminable indeterminacy (*PP*, 172, 347, 360). Yet the equivocal and indeterminate are not in the main 'bad ambiguities', for they motivate us to engage in exploration and to understand more adequately without completion or closure. We even display a 'genius for ambiguity' in so far as our expressions of ourselves and of things are prompts for still further acts of expressive articulation (*PP*, 195, 401; *PrP*, 11). Only within the frame of objective thought is ambiguity something to be ironed out or dispelled.

Ambiguity is set against a generalised and misplaced ideal of exactitude rather than rationality itself. The authentic philosopher 'is marked by the distinguishing trait that he possesses inseparably the taste for evidence and the feeling for ambiguity'. He or she will work to sustain a productive play or movement between them 'which leads back without ceasing from knowledge to ignorance, and from ignorance to knowledge'.[14] Evidence has a peculiar signification for phenomenologists in that they systematically seek to foreground a priori structures of experience that are prereflectively present in experience, to show them forth *in* their evidentness as distinct from unearthing evidence for the hidden. In his theory of the body schema Merleau-Ponty posits an a priori and schematising intentionality that is not even marginally present in experience but *for* which he finds compelling evidence. I have opted for a narrative and reconstructive exposition of his book that does not always match the order of his chapters and sections, and this is to show more clearly the development and character of his theory. I draw on formulations from his other works where these are consistent with his big book and illuminate it more clearly, and where they can be extrapolated from it justifiably.

The title of this monograph picks out the body that is immanently informed from the outset (already being more than a sum of causal processes) and that is reciprocally determined by the act intentionalities and cognitions that it founds and shapes (in giving them their purchase on the world). In Chapter 1, I provide an initial explication of Husserl's phenomenology, a story about how Merleau-Ponty appropriates his

---

[14] Merleau-Ponty 1963b, 4–5.

methodology and another story about objective thought and its genealogy. In Chapter 2, I outline Merleau-Ponty's critique of first-generation empiricism and suggest how he might criticise some second-generation variants. In Chapter 3, I set out his critique of intellectualism and show how he takes up ideas from Kant that are not tied to its suppositions. Chapter 4 begins with an exposition of Husserl's phenomenology of embodiment, which is oriented around his fundamental distinction between the body as object and the body as lived. I show what Merleau-Ponty takes up from Husserl and adapts for his own purposes, and also what he gets from Uexküll's ethology and Heidegger's account of our being involved in the world projectively. In this light, I say more about his own approach, providing a more detailed preamble to his positive account.

In Chapter 5, I start to explicate his theory of the body schema through which our skills are deployed, focussing on his understanding of the phenomenon of the use-phantom limb. I then show what the schema can exclude and incorporate and why it is an a priori condition of cognitive distanciation and of readily reckoning with the possible. Chapter 6 is devoted to his view of motor intentionality as silhouetted by the Schneider case. Such an operative intentionality is interpreted as the work of the body schema organising both postures and phenomenal fields towards outcomes. I suggest that skill transpositions can be extrapolated from Merleau-Ponty's theory, but also that he neglects shorter events of reflection in the flow of action. In Chapter 7, I turn to his account of the way we experience others in and through their attitudes and engagements. He is highly attentive to the expressivity of others and to our enculturation, and he maintains that we can never be objectified as Sartre thinks we can. In Chapter 8, I traverse the account of language as the medium of thought and as existentially significant and creative. This is followed by an outline of his views of our affective lives in knowing and loving. In the final chapter, my initial concern is with the theories of immanent temporal awareness and existential temporality that Merleau-Ponty inherits from Husserl and Heidegger and qualifies with his account of body temporality. I then set out his stories about the tacit and spoken cogito and about the concrete subject or person with its original union of conscious and cognitive awareness and a certain body. I conclude by examining some objections to his view, chiefly to the effect that his active and proficient body is an idealisation from an ageist and ableist perspective. These objections carry weight, though Merleau-Ponty's theory can be reworked to accommodate them. In any event, his idea of a radical reflection on reflection and on the unreflected shows his loyalty to the phenomenological enterprise. It is of its essence to be revised and reworked, and the directions it is yet to take are unforeseeable.

Maurice Merleau-Ponty was born in Rochefort-sur-Mer in 1908 and raised in Paris by his mother following his father's death in 1913. He studied first at the renowned Lycée Louis-le-Grand and then at the equally renowned École Normale Supérieure, where he became a friend of Simone de Beauvoir. Some years later he befriended Jean-Paul Sartre. This was followed by a research fellowship and teaching posts, first in the Lycée de Chartres and then back in the École Normale. After army conscription from 1939 to 1940, he taught in the Lycée Carnot and Lycée Condorcet in Paris. *The Structure of Behaviour* was published in 1940, five years before *Phenomenology of Perception* (which gained him his higher doctorate from the Sorbonne). In 1945 he also founded the journal *Les Temps modernes* with Beauvoir and Sartre and became a lecturer at the University of Lyon, being promoted to professor in 1948. He was appointed to the Chair of Psychology and Pedagogy at the Sorbonne in 1949, and to the Collège de France in 1952, the summit of his academic career. Other important works include *Humanism and Terror* (1947), *Adventures of the Dialectic* (1955) after breaking with Sartre and *Signs* (1960). He died from a heart attack in 1961, leaving unfinished the posthumously published *The Visible and the Invisible* (1964). If the anglophone reader wishes to learn about Merleau-Ponty's character, the course of his life and Parisian milieu, Sarah Bakewell's account is to be recommended. She gives a fine overview of his network of relationships and of his philosophy from early to late, and a rich sense of how his style is echoed in his thought. For most of his life, he was consummately what she says he was, the happy and dancing philosopher of the things as they are.[15]

---

[15] Bakewell 2016, 111–12, 228–41, 325–6. See also Robinet 1963, 1–65.

CHAPTER I

Phenomenology and Objective Thought

1.1 Introduction

On the opening page of his preface to *Phenomenology of Perception*, Merleau-Ponty remarks that phenomenology is a study of 'essences', of the essential features and underlying structures of perception and of consciousness. All of its problems come back to the definition of essences, yet it is also a philosophy for which the understanding of existence demands a return to its humanly lived and engaged factuality or 'facticity'. It seeks to place essences back into existence, finding them interwoven inextricably with our being in the world. We find a strange tension in a philosophy aspiring to be a pure, disengaged and exact science while also showing a remarkable concern with our pre-scientific and taken-for-granted space and time and lived world or lifeworld (*Lebenswelt*).[1] Most of the preface is promissory, signalling how Merleau-Ponty will adopt and adapt what he understands as Husserlian phenomenology. In its course, he characterises Heidegger's *Being and Time* as nothing more than a development of Husserl's explications of our natural conception of the world and lifeworld (*PP*, lxx–lxxi).

From the outset, Husserl regards phenomenology as a science of consciousness by way of its appearances. It commences with the description of our psychologically lived experiences and works back to the universal, invariant and recursive features and significations that the experiences must exhibit to be what they are. We must return to the things or the matters themselves, which means that at every step of the way our word meanings must be clarified and their referents rendered self-evident in fully fledged intuitions or actually lived experiences. And only by tracing what

---

[1] Merleau-Ponty is wrong to state that Husserl characterises phenomenology as a discipline aspiring to scientific exactitude. It is instead a rigorous science of essences grasped in cognitions warranted by direct lived experience. 'Philosophy as Rigorous Science', trans. Quentin Lauer in Husserl 1981, 166–8, 196.

we purportedly know in our utterances and inscriptions back to lived experience (which is in the first instance perceptual experience) and by describing it rigorously can we uncover the essential forms and laws that warrant knowledge claims (*LI 1*, 168, 178; *LI 2*, 112, 343). When he goes on to take his transcendental turn, Husserl seeks to uncover the a priori structures or conditions of possibility of perceptual and epistemic life as described systematically. It is at this stage of his philosophical career that he thematises our 'natural attitude', or natural belief in the world.

In Merleau-Ponty's view, transcendental phenomenology as formulated by Husserl can be shown to pass more or less seamlessly into existential or humanly situated phenomenology as developed by Heidegger and others (*PP*, lxxvii–lxxviii). I begin this chapter by running through Husserl's account of the natural attitude and his methodology of bracketing and reduction. This proceeds from descriptive to eidetic to transcendental phenomenology, finally questioning back to constituting subjectivity and to constituting sub-consciousness. After outlining Husserl's conception of the transcendental phenomenology of active and passive constitution and explicating some of its initial deliverances, I indicate how Merleau-Ponty takes up this approach and recasts it as an existential project. Phenomenology is humanly situated, begins descriptively and ought to proceed genetically. It is the fundamental antidote to the scientistic incarnation of objective thought common to empiricist and intellectualist theories of perception, distorting the descriptions and conclusions of both. Finally, I set out Merleau-Ponty's genealogy of objective thought. In this story he seeks to show why it is so persuasive in its everyday as well as scientific variants.

1.2   From the Descriptive to the Transcendental

When I consider the world in ordinary reflective fashion, according to Husserl, I take it as spread out endlessly in space and having endlessly become in time. In this world, both things and living bodies (those of animals and people) are there for me. Some of the things are immediately present to me – a being who has certain habits and who pursues certain interests – as objects of use and beauty, like the glass for drinking, the vase for flowers and the piano for playing. Other people are present to me as friends or enemies, relatives or strangers or colleagues and students and so on. As I write, I am marginally conscious of the existence of the unseen parts of the room in which I am sitting and of the children playing and chattering out in the garden. By switching my attention and moving, I can successively bring these people and things into view, converting vague background experiences into more or less clear and focal awareness. In this room, I can assume an aesthetic attitude as a musician or listener, or an arithmetical attitude when working through a mathematical proof, but these particular attitudes exhibited by myself and others are nested within a natural attitude or natural belief in the world as existing for all of us (*Ids1*, 51–6).

This naive attitude is often given a strongly naturalistic slant when explicitly formulated as a thesis. It is not just that the world is taken to have existed before my birth and that it is expected to persist after my demise. For physicalistic naturalism, it is at root the world of matter and is therefore best dealt with by the natural sciences. Husserl now makes the first move in his transcendental phenomenological method. The natural attitude is thematised by being placed in parentheses or brackets and put under suspension (*epochē*). This term was used by Pyrrho of Elis and Sextus Empiricus, who held that a consistent scepticism must be sceptical about its own claims, since we cannot even know when we know and when we do not. For Husserl, I must not precipitously claim that I can address the question of the world's existence by providing an unprejudiced answer one way or another. To place the natural attitude under suspension is neither to affirm nor deny that there is an external world that exists apart from me and all of my thoughts. In bracketing the attitude and putting it out of play, I am deliberately *neutral* about its status, which looks like a sceptical move. But this is only done to put it at a distance, so that the overall belief can be silhouetted or shown forth in its full relief. Husserl realises that we must first get the character and sense of the attitude right, and we must also foreground and explicate what it presupposes (*Ids1*, 56–62; *Ids2*, 189–93).

In this way, bracketing and suspension (which Husserl often telescopes into the nomenclature of reduction) lays the ground for descriptive phenomenology, which is carried out in the descriptive reduction (reduction as understood in the sense of *re-ducere* or leading back). The natural attitude is silhouetted so it can itself become a phenomenon for elucidation; I go back to what has been placed at a distance in order to bring out its character and implicit sense for me. Revealing the tacit senses and meanings of phenomena behind the explicit ones is the royal road – and indeed the sole road – to a rigorous science of consciousness. But only at the theoretical level can I put the attitude out of play and return to it. Only in the 'transcendental attitude' can I be a philosophically reflective and disengaged onlooker of my ordinary believing experience. And to elucidate the sense of the attitude is to describe the way it is adhered to unthinkingly. Over the whole time I seek to uncover its significance, notes Husserl, I am living within it. What is most important are not the explicit and affirmative judgements that I sometimes make about the world's existence, but my ongoing and pre-reflective world-belief. Even if a particular thing turns out to be different from what I thought, to the extent of being a hallucination, I do not doubt the wider world in which it appears. Through the flow of background appearances the world's existence is assumed continually. The character of the attitude is that of a fundamental belief or faith in the world's existence, with the implicit sense of it being utterly unquestionable. This leads me to take its existence as absolute and independent whenever I think about it in everyday life, whether or not I posit that existence as physical at its most real (*Ids1*, 56–7, 129; *Ids2*, 192–3).

More than the natural belief must be put in parentheses, since it is only held by a consciousness by virtue of appearances for that consciousness. For this reason, the entire phenomenon of the experiencing being who lives believingly in the natural attitude and who can put it forward in a thesis has to be bracketed. Put another way, its flow of awareness with its memories and imaginings and perceptual objects and perceptual fields must be placed in parentheses, and with them its lived body and everything perceived in and on and from it. Everything must be placed under the *epoché* so that nothing is lost for the descriptive reduction (*Ids1*, 112–3, 125–6, 172). Whatever I perceive thematically is something that is implicated in a state of affairs or situation, such as the steep hill that I am seeing in front of me and above me and feeling under my feet, and that I am ascending with some difficulty to get exercise and to enjoy a panoramic view from the summit. What is bracketed for elucidation is the whole experience, the phenomenon of the seen hill and anticipated panorama within the world for this conscious existent *and* the attendant phenomenon of my body as engaged in the climbing activity. Perceived and believed and perceiver and believer are preserved as correlates of each other. The conscious embodied existent for whom objects and world come to appearance and claim being must itself be a factor in their description (*CM*, 33–5; *CES*, 99–100).

Husserl is well aware that the route to phenomenological description looks deceptively simple. In the 'splitting of the ego' consequent on the suspension of the natural attitude, one has to reach the level of disengaged reflection while at the same time endeavouring to capture one's I and everyday flow of acting and believing life. Given that all of us have our individual habitualities, interests and inheritances, moreover, it is difficult to avoid importing hidden hypotheses and inferences into description. The performance of the *epoché* and reduction requires extensive training in the avoidance of over-interpretation. We cannot actualise the ideals of freedom from prejudice and disinterested knowledge in one fell swoop (*CM*, 35–6; *CES*, 154–5); and of course description presupposes language. We can never eliminate all vagueness and ambiguity from natural language, with its indexicals or essentially occasional expressions whose meanings are bound up with the contexts of utterances or inscriptions (*LI 1*, 223–4). Yet we can employ terms that are warranted experientially. We can also examine whether a term that was fixed in earlier contexts of use has the same sense in a new context (*Ids1*, 66, 151–2).

These strictures also apply to the subsequent stages of the phenomenological reduction. When description has done its work, I proceed to the eidetic reduction; I go back to a foregrounded phenomenon to discover its essential characteristics. An essence or *eidos* is a characteristic it must possess to be a phenomenon and to be the type that it is. It is revealed when I work over the appearance through a systematic process of free imaginative variation. If I am looking at my table, I think and imagine that it need not be a deep and rich walnut colour to count as a visual phenomenon. Nor does it have to be rectangular or have four legs. But free imaginative variation reveals that it must have some colour and shape, which tells me that colour and figure and extension are not only interdependent parts or moments of a visual phenomenon, but essential to it. Once I discover that they cannot be removed without destroying the very possibility of this type of appearance, I have apprehended at least part of its essence in an eidetic intuition (*CM*, 70–1; *LI 2*, 5–7).

When I turn my attention to the overall lived experiences (*Erlebnisse*) of seeing and valuing and imagining and judging, Husserl observes that those which are describable in the everyday first-person and phenomenologically purified perspectives possess the essential feature of being intentional experiences. Intentionality is the directedness or 'aboutness' that is characteristic of all these episodes:

> Intentional experiences have the peculiarity of directing themselves in varying fashion to presented objects, but they do so in an intentional sense. An object is 'referred to' or 'aimed at' in them in the manner of a presentation or likewise a judgment and so on. This means no more than that certain experiences are present, intentional in character, and, more specifically, presentationally, judicatively, desiringly or otherwise intentionally. There are (to ignore certain exceptions) not two things present in experience; we do not experience the object and beside it the intentional experience directed upon it. There are not even two things present in the sense of a part and a whole which contains it: only one thing is present, the

intentional experience, whose essential descriptive character is the intention in question. . . . If this experience is present, then eo ipso and through its own essence (we must insist) the intentional 'relation' to an object is achieved and an object is 'intentionally present'; these two phrases mean precisely the same.[2] (*LI 2*, 98)

Expressions to the effect that something is 'within the mind' or 'immanent in consciousness' are highly misleading, for they suggest that consciousness is a sort of container that has or comes to have things inside itself. Husserl stresses that there are not at first acts that go out to objects (things in states of affairs and truths) and then internalise them. Rather, the conscious acts only exist in their having gone out; they do not enjoy original separation from their objects (*LI 2*, 98, 100). All objects are irreducible to the acts of intending them, which is to say that they transcend or go beyond consciousness, whether they are mathematical truths or mythical beings or the blossoming trees in front of me. The relevant objects can still be described (*LI 2*, 99, 126–7), and in the case of worldly things, it cannot cease to be emphasised that their transcendence in the fullest sense must be preserved by the *epochē* as a phenomenon for explication through all the reductions. And the thing perceived is not a second object 'out there' that lies behind an intentional object 'in here'. There is no need to representationally duplicate an object into image and reality, since the intentional object is the same as the actual one. The point is that consciousness has reached the latter perceptually (*LI 2*, 126–7; *Ids1*, 218–20).

The terminology of reaching an object is not univocal, since acts of memory and imagination have by definition reached their objects in their own ways, which cannot be supplanted if the relevant objects are only accessible through these modes. But memorial and imaginative determinations are surpassed when things and states of affairs perceivable empirically come to be perceived. These considerations help to ground the crucial distinction that Husserl makes between signitive intending and intuitive fulfilment. To intend a worldly something signitively is to aim at the relevant object without that object as yet being present perceptually, that is, given in flesh and blood in sensuous or empirical intuition. To the extent that an intention is signitive, it is *empty*. I am more obviously intending in this mode when frantically looking for my house keys before journeying to an urgent appointment. I imagine where they might be and retrace my steps, trying to remember where I put them. When I eventually

[2] Translation emended.

track them down, the signitive and empty intending gives way to intuitive givenness or fulfilment. It is filled by a direct perceptual presentation. To the extent that empirical emptiness gives way to direct presence, the presence is *fulfilling*. The finding of the keys is a case of dynamic fulfilment, since there is a temporal stretch between the initial intending and its satisfaction. In cases of static fulfilment, the intention and its fulfilment occur together. When out walking, I was not thinking of rabbits before one dashed out onto the path in front of me (*LI 2*, 206–7, 218–20).

Descriptive and eidetic phenomenology would fall short badly if intentionality were taken as a simple two-term structure; we can and should discern three essential characteristics of every conscious or act-intentional experience. In a perceptual act most notably we can distinguish the real act with its qualities, the act matter or content and the relevant object intended and intuited. The real act is the conscious experience itself as a transient event in the flow of awareness that will never be again. It has qualities of believing and valuing and is sense-giving or meaning-conferring (*LI 1*, 192; *LI 2*, 113, 119–22). The act matter is the complex of sense and meaning that the act carries and confers on sensory deliverances. It is the interpreting content through which we are presented with an object as a significant unity. At the outset, it is a pre-predicative 'apprehending sense' (*Auffassungssinn*) established in early infancy, which soon comes to be worked over with meanings or expressive significations (*Bedeutungen*). Meanings articulate objects conceptually and predicatively when we enter the cognitive realm in language (*LI 1*, 214, 280–1; *LI 2*, 121–2, 161–2; *APS*, 33). The earliest acts with their apprehending senses are founding, whereas the later acts of conceptualising and judging are founded. They articulate objects into general types and their component parts. Because of these expressive articulations, we encounter objects in developed awareness as unities of sense with reportable meanings (*LI 2*, 116, 284–7; *Ids1*, 297; *APS*, 296). The contribution of the interpreting content can be brought out by explicating, not just why we perceive, but what we perceive, the way we perceive and how we perceive.

Why we perceive is initially answered in the naïve attitude. When others and things do not break in through our senses, they are sought out for essential purposes and because they attract us in other ways. If harmful or repulsive we avoid them. But the question of *what* we perceive shows the descriptive reduction employed more extensively. For Husserl, we do not see or hear or touch bare sense data. Hence one is not confronted with red and yellow patches on grey, or rising and falling tones, or a green expanse flecked with purple and white and surmounted by a blue expanse, with everything bobbing up and down. It is rather that I see the matchbox on the mantelpiece, or hear the singer's song on the radio, or see and feel the flower-strewn hill that I am ascending under the sky (*LI 2*, 99; *APS*, 121–2). Because the interpreting content is at work, I do not first look at and hear my sensations and subsequently turn them into perceptual objects. In this direct empirical realism, sense and meaning are given *with* the sensations they inform, not plastered on afterwards. Intentional acts of perceiving are directed towards already significant unities, which tells us that the sensations are not themselves intentional. Without doubt they are essential moments of perception, but what we aim at and experience are the objects that they present. This is why we should say that we do not perceive our sensations, but *have* them. We can zone in on patches, colours and tones as such, but these presentations presuppose earlier experiences from which they have been abstracted as derivative parts from original wholes (*LI 1*, 214; *LI 2*, 99, 103–4).

The *way* that we perceive empirically is unavoidably perspectival. Each of us experiences from only one standpoint, and our objects are apprehended as spatially exterior to us. Their mode of givenness is therefore partial or inadequate. In vision, for example, what I see of the matchbox or hill is that aspect or profile (*Abschattung*) of the object that presents one or more sides from this or that standpoint – several sides of the matchbox or one prospect of the hill – while its other sides remain hidden. We typically think that, if a supreme and infinite being exists, then such a divinity will enjoy the complete and adequate perceptual grasp that we lack because of our finitude. Husserl's reply is twofold; we cannot even imagine what it would be like to have an all-in-all experience of something, and if God could have that adequate grasp of the thing that we lack, then the transcendent existence of a thing would lose its significance in fact and principle. The second proposition is a contradiction or countersense (*Widersinn*), for it implies no essential difference between something immanent or transcendent. Were God to have this totalising grasp, the thing would be actually and not just intentionally immanent, a mere moment within a divine flow of awareness encapsulating it fully (*Ids1*, 92; *APS*, 48, 56).

If a worldly object is always given inadequately, it is nonetheless a truism that in sensuous perception we take ourselves as experiencing the entire existent. We are not surprised when something reveals further aspects in rotating or when we move around it. Over the course of the perception, we tacitly interpret every aspect that is directly present as a part of a wider whole. This implies we are signitively intending other aspects of the object – the ones not directly present right now – as potentially present in the future. Here as so often elsewhere, Husserl is careful to keep his descriptions faithful to the phenomena. We do not expect that one or other hidden side *will* be there if we go around the object, for it is 'co-intended' as *already* there, as another extant part of the whole. Rather, we expect that it will come into view. In co-intending it is 'appresented' as indirectly on the scene yet available. As a new aspect comes into direct and fulfilling presence, furthermore, the earlier aspect becomes hidden in its turn. What was the front side is now the rear side. There is thus an ongoing interplay of gain and loss in perception, and it is of particular note that signitive and empty intending never becomes redundant. No matter what standpoint one may come to assume, the aspects that remain hidden are being signified all the time. We discover that it is essential to the apprehending sense of perceptual awareness, not merely to make direct presentation significant, but in so doing to be co-intending *beyond* what is directly present towards potential fulfilments of what is occluded. Conscious or intentional awareness in interpreting what we call the given reaches beyond itself and beyond the given. Intentionality of its very nature points forward into possibility (*LI 2*, 211, 227–8; *CM*, 46).

In Husserl's later terminology, the real act or the conscious experience is the noesis, and the apprehending sense (and later the meaning) along with the interpreted sensations the noema. The noema is the thing *as* it is intended significantly (*Ids1*, 213–8). Everything emptily intended in the noematic sense of an object as also there and as a possible appearance comprises its *horizon*. Perception is intrinsically horizonal, and its acts in their signitive co-intendings are never completely empty. On foot of past fulfilments we remember other aspects of things and of living beings. In pointing forwards, we unthinkingly project the colour of the vase into its hidden aspects, and we take the carpet as soft and deep and pleasant to kneel on. Even when we have not seen an object of a certain type before, we read its visible qualities into its invisible ones. Accordingly a horizon is a predelineation of potentialities, a fore-sketching in which we do not merely appresent hidden aspects as already there, but anticipate what they will look like and feel like and so on (*LI 2*, 211, 241; *CM*, 44–5, 48; *APS*, 42, 79). But we must qualify this, for the predelineating projection of certain qualities into the rear side of an empirical thing does not involve imagining that side as seen. If we could form a head-on image of the rear in attentively seeing the front, this imaginative picture would itself be perspectival and horizonal, referring back to the front side. We would be faced with a regress, and in the first instance the imagined far side of the imagined rear would be an image mysteriously superimposed on the aspect that is directly present perceptually (*TS*, 47–8).

The intuitive and signitive and horizonal are blended together in unified perceptual intentionalities (*LI 2*, 224). The predelineation of potentialities does not for all that pertain to an isolated thing, and Husserl distinguishes the inner and outer horizon of an empirical object. The first is everything co-intended of the object itself, while the second includes the perceptual field or background around it and by implication where and when it will typically appear. In concert they point forward to a determinable indeterminacy, where fulfilment makes more determinate the inevitable vagueness of memory and imagination (*Ids1*, 52; *APS*, 42). Because perception is on ongoing as against a momentary act, however, we should refer to an on ongoing synthesis of fulfilments that successively fulfils and confirms what is signitively co-intended and predelineated. Yet there is always the possibility that what comes to be viewed or touched will turn out to be different to what was expected. The rear of a vase may be a different colour, and a carpet hard and grainy rather than soft with a deep pile. A synthesis of fulfilment of horizonal expectations can become a synthesis of frustration. The perceptual certainty we enjoy in the natural attitude is therefore a contingent certainty, since it is dependent on a course of experiences continuing to confirm and enrich what came before. Perception is always inadequate, and its sense and meaning open to correction by subsequent perceptions, so the indeterminacy of its objects cannot be made fully determinate. There is always something more and it may turn out otherwise (*LI 2*, 212–3; *CM*, 15–7; *APS*, 43, 64–5).

Certain experiences of frustration bring such claims to even better evidence, showing that a phenomenology of 'nullifying illusion' is utterly indispensable for a phenomenology of genuine actuality (*Ids1*, 364). One of these is recounted by Husserl following a visit to a waxworks museum. As he goes through the entrance doors, he sees a woman descending the grand staircase and smiling at him. But as he advances further, things start to jar and look discordant. Her face is frozen and so is her out-stepped foot. Then he realises that 'she' is a wax figure put there to deceive the new visitor. The experience of frustration is the 'explosion' of the noema's horizonal predelineation. The core noematic sense of encountering an enduring pole of identity remains, but the rich sense and conceptual and reportable meaning significations of a real woman have been destroyed. This tells us that the significance of the perceived is not indifferent to the co-perceived or co-present background. In his outer horizon of a waxworks figure, Husserl expects to see it on a pedestal in a gallery, and in his outer horizon of a real woman descending a staircase, he expects to see her hands and feet synchronised with the balustrade and stairs, whether or not she sees him and smiles. Where the figure is placed and when it comes into view contributes to the success of the deception (*LI 2*, 137–8; *Ids1*, 313–5, 332; *CES*, 162). On further examination, we find that inner and outer horizons usually confirm each other without interruption. If confirmation were lacking there could be no world – it must be negotiable for and negotiated by consciousness to be known (*Ids1*, 109–10).

This waxworks example also shows that expectations are socially and culturally mediated – with the help of others, we already learned to search for effigies in certain places in turn-of-the-century Europe. Prior to a phenomenology of a familiar world, however, is the basic question of *how* we perceive, of how we can take ourselves as perceiving whole things and events in a world in the first place. If the predelineation of things brings in an external horizon, the predelineation of the latter as a field of co-present experiences means that we co-intend beyond it in turn. The very sense of a field entails a reference to something larger and more encompassing. Consciousness implicitly takes the current perceptual field as a sector of a world that stretches beyond it, and that promises a larger and indeed unlimited multitude of possible experiences. No matter how hazy and indefinite it may be in its far distances, we have the awareness that it offers ever more determinable indeterminacies (*Ids1*, 52–3; *CES*, 162). This brings us to the third and transcendental reduction. We must ask how we can have the sense and expressible significance of a wider world that we distinguish from ourselves as radically transcendent. Within the immanently flowing stream or flux of awareness, we must also ask how we can intend objectivities as abiding unities in the world, and be confident that we can continue to do so (*CM*, 48–9).

1.3 Active and Passive Constitution

All these questions lead Husserl back to an archaeology of noematic horizons. To ask how things and states of affairs and world are taken as actual *by* us and as prospectively accessible *to* us is to ask how we establish noemata and predelineate potentialities. Transcendental phenomenology is devoted to showing the intrinsically productive and 'constitutive' functions of consciousness. Constitution is what Kant calls synthesis; through it significant phenomena emerge, configurations that are progressively stabilised and re-identified, first being sensibly and then cognitively articulated in the stream. It does not literally create phenomena, but systematically endows things with senses and meanings in ways that can be shown to be appropriate to them and yet ineliminably necessary.

Problems of constitution are the fundamental ones for phenomenology (*Ids1*, 128, 207–9, 291; *CM*, 51–2). Its studies in constitution are 'transcendental' in working from the essential features of phenomena back to the essential structures or conditions of possibility for revealing them. Though the structures are physically founded, they can only be uncovered from the first person and interpersonal perspectives and cannot be reduced to their causal underpinnings. In Max Scheler's words, some a priori structures are 'material' rather than 'formal', not being imposed from above.[3] Material a prioris are immanent in somatic experience. In doing their work and as registered marginally in the flow of awareness, they articulate empirical things to make them intelligible (*TS*, 119; *EJ*, 107–8). In Chapter 4, we shall see how they must be those of a certain body.

In this third and ultimate stage of the reduction, Husserl also turns his attention to the egoic character of consciousness itself, which has endured through all the previous steps – albeit considered from a different attitude – without having its own being placed in parentheses. Embracing self-aware and reportable experience and sub-conscious awareness, consciousness is the residuum surviving the procedure, with everything else now coming into view as relative. All of its objects have been shown to be indubitable phenomena *for* it, with the focus having turned from the table or matchbox or hill to the entire experiences in which such objects are implicated. Through the experiences, consciousness is an enduring and egoic pole of awareness. In its current phase, it both retains earlier experiences and anticipates later ones. Kant famously remarks that the 'I think' must be able to accompany all of my presentations. If I could not grasp the multiplicity or manifold of presentations in one consciousness through time, I would be unable to call them mine. By the same token, I would have as many-coloured and diverse a self as I have presentations of which I am conscious to myself, which is to say that I would have no self at all (B 132, 134). Husserl agrees, and what he calls the 'pure ego' is my persisting pole of self-awareness in abstraction from my individual personality with its peculiar inheritances and habitualities and motivations (*Ids1*, 65, 132–3, 190–1).

In its constitutive role, the ego is a transcendental ego or transcendental subject, and I constitute reciprocally with other such egos in one 'transcendental intersubjectivity' (*CES*, 172, 255). The world of the natural attitude and all the objectivities thematised within it are not ready-made givens that I merely stumbled upon. Rather, they are achievements or accomplishments

---

[3] See Scheler 1973, 49, 54, 65–6.

of constituting subjectivity and intersubjectivity. Because daily living is naively immersed in the world, however, I knew nothing of these functions that had already done their work anonymously or pre-reflectively (*APS*, 57; *CM*, 153; *CES*, 204). What is wrong with ordinary thought about the natural attitude and naturalistic views is what they leave out of account. We have illegitimately absolutised the world's existence and have often attributed its ultimate significance to what we call physical being. In so doing, we have mistakenly interpreted consciousness as one more item within that world, conceived as containing some bodies that *have* minds. We may even follow Descartes in holding that the *ego cogito* exists apodictically or indubitably, but pass over the transcendental subject by regarding the ego as a piece of mundane being that is fully explicable in terms of physical and causal processes (*Ids1*, 128–9; *CM*, 24–5).

These considerations lead Husserl to conclude that the very terms 'reality' and 'world' are names for constituted unities of sense. They presuppose ordered and productive concatenations of awareness through which they emerge. To be consistent we must therefore espouse a transcendental idealism. Without essential contributions from consciousness, there would be no world. Against the charge that this is one more subjective idealism collapsing the world into the mind, it can be responded that nothing is taken away from the environment all around us. Its real actuality is not diminished or reinterpreted – all that is affirmed is the transcendent reality and validity *senses* that it comes to possess for consciousness. This is consonant with a direct empirical realism in which constitution is not a creation or production *ex nihilo*, in which we intentionally and actually reach things themselves, and in which informed empirical experience alone can validate or frustrate earlier empirical experience. As the sense-giving (*Sinngebung*) source of significance, however, we must affirm that consciousness is absolute and originary. It is presupposed in every phenomenon that claims existence, and in this strict sense is the sphere of absolute origins (*Ids1*, 128–9; *CM*, 26, 62, 86). In Eugen Fink's phrase, phenomenology is a philosophy that knows 'the origin of the world', the ultimate source of all intra-worldly knowing of phenomena as actualities. But just as the world is only what it is for its 'origin', so the origin is only what it is in relation to the world.[4]

We are nonetheless left with what Husserl calls 'the paradox of subjectivity'. How can a component of the world, an embodied being with its own

---

[4] Fink 1970, 98, 99–100. For a very well-argued reading of Husserl's transcendental idealism and of his opposition to specifically *naturalistic* realism, see Hopp 2020, 270–92.

subjectivity, constitute the whole world if it is only one formation in the total accomplishment? How can everything count as meaningful phenomena *for* the transcendental subject presupposed in such appearances when the subject is *inside* the world of empirical phenomena? The answer lies in adopting and adapting Kant's distinction between the transcendental and empirical subjects (B 152–3, 155–9). So far as I have the everyday phenomenon of myself with my peculiar personality and habitualities in the world with other humans, I am an empirical subject constituted by the hidden transcendental subjectivity that is its condition. The latter is accessed by way of the philosophically reflective reductions after the *epochē*. I learn that I am a double-sided subjectivity in and for the world and others too. Yet this is discovered in *my* awareness, and *I* must recognise that *we* anonymously constituted the essential sense of the world as being *our* world in transcendental intersubjectivity (*Ids I*, 124–6; *CES*, 179–86). Within it '[a]ll real mundane objectivity is a constituted accomplishment, including that of men and animals and thus also that of the [egoic] "souls"' (*CES*, 204). Personhood and transcendental subjectivity are not thereby exclusive, for each of us constitutes as an embodied and habitualised ego. Constitutive acts are achieved in and between and contribute to every singular awareness (*CM*, 66–8, 139).[5]

As Husserl develops his transcendental phenomenology, notes A. D. Smith, he stresses that constitution is not the sole or original preserve of transcendental egos or subjects.[6] In developed and waking perceptual life, we engage in active or egoic syntheses, turning attentively to worldly things and at once objectifying them intellectually. This is the aforementioned stage of informing them in noematic and predicative acts, of apprehending objects and of articulating them by means of concepts and judgements. Here we actively constitute reportable wholes and parts, cognitively intending re-identifiable particulars and their various features (*APS*, 33, 276–7, 278–80). But all this is founded on earlier and ongoing operations of 'passive' or sub-egoically constitutive syntheses. Primary passive syntheses first awaken the ego and solicit its activity (*CM*, 78–9; *APS*, 118–9, 280, 312–13). Through the work of a transcendental sub-consciousness, patterns that are most consonant with our interests are discerned associatively within our perceptual fields, exercising an allure or affective pull on egoic awareness leading to their noematic

---

[5] The constituting ego is not a formal or universal subjectivity, but factical and unique. See Taipale 2014, 10–11.

[6] Smith 2007, 8–11.

objectification. Sensations are proto-objectively configured, so sensibility is never the sheer receptivity of bare or formless data. It already discerns and is motivated to discern particular arrangements. As we shall see, the enduring unity of the ego pole is a product of a passive temporal synthesis – there is a pre-constitution of perceptual object and constituting subject. We shall also see that our sense of things in space needs both constitutive syntheses, and that all activity works with passivity. As awareness evolves, moreover, active and egoic syntheses become sedimented beneath reportable awareness. Yet these forgotten acts and judgements still function as convictions that motivate us in various ways. These acquisitions are secondary sub-egoic passivities. Unlike the primary passive syntheses that they come to colour, some can be reactivated, that is, brought back to conscious presence and evidence (*APS*, 93, 287; *CM*, 66–7).

Explicating the experience of a familiar house brings us to the beginnings of transcendental phenomenology of constitution. We see it from without and then from within, and in such explorations we depend on a passive synthesis of temporality. Each present and direct appearance is informed by immediate memories of the earlier appearances and immediate expectations of future ones. The successive views involve a sliding transition of perceptual manifolds or multiplicities, since each visual presentation slides smoothly into the next one. There are no staccato breaks as in a slideshow of stills. We also apprehend these successive presentations as showing different aspects of one object. An identity is apprehended 'longitudinally' between the manifolds and 'transversely' within each manifold. In the sliding transition from appearance to appearance, transcendental sub-consciousness achieves a 'transition synthesis' and 'synthesis of identification' that subjectivity will draw on. Longitudinal temporal synthesis retains in memory the earlier visually and transversally tracked appearances as one turns and moves around. The transition synthesis is their joint delivery of the experience of the sliding succession of visual contents. This is a logically prior condition of the synthesis of identification, which does not discern a discrete identity within each presentation and then establish an enduring identity-sense or noematic pole between them. It is *by way* of the transition between manifolds that an identity-sense is constituted across them and thence within each of them. Identification presupposes a holding on to differences, and the evidence lies in the tacit apprehension of the figure in each new manifold as an aspect of a multi-faceted whole that is remembered, signitively intended and horizontally predelineated. In early infancy, such a synthesis is passive and performative without as yet being meant (*TS*, 22–6, 131–2, 165–6; *LI 2*,

284–5; *EJ*, 59). And only on foot of having the noematic and horizonal sense of a whole can conceptual or meant identification grasp that whole explicitly as a certain type of thing (in this instance a house), and thematise its aspects and component features in propositional articulations or linguistic expressions. Each aspect and its subsidiary features as revealed from each perspective are cognised as the actual determinations of a determinable something.

For Husserl, the a priori structures revealed by transcendental phenomenology must not be peculiar to our own species. If this were the case, they would be contingent on facts concerning human consciousness and embodiment. Thus he will never renounce his early critique of individual and species psychologism or anthropologism. All such theories conflate the psychological acts of judging with the ideal and invariant objects of scientific judgements, and forget that truth is one and the same, whether appended by humans or angels or gods. Husserl contends that psychologism is as pernicious in a priori analyses (as transcendental psychologism) as in its purported applicability to logical laws and truths (*LI 1*, 49, 78–83; *CM*, 32; *CES*, 206–7). The constitutive functions of a rational subject having a world must belong to an eidetically universal ego, even if a species or consciousness takes them up in its own manner. After the transcendental reduction, 'the uncovering can become genuinely scientific only if I go back to the apodictic principles that pertain to this ego as exemplifying the eidos ego' (*CM*, 72; *CES*, 183). Transcendental sub-consciousness enjoys the same status (*CM*, 80–1, 85).

There is no doubting the ambition of Husserl's transcendental project, which if not ignoble nonetheless looks unfeasible. A ready objection in theoretical terms is that we can conceive of conscious beings whose constitutive capacities and correlative world are utterly different to ours, a criticism that Husserl quickly moves to address. A world completely outside ours seems a perfectly logical hypothesis, for there is no discernible countersense involved in asserting its possibility. On further examination, however, this possibility turns out to be completely empty, though it is often accepted uncritically. To assert it in the very first instance is to imply that the relevant subjects and their world could come to be recognised by us, which means that they are recognisable. In principle it would have to be the case that some mutual and empathic understanding could occur, so that 'the worlds of experience separated in fact become joined by concatenations of actual experience to make up one intersubjective world, the correlate of the unitary world of mental lives' (*Ids1*, 108). Once we take this into consideration, we see that the formal-logical hypothesis of a reality *utterly* outside our world is a material countersense devoid of content. If there is 'another' world, the experiences by which it is constituted must be able to extend into my experience and that of every ego, and it can be shown that certain a priori conditions of having that world on the part of its inhabitants must also be ours.

1.4   Existential and Genetic Phenomenology

In Merleau-Ponty's eyes, the entire effort of the supposedly detached spectator that has performed the *epochē* is devoted to rediscovering our naive contact with the world that is always already there in order to raise this contact to a properly philosophical status (*PP*, lxx). When the reduction begins, however, he stresses that great care must be taken not to import causal theories into description. One must sift out of the natural attitude and its conceptualisation everything that makes it naturalistic, zoning in on pre-scientific experience alone. Everything that I discover about science I know from my own perspective and from my prior experience of a meaningful world, without which the symbolic notations of the sciences could find no application. Scientific (or rather scientistic) attitudes according to which I am a mere part or moment of the world are for this reason naive and hypocritical, for they imply and make use of the perspective of consciousness without ever mentioning it. Each of us has a point of view on and engagement with the world that cannot in fact or in principle be collapsed into the latter. It is in my inescapable awareness that a world first arranges itself around me and begins to exist for me. In relation to the lifeworld, every scientific determination of objects is not only derivative but abstract, signitive and dependent, 'just like geography with regard to the landscape in which we first learned what a forest, a meadow or a river is' (*PP*, lxxii).

There is probably no other question, states Merleau-Ponty, that Husserl spent more time trying to understand than the reduction (or more precisely the *epochē* and reduction). Whereas a thoroughgoing transcendental idealism implies that all determinable indeterminacies can be determined fully and rendered totally intelligible, Husserl's procedure does not strip the world – and the significance of the world – of its opacity and transcendence (*PP*, lxxv–lxxvii). While his method recognises my thought as an inalienable fact, it simultaneously reveals me as a being in the world, a world paradoxically within and beyond the hold of intentional awareness:

> Because we are through and through related to the world, the only way for us to catch sight of ourselves is by suspending this movement . . . Reflection

does not withdraw from the world toward the unity of consciousness as the foundation of the world; rather, it steps back in order to see transcendencies spring forth and it loosens the intentional threads that connect us to the world in order to make them appear; it alone is conscious of the world because it reveals the world as strange and paradoxical ... Husserl's entire misunderstanding with his interpreters, with the existential 'dissidents', and ultimately with himself, comes from the fact that we must – precisely in order to see the world and to grasp it as a paradox – rupture our familiarity with it, and this rupture can teach us nothing except the unmotivated springing forth of the world. The most important lesson of the reduction is the impossibility of a complete reduction. This is why Husserl always wonders anew about the possibility of reduction. If we were absolute spirit, the reduction would not be problematic. (*PP*, lxxvii–lxxviii)

Husserl's positing of a disengaged and disinterested onlooker in the transcendental attitude has scientistic overtones, and it often reads as if the reduced world could be displayed in its totality before such an awareness (*PP*, lxxiv–lxxv). Yet everything in his descriptions strains against the conception of an absolute spectator with its fully objectified world, which tells us that his view of the onlooker should conform with its actual situation, as his existentialist successors emphasised. He himself realises that there is never just one bracketing and describing and uncovering of essential features and constitutive conditions performed once and for all. Phenomenology is the province of a perpetual beginner who must incessantly retrace steps already taken. In trying to elucidate the horizons of a finite existent living in the natural attitude, we must proceed backwards and forwards in a zigzag fashion (*CES*, 58, 188; *PP*, lxxviii). We might conclude that a progression from descriptive to eidetic and transcendental phenomenology has uncovered a horizon of anticipation dependent on a lived body in general, for example, but it could transpire to be specific to one epoch or sex. But if revisions may be requisite, we cannot claim to have attained a purely disinterested standpoint from which to put phenomenology to work.

Espousing a view associated with Heidegger, Merleau-Ponty maintains that our human situation and interests always slip into theoretical reflection. Even repeated revisions of the reduction cannot finally get behind them. Its very performance is interested, and the motivation to perform it is perhaps best formulated by Fink when he writes of a wonder (or better an astonishment or *Verwunderung*) before the world (*PP*, lxxvii, 309).[7] Far from leading to an idealist position, continues Merleau-Ponty, the

---

[7] See Fink 1970, 109; and Landes' remarks in *PP*, 494–5.

phenomenological reduction is in fact the formula for an existential philosophy. What Heidegger calls our being in the world as being involved can only appear against the background of a procedure that has taken the entirety of intentional life as its theme (*PP*, lxxviii, lxxxii). Letting us show that intentionality arcs forwards into possibility, the reduction opens the way to an account of consciousness as a project of the world that it is destined towards without being able to possess. In this light, we must reject the possibility of a fully detached standpoint without abandoning the ideal of faithful and renewable description. Phenomenology cannot make our involved existence completely explicit, but this is not its failure. Rather, it indicates its abiding concern with the mysteries of an inexhaustible world and a historically situated reason that can responsibly choose to respect that world and the awareness interwoven with it. And if we cannot achieve total separation from our human lives, this does not stop us working back to what is essential and necessary in them. We can bring out a priori structures or conditions of meaningful actuality that go beyond psychological curiosities and causal facts (*PP*, lxxviii, lxxxv, 60–1, 64–5, 97–9).

The task of disclosing our projective being in the world, as Merleau-Ponty sees it, demands a transcendental yet existentially situated phenomenology of our engaged perception (*PP*, 61, 64–5, 454). But this would seem to open him to the charge that Husserl levels at Heidegger, of having restricted himself to intramundane analyses that can only culminate in transcendental psychologism or anthropologism. Now Merleau-Ponty agrees that angelic or otherworldly thoughts and evidences closed off from us are empty possibilities. If the intentional acts of other beings and correlative fulfilments within their world are to be recognisable as such, an absolute difference between our worlds is precluded. So long as we can access their world it cannot count as a second one, and if we did access it then the significations, conceptions and evidences that we have or could come to have would envelop those of the others. We would still apprehend those from the perspective of *our* perceptions and horizons (*PP*, 418–19). But transcendental work would then reveal conditions of actuality of our common world without having to uncover conditions of possibility of each and every world (*PP*, lxxx–lxxxi, 40, 417, 419). It should be emphasised that every a priori necessity we can apprehend is situated within our human realm:

> From the moment in which experience – that is, the opening onto our factual world – is recognised as the beginning of knowledge, there is no longer any means of distinguishing a level of a priori truths and a level of

factual ones, or between what the world ought to be and what the world actually is . . .. [t]he a priori is the fact as understood, made explicit, and followed through into all the consequences of its tacit logic; the a posteriori is the isolated and implicit fact. (*PP*, 229–30)

This is of little concern, for what we explicitly identify as requisite for the constitution of our common world remains undiminished by anything intended emptily. It might be objected that truths evident to us are not irrevocably evident, since only an absolute spirit could enjoy the indefeasible certainty of having avoided psychologism, knowing what is requisite universally and not merely for us (*PP*, 417–18). Merleau-Ponty might also be accused of inconsistency in stating that one's body with its perspective and operatively intentional movement is 'the condition of possibility' of thematic act intentionality, of geometrical synthesis and of all the expressive operations and acquisitions that constitute the cultural world (*PP*, 408, 453). He would reply that we can still speak of a condition of possibility on the proviso that it is a condition of actuality of this world, the only one we can assign importance to because it is the only one that is important, that has real significance. We are what we are on foot of factical and structural conditions of embodied and agential awareness. These we take up and make our own and may come to recognise (*PP*, 98–9, 105, 174, 229). More than this, our recognition of an a priori necessity is sufficient onto itself. As warranted by all the evidence from intentional analysis, it needs no extra-worldly justification. It is a hardly a strong objection that our factical truths can be considered inadequate – and that psychologism can persist as a serious concern – in relation to the idea of an absolute and omniscient spirit (*PP*, 59, 205, 418–19).[8]

Though we can access being solely through what appears to us, intentional investigation as taken over from Husserl does not presume that we generate the form and unity of the object. Rather it seeks to make the object's primordial form and unity explicit. In Merleau-Ponty's eyes,

---

[8] If we cannot transcend facticity in any way, according to Andrew Inkpin, then our so-called necessity will be conditioned because it is determined by underlying facts. Our bodies could be different, lacking various parts and organs, but if we cannot separate what is contingent and necessary about them, then we effectively abandon the idea of necessity. If it is responded that Merleau-Ponty's transcendental account is novel although weak, the problem with his redefinitions is not his terminology, but their failure to yield intelligible distinctions and a distinctively transcendental mode of validity (Inkpin 2017, 40, 42, 44–5). Yet the claim that everything about our bodily organisation is necessary (*PP*, 174) does not preclude material a prioris. On the necessity of having an upright posture and opposable thumbs, see Chapter 4, and of a schematised posture, Chapter 5. Even the forms of our lungs, ears and nails are taken as necessary (*PP*, 455), presumably for speaking and hearing and fingertip work with precision and protection. We have to recognise that 'human existence is the change of contingency into necessity through the act of taking up'. *PP*, 174.

synthesis is a productivity of revelation more than creation that is forever incomplete. But for this very reason, the term 'constitution' is problematic, since it is all too strongly suggestive of an omnipotent transcendental subject doing its work from on high (*PP*, lxxiii, 61–2, 148, 215). The connotations of the term are nevertheless ameliorated by Husserl's later formulation of a genetic phenomenology as distinct from a static one. The static approach carries out its descriptive, eidetic and transcendental analyses in a synchronic and ahistorical manner. It isolates essential and a priori structures by abstracting them from a developed awareness, without asking how they successively came into play. A genetic approach is diachronic and historical; it is concerned with the development of awareness from primary passive syntheses through to the constitution of the first noematically apprehending senses, followed by explicit cognitions in which concepts, language and judgements are doing work (*APS*, 629; *CM*, 106).

It could be retorted that a static phenomenology when properly executed will reveal the same essential features and constitutive conditions as a genetic one, albeit in isolation from their antecedents and subsequents. But this divorce from a genetic and historical progression compromises the procedure. In neglecting the progression, the static approach underplays the interrelations of the founding and founded stages of awareness. Each stage demands an understanding appropriate to it, but also an appreciation of how the higher stages reciprocally influence the lower ones upon which they remain dependent. The genetic approach is best placed to show how awareness must itself evolve through its worldly engagements. The task is to reveal how our own development is bound up with our articulating of the world (*PP*, lxxxii, 127–8, 414). Husserl holds to the end that genetic phenomenology must uncover the constitutive progression necessary for any conceivable awareness, whereas Merleau-Ponty stresses that the former's essences cannot be separated from human existence, and 'must bring with them all of the living relations of experience, like the net that draws up both quivering fish and seaweed from the seabed' (*PP*, lxxix). On Merleau-Ponty's construal, the former's descriptions point back to concrete essences, definitive features of lives, lived experiences and objects inseparable from their factical situations. The concrete essence of the triangle is its actual physiognomy as first set down on paper for the gaze, even if the geometer will contend that this only illustrates its ideal essence. The concrete essence of the pen is discernible in the way of holding and using it, while the concrete essence of drawing lies in part in the smooth and unthinking flow of movement shown in the skill's deployment. Such definitive features of the action cannot be abstracted from the actual performance, since the proficiency expressed is indissociable from its peculiar mode of expression (*PP*, 133, 151–3, 406). Because the flow of movement is an achievement, a genetic story lies behind it. Once told material a prioris will have been uncovered, structural conditions of the skill's deployment immanent within it.[9]

When he shows how somatic syntheses are conditions for having a world, Husserl will also show that the natural attitude is what we live unthinkingly. The uncovering of a deeper and operative intentionality will add the insight that the world is not just what I reveal with my body, but what I am geared into through it (*PP*, lxxxii, 131–2). Once 'sense-giving' is qualified by a story in which its syntheses of revelation are dependent on and shaped by a body that is responsive to others and to the contours of the world, it will remain transcendental without having to entail a transcendental idealism.[10] And this operative body is as socio-culturally coloured as my consciousness. Both are moments of an integrated existence with an historical genesis, an unfolding drama condemned to sense and meaning (*PP*, lxxxiii–lxxxiv, 174, 195). There is no closed-off 'inner man', as Husserl misleadingly suggests at one point (*CM*, 157). We are in and towards the world, and only through it do we know ourselves, such that our certainty of the world is never the certainty of our thought about it.[11]

---

[9] Merleau-Ponty affirms material a prioris early on, holding that our conception of consciousness must be profoundly modified as a result. *SB*, 172.

[10] In Merleau-Ponty's view, idealism falls down for at least two reasons. It cannot encompass the transcendence and richness of the world, and embodied and projective awareness gears us into the latter before self-consciousness can arrive on the scene. The theory of the body schema is of a sub-conscious awareness that is an accommodation to others and to the world and that inhabits so-called sense-giving, which is as much centripetal as centrifugal (*PP*, 131, 452–3, 466, 474). All this must be in place for me to *posit* a world and have the composure for positing. See the last section of Chapter 5. Though I read Merleau-Ponty as a transcendental empiricist and realist, because of the precedence of material a prioris and the forms discerned in the world (albeit from our perspective), his portrayal of idealism is too sweeping and its dismissal too brusque. Some of his theses are shared by transcendental idealism, notably that perception and subjectivity are not mere facts in the world. For an account of Merleau-Ponty as a pre-objective idealist, see Gardner 2015, 312–15.

[11] This can be read as a criticism of Husserl's earlier and Cartesian claim that the being of anything transcendent is open to doubt, unlike immanent experience. Even the world of the natural attitude can be doubted in that its non-existence is conceivable. And if certain concatenations of experience were to collapse such that the empirical order of the world were annihilated, consciousness would still survive as a residuum able to enjoy other lived experiences (*Ids1*, 100–4, 109–12). Rudolf Bernet has shown that Husserl later rejects the annihilation hypotheses because it severs the essential correlation between a subject of intentional experiences and a world, or between the possibility of an interested awareness with its worldview and the possibility of a world (Bernet 1990, 5–7). An awareness with actualisable interests must be capable of habitualisation and personalisation and cannot be a soul-substance. It exists in reciprocal dependence with a body and social community. *Ids1*, 127–8; *Ids2*, 139–43.

I can never find myself as a discrete existent, for the world runs inside me and I am outside myself. At the core of the subject we will reveal body and world as more than the objects of our ideas. The world is to be uncovered by way of the 'hold' that the knowing body has on it, and 'knowing' and 'understanding' will take on a wider and a deeper sense (*PP*, lxxiv, lxxvii, 430–1).

1.5   Objective Thought and Its Genealogy

Merleau-Ponty stresses that everything in phenomenology hangs on its descriptions. If these go wrong, so will genetic accounts and the conclusions drawn from them. Description as framed by Husserl is the endeavour to avoid over-interpretation and under-interpretation. We must be careful not to read too much sense and meaning into phenomena, lapsing into metaphysical speculation and construction. Nor must we take too much away, lapsing into reductionism (though these mistakes more commonly come together and mark each other). Against the backdrop of Husserl's genealogy and critique of physicalistic naturalism (*CES*, 51–3, 60–9, 127), what description must escape is the objective thought found in explanation and in analytic reflection (*PP*, lxx, lxxii). The endeavour to explain perception defines empiricism, which for Merleau-Ponty is the empirical psychology of his time rather than the philosophy of a Locke, Hume or Russell. The explanatory procedure of empiricism as he finds it is far more severe and ambitious than in the classical philosophical versions, for perception is to be completely translated into the causal explanation definitive of natural science. Empirical psychology seeks to reduce experiences to simple sensations or feelings registering simple stimuli, and to the reflexes reacting to them. Every such theory espouses scientific realism. We may have a common-sense belief in the everyday world, but what are genuinely real are the underlying physical and chemical processes and their constituents. In impinging on us causally they determine completely our sensations, feelings and reflexes (*PP*, 7–9, 24, 48).

Analytic reflection or regressive analysis is the approach that is employed by intellectualism or rationalism, the predominant alternative to and antithesis of empiricism. It originated with Descartes, who argues that the understanding of what he calls mental and physical things and of their persisting identities through changes can only be confirmed through the power of judgement, by which the intellect affirms their essential properties as cognised clear and distinctly.[12] It was refined greatly by Kant and

---

[12] Descartes 1984b, 20–3.

reappears in many cognitive psychologies. The task of analytic reflection as the philosophical intellectualist sees it is to reconstruct the table of transcendental or a priori concepts, together with the rules for their application in judgements. These are what render our scientifically intelligible world possible, and we can also identify principles and concepts for the practical world. Knowledge may be related to its object in two ways, by determining it theoretically or by making it actual in practical or moral action. The world of phenomena capable of scientific determination is a product of a transcendental or constituting subjectivity, which brings them under concepts such as substance and causation (B ix–x, 212–33). Positing the work of an autonomous rational subject that generates the unity of the object, intellectualism typically entails some form of idealism. The world proper and all its constituents are constituted in consciousness (*PP*, lxxiii, 41, 45).

Merleau-Ponty notes that in a profound respect empiricism and intellectualism are in agreement. One sees the world as existing independently of a purely mundane consciousness contained within it, and the other that world as the outcome of transcendental syntheses, but they share a view of its essential nature. Hence anti-naturalistic intellectualism is ultimately a divergent outgrowth of objective thought. In their common scheme of things, every entity within the world is a fixed and comprehensive totality. The world for investigation is the sum-total of identified or identifiable entities – atoms and molecules up to the largest things – that have a definite location in space and duration in time and that obey invariable laws. These laws are ahistorical and atemporal and have been uncovered by natural science (*PP*, 41–2, 73–4). As Russell Keat has pointed out, this is a model in which bodies have a determinate shape and magnitude and mass. Each possesses a set of parts and determinately specifiable properties that can be explained in purely causal terms.[13] The thing is defined as an intersection of properties whose parts are exterior to each other, and the only relations recognised between entities are external and mechanical, in the narrower sense of a motion imparted and received or the wider sense of a function and variable. A function is some recursive operation yielding a recursive result that can be modified by some variable (*PP*, 41, 55, 122).

A variable is any changeable factor in an operation or state of something that can be measured so as to grasp its causal contribution to or influence on that operation or state. If we examine atmospheric pressure, we find that it varies according to altitude, temperature, concentration of water vapour

---

[13] Hammond, Howarth and Keat 1991, 130.

and wind, which affects air density. A cardinal discovery of objective thought in modern science is that we can pin down these changeable factors, demonstrating how the precise altitude or precise concentration of water is affecting atmospheric pressure in some locale. We do not merely enumerate the number of variables with this detached and third-person approach, but isolate the specific causal contribution of each to the operation or state. It can be determined from outside independently of all the other variables. Such a procedure is clearly adequate to the regions of macroscopic physics and chemistry and closely associated disciplines. But its undoubted coherence, explanatory value and sheer utility does not entail that the human world – or the environment of the animal – can reasonably be accounted for in its terms. In these milieus we do not encounter fully determined or fully determinable entities in states or functions that exhibit merely external relations. Objective thought gives us a different reality to the one we actually live within and negotiate. Its so-called world is really the idea of a scientific universe, of a complete totality where all relations are reciprocally determined. The notion of a world, by contrast, is that of an open and indefinite multiplicity where relations are reciprocally implicated (*PP*, 73, 122).

Before explicating our being in the world, it will be helpful to show that objective thought is already at work pre-scientifically. We can begin by revisiting the achievements underpinning ordinary perception. Following Husserl, their anonymity amounts to a ruse through which we miss its constituted character, motivating us to believe that an object is the fully accessible source of its significance. This prepares the way for the theoretical 'perceiving' that asserts a total command of the perceived (*PP*, 57, 69). Objective thought commences with an idea going beyond actual perception, that of the thing in itself. To show its genealogy, Merleau-Ponty comes back to the aforementioned example of a house. We have perceived it from many perspectives, from the road, hillside, riverbank and aeroplane. We have also walked around and through it. In these interested and horizonal episodes we have achieved a transition synthesis (*PP*, 70, 72, 340, 344). On foot of it, meant or conceptual identification grasps the intended as a certain type of thing.[14] Each aspect and its subsidiary features as

---

[14] Here Merleau-Ponty does not discern a synthesis of identification, which on his view would link different aspects of an object through an intellectual act that can be reproduced in recollection. But no such act could link sensations and then perspectival appearances of the object together from outside. The epistemic subject's act of connecting must draw on a prior unity, which is not the unity of a substratum of properties or 'empty X' to be posited behind appearances, rather a unity to be found in them or constituted in their flow (*PP*, 250, 286, 333, 340–1, 442–3). The thing's spatial

directly revealed from each perspective are cognised as actual determinations of a determinable something. In our naïve attitude, we hold that
there is a persisting truth in our perceptions. We believe we have reached
the thing in itself by way of its visible properties (*PP*, 33, 70, 72, 277).

But what do we mean by the house in itself with its properties, some in
front of us, some immediately retained and many remembered when we
are elsewhere? In our everyday and naïve living, we would answer that the
house is not itself any single perspective, or even a series of perspectives, but
something that is independent of any perspective, since it exists apart from
us. But this would be the house as seen from nowhere. There would have
been no intentional acts having it as their correlate, so it would never have
been perceived in the first instance. The obvious retort is that we grasp its
independence in commencing our successive experiences of it. What we
really mean on examination is that the house in itself is something that can
be seen from everywhere, so long as it remains within perceptual range
from further along the riverbank or road or higher in the sky. We may have
journeyed far away from it, but we can always revisit it so long as we are
able, assuming that it has not collapsed through age or undergone demolition. What we come to intend and explicitly posit in our statements is an
enduring, re-identifiable empirical particular capable of further determination by us. It is an existent-in-itself that we can explore and articulate ever
anew. In a more familiar language, the house exists an hour away from us,
and is waiting should we be interested in returning. Its features are available
to all, though each of us will be attracted to different ones (*PP*, 69, 71, 72).

Most of us are never aware of syntheses of transition and of horizons,
though we sometimes realise that perception is perspectival and temporal,
that we always see from a single if changeable standpoint and over
a duration. Yet we ordinarily forget its perspectival character, and the
positing of the house as a thing in itself goes beyond the limits of perceptual

---

identity in a sliding transition is found via the identity of the perceiving and exploring body, and its
interdependent temporal identity via the synthesis of time, with both effecting a transition synthesis
(*PP*, 191, 440–3, 446). Richard Zaner has argued that such a synthesis cannot do all the work
Merleau-Ponty wants it to, since a single identity is apprehended in and between successive aspects.
They are all apprehended as the thing itself seen at different times. The synthesis of transition has to
run with a noematic synthesis of identification. Otherwise there could be no differentiation of the
object as intended and the intended object (promising still more appearances). More than this,
Merleau-Ponty gets the identification wrong (Zaner 1964, 176–9, 226–30). Because the performative
synthesis of identification is a passive synthesis on the part of a pre-egoic pole of awareness, the
apprehending sense or perceptual noema of the perceived object at this pre-predicative stage does
not have a core or determinable 'X' apart from its apparent qualities. Rather, it is aimed at in the
sense as the enduring thing the qualities are determining. Only at the expressive stage of intellectual
positing is it set apart as the bearer of these appearances as predicates. *Ids1*, 310–14; *CM*, 41–2.

experience definitively. It is an idea, and more specifically the idea of the thing as the absolute, self-contained pole of all experiences. We regard it as a plenitude that is already the sum-total of what any possible perspective on it might reveal. When we posit the house as seen from everywhere, we are referring beyond its visible walls and gables and windows. The idea includes its invisible foundations and water pipes and hairline cracks spreading in its ceilings. They are not seen or otherwise perceived by us, yet we believe that the house *has* them. That we genuinely reach the thing in perceiving it is a warranted belief, but the thought of the thing in itself is different in kind. It is the conception of a finished object that is utterly translucent, capable of being shot through by an infinity of gazes that simultaneously intersect at its innermost depths, comprising a comprehensive 'x-ray picture' from all angles that leaves nothing hidden whatsoever. We forget that we can have only one standpoint at a time, and that our memory of perspectives only builds up gradually and fitfully. Thinking that memory has captured aspects of the thing, we are often surprised when new perceptions reveal its fallibility. We remain in thrall to the notion that the object is a crystalline being to be exhausted by the adequate perception that we fail to enjoy because of our finitude (*PP*, 71, 72–3).

In this way, we are perpetuating the idea of a supreme awareness for which everything lies in full and open view. As noted earlier, Husserl maintains that we cannot even imagine what a panoptical grasp would look like, and it cannot be reconciled with the transcendence of an empirical thing. Yet its possibility is more often accepted without examination, which points to the ongoing influence of a certain theology and which Merleau-Ponty could say more about. But one way or another, the notion of the thing grasped through and through in an elevated and incorrigible vision founds the ideal of explicit and fully objective knowledge first developed in logic. In the same blow, it prefigures the modern idea of the universe, regarded as a thoroughly surveyable totality (*PP*, 62, 73, 173). Natural science is the sequel and amplification of the pre-scientific idea of the fully accessible thing in itself. The scientific concept of nature is taken as the way of finally fixing and objectifying the phenomena, whose true being is the invariant in all perceptual fields for all properly trained perceivers. With the concept we can come to eliminate indeterminacy and individual bias (*PP*, 54, 74).

Early modern science worked with the ideal model of a homogeneous and geometrical space indifferent to what it contains, and of a pure movement that does not change the properties of the object that is moving. Galileo conceives of a perfect sphere on a frictionless plane, which if pushed will move in a straight line to infinity. In Newton's first law of motion, a body continues in its state of rest or uniform motion in a straight line unless it is compelled to alter this state by forces that are impressed on it. Phenomena could be measured against a completely inert milieu of existence, such that each event could be linked to the conditions responsible for intervening changes (the aforementioned variables), and where each event contributes to the physical determination of being. With Lavoisier and Dalton, it was realised that the chemical properties of bodies could be established statistically. A certain conception of 'the thing' came to predominate – it could be comprehended without any remainder. Even those who asserted that the scientific determination of the empirical thing would never be complete agreed that there was nothing to say about it beyond what natural science can tell us (*PP*, 54–5).

Given this view of the thing in general, the living body was not to escape determination through physico-chemical properties. It came to be understood as a machine that could be studied from the outside, through an objective and third-person study. Conceived as such, it was an assembly of sensory functions related externally and mechanically, and therefore capable of being studied individually. Sight could be determined apart from hearing and apart from the functions of affectivity and motility. The receptors convey separate sensory qualities that are purely visual or auditory or tactile and so on. Though these are brought together in the brain, we can isolate the different modes of received data before this happens. And as with sensing, so too with our being in the world, which was called 'behaviour' and attributed to the intersecting of multiple causalities. These determine my body and psyche (*PP*, lxxi, 10–11, 55–6). Some thinkers were satisfied with this physicalist characterisation, whereas others wished to preserve a domain of reason, freedom and purpose. This led them to posit a mind or soul above the mechanical body, a consciousness radically distinct from the physical in being thinking and unextended. Consciousness can comprehend itself objectively, if not pictorially, for its modes of thinking can be introspectively isolated and explicated in their own terms (*PP*, 25, 57–9).

It had to be claimed that physical actions come from free acts of will in the realm of reasons, for otherwise they would be determined causally. But to the will only an instantaneous fiat was allowed. In this way, a peculiar slant was given to the view of human action set out by Edith Stein, which has three distinguishable moments. There is the *fieri* or what may be done, which involves the envisioning of the outcome of an action. When I consider doing something, I frame a scenario imaginatively. I represent to myself what the result would look like and feel like, and in a broad and loose sense I may even imagine the course of action. The *fiat* is the act of will that it be done, the decision to embark on and complete the course of action. Integral with it is the *facere* or the making real, the bringing into actuality of the being-willed.[15] On Merleau-Ponty's reading, Cartesianism recast these moments in terms of what I call a representation, decision and implementation model. Choices are made immediately (if sometimes after deliberation) and imposed on the body from above. After the discrete decision, the body moves without delay, making it real in the world. Once I have chosen to pursue what I have imagined, it is left to my mechanical system to promptly implement the decision and to therefore realise the representation. Intelligent movements owe all their intelligence to the mind.[16] It is accepted that many movements are due to physical causes, either directly or by way of the passions that some of these excite. But so long as there are actions in the proper sense ensuing from free decisions, the body is an indifferent servant of the mind and will. It places a huge range of possible movements at their disposal, but these possibilities are not internally related to the decisions and actions (*PP*, 55–6, 452). In Rasmus Jensen's rendering, the extended and physical body is taken as agency-neutral. Its movements are bare occurrences fully amenable to scientific explanation.[17]

Because all sensing and moving had been placed within physical nature, the conscious subject's practical stance towards the world (from which it had been sundered) was absorbed into the body. In working through its parts scientifically, we could follow the transmission of sensory data from the inner and outer receptors into the brain and central nervous system, explaining both empirical presentations and the mechanical reactions to them (*PP*, 55–6). The consequence was that:

> The living body thus transformed ceased to be my body, that is, the visible expression of a concrete Ego, in order to become one object among all others. Correlatively, another's body could not appear to me as the envelope of another ego. It was nothing more than a machine, and the perception of another person could not truly be of another person, since it resulted from an inference and thus only placed consciousness in general behind the automaton, a transcendent cause and not someone actually inhabiting its movements . . . Thus, while the living body became an exterior without an interior, subjectivity became an interior without an exterior, that is, an impartial spectator. The naturalism of science and the spiritualism of the

---

[15] Stein 1989, 54–5.   [16] Descartes 1984c, 343–4.   [17] Jensen 2009, 376–7.

universal constituting subject, to which reflection upon science leads, share
in a certain levelling out of experience: standing before the constituting I,
the empirical Myselves are merely objects. (*PP*, 56)

To all effects, Cartesianism (and intellectualism more generally) posited an
impersonal awareness, since it was no longer individuated or particularised
by the body, having nothing in common with the world. On this picture
there could be nothing in common – that consciousness can have no integral
relationship with a purely physical and mechanical body and a wider environment is something that Cartesianism is quite correct to affirm (*PP*, 56,
367). Hence the picture must be abandoned as a fundamental distortion of
our projective and expressive being in the world. And in doing this, we will
realise that the transcendental field of possibilities intended and co-intended
in every perceptual or phenomenal field is founded on a somatically limited
power and a certain point of view (*PP*, 62, 65, 93).

Merleau-Ponty notes that natural science has already begun to move away
from first-generation objective thought, and is thoroughly reworking its
foundations. The completely determined natural object was the first to give
way, since the new physics deals with quanta of energy with fields of influence,
predicting their effects in terms of statistical probabilities. It has also been
recognised that natural space is not geometrical, only appearing as such to the
theorising observer limited to certain macroscopic givens (*PP*, 57, 414). Even
more interesting are developments in current biology, which have led to a new
conception of organisms in their lived milieus. And when we come to look at
human society, we find that it is not of itself a community of reasonable
spirits. Such a conception could only get off the ground 'in privileged
countries where vital and economic equilibrium has been established locally
and for a certain length of time' (*PP*, 57). But there are two good reasons why
our concern has to remain with philosophical and psychological theories. The
contemporary revision of basic scientific concepts and suppositions still can
and often does run with a scientific realism and naturalism in which the
physical processes are understood as more real than our experiences in the
lifeworld, as the new fundaments of true and independent being.
Furthermore, many of the theories still show an attachment to the first-
generation framework of objective thought. Phenomenology has to overcome
their unquestioned belief in a determinate world without recourse to intro-
spection. It must reveal the pre-scientific life of conscious and sub-conscious
awareness by way of intentional analysis, but only after we criticise empiricism
and intellectualism. The critiques are necessary detours before presenting the
alternative.

CHAPTER 2

Sensations, Associations and Explanations

2.1 Introduction

When we begin to reflect on perception, according to Merleau-Ponty, we immediately run into the word 'sensation' with its seemingly clear and unambiguous meaning. We sense red or blue or hot or cold. In saying this, we believe we know perfectly well what it is to see, to hear and to sense, because in giving us sensations, perception has given us coloured or sonorous objects that we transport into awareness (*PP*, 3, 5). Modern empiricists may not accept such an everyday story in its totality, but do seek to begin with the simple sensation or impression or sense-datum, contending that it is an immediate and incontrovertible given. In their procedure, as they see it, they are going back to what is most basic in perceptual terms, and in this way are avoiding extravagant metaphysical speculations and other unwarranted constructions. We progress by associ-ation from simple to complex sensations, and from there to still further associative mechanisms. These build up the world of everyday phenomena that natural science is comprehending in its depths. A purely empirical psychology avoids distortions and contributes to scientific advance. It appreciates that the data that are perceived are outcomes of a process beginning with the efficient causality of outer stimuli. These act on the peripheral organs of reception before being carried inwards and converted into representations.

Merleau-Ponty argues that the very idea of a sensation is confused, and that, in accepting it, the empirical psychology succeeding empiricist phil-osophy emerges as the one that is least able to give an account of percep-tion, since it does not reveal what experience actually delivers, to the extent of having missed the phenomenon of perception (*PP*, 3, 27). A large part of his critique of empiricism is an elaboration of the phenomenological claim that we do not see or hear sensations, but what they present. I commence this chapter by running through the empiricist notion of the simple sensation of a determinate quality and the constancy hypothesis. Merleau-Ponty rejects both the simplicity thesis and the revised view that in good conditions we encounter complex determinate qualities mirroring the thing as it is in itself. All perception is intentional or proto-intentional, does not entail constancy with stimuli, and does not purge its objects of their indeterminacy. Gestalt psychology's retention of external association as an autonomous process is also rejected, since it fails to give due weight to the original patterning of 'data' in a significant fashion within the perceptual field. In its examples, moreover, empiricism privileges vision and neglects the intermodal nature of perception. I go on to consider the objection that Merleau-Ponty's critique does not bear on contemporary or second-generation objective thought. The descriptive priority of lived intentional awareness for phenomenology must give way to the explanatory priority of the physical processes discovered by the new sciences. Merleau-Ponty would respond that the new scientist never departs from the natural attitude in the midst of theorising and in practice works with ineliminable and eminently justified beliefs concerning the lifeworld.

2.2 On Sensations of Determinate Qualities

For empiricism, the simple sensation or sense datum of a determinate quality is the fundamental unit of explanation, for everything else in perception is built on it. A pure sensation is the experience of receiving or undergoing an undifferentiated, atomic and instantaneous impression, and this is what scientific analysis must recover. Each self-standing organ of reception picks up and convey inwards the sensations that it is uniquely equipped to register. An anatomical trajectory leads from the peripheral and determinate receiver through a definite transmitter to the final recording post that is itself specialised. The process occurs prior to the qualities registered from the different sense organs being brought together in the brain. The existence of a determinate world being accepted as a given, it is assumed that the world confides messages that, following their reception and transmission, are finally decoded in such a way as to reproduce in us the original text. The reproduction will of course be distorted by variable conditions of observation. We have only to think of a sense organ that is damaged, of fog or excessive brightness or the distance of observation. But there is in principle if not always in fact – or even ordinarily – a point-by-point correspondence between the stimuli out there and the elementary perceptions in here. Empiricism works with a constancy hypothesis to the effect that there is an identity of form or isomorphic constancy between the causal original and derivative presentation in the absence of extraneous influences (*PP*, 3, 6, 7–8).

For Merleau-Ponty, it is understandable why one would initially posit a bare sensation that comes from without, such that one is a passive recipient of this causal impingement. There are without doubt situations in which our experience seems to be close to the pure experience of a pure quality. We might think of those intervening moments when our waking perceptual life is shutting down or not properly booted up. There is the greyness onto blankness that envelops us when we are dropping into sleep, and the vague noise or hum that is not clearly identifiable when we are gradually waking up, still in that strange half-life between sleep and wakefulness. With a confused and disoriented feeling that the unfamiliar has forced itself into awareness, we find ourselves scrabbling to pick out what it could be. When we perceive wakefully, however, we predelineate what is impinging on us when it does, unless it is a loud noise or dazzling light so painful as to invade us. Far from being passive recipients, we zone in on something actively and intentionally. Yet the terminology of picking out and zoning in on something presupposes a contrast within the perceptual field that lets us apprehend a certain configuration in the first place. A simple visual example is a dark patch on a white background, already complex as the product of a colour contrast. And as I pick it out the configuration it is already charged with a sense. It points beyond itself in that it has triggered signitive and horizonal expectations going beyond what is directly present. Because even a simple patch of colour appears *on* the background rather than merely interrupting it, it is referring beyond its visible surface (*PP*, 3–4, 221, 329).

Everything in describable experience speaks in favour of the conclusion that what is most basic in the most elementary perception is the figure and background structure. What I perceive is always a configuration in a field.[1] This is an essential structure of perception itself, not a contingent fact. More than this, the figure is internally related to its surroundings. A red patch on a carpet is affected by the wider figure or wider background within which it is located. Apart from needing light to be a phenomenon, it must be a certain size in a pattern to stand out from the latter, and it must contrast strongly enough with the adjoining colours. If these were dark orange or light purple, for example, it might not be possible to see the red. If surrounded by white or blue, moreover, it would not be the same shade (*PP*, 3–5). The empiricist might object that none of this shows the essential

---

[1] Köhler 1938, 23, 35–6.

necessity of the figure and background structure. Even as a developed perceiver, I can imagine myself floating in a blank or featureless environment, as if in the middle of a cloud, yet I would still be seeing the white or the grey (in adverbialist language, I would be seeing 'whitely' or 'greyly'). Lawrence Hass has rejoined that a figure would nonetheless be implicated in the experience. The empiricist presumption is that a figure in a perception must be *in front* of me. Even in the seeing of the white or the grey, my own body, real or imagined, comprises the figure. I am thrown back on it, coming to focally feel and see myself as the perceiver visually traversing the blank expanse from just here. The figure–background structure cannot exclude a causal story, but it does make what is apprehended more than a causal representation.[2]

These descriptions do not remove the worry that what are being referred to all the time are the contents of developed perceptions, when simple sensations have come to be worked over extensively by empirical associations, explicit identifications and imaginative experiences based on memories. Today the sensations are informed by the acquired capacities of a mature awareness, but did not look the same in their primal forms. Merleau-Ponty would seem to have succumbed to what empirical psychologists and psychophysicists have entitled 'the stimulus error'. The empiricist can defend the occurrence of simple and determinate sensations, while readily granting that their recovery is not easy to accomplish, since in giving a report about the experience of a sensory quality we make the mistake of reading into that report what we know from our subsequent associations and educations. The sensation is confused with the stimulus, with the larger object out of which it is built in concert with other sensations, and with the acquired meaning assigned to the object. It is an error that occurs unconsciously and unavoidably, but through controlled observational conditions and the special training of observers it can be surmounted. By employing every means of precise experimentation at our disposal, we shall reveal sensations of determinate qualities purged of anything equivocal.[3]

In response, Merleau-Ponty argues that the pure sensation of a pure quality could not count as a perception in the first place, for the perceiver and the perceived would then coincide perfectly, to the extent of being utterly indistinguishable. Not to sense anything is not to sense at all. The empiricist has tacitly converted an element of awareness – a necessary moment of a perception's empirical content – into an object of awareness,

---

[2] Hass 2008, 30–1.   [3] Boring 1921, 450–1, 469–70.

while simultaneously affirming that this 'object' is a mute impression signifying nothing. And even if we were to grant that an element can be isolated in and for itself, we cannot conclude that it would remain unmodified in the process. Its revelation would only be possible because the observer has been artificially detached from his or her everyday commerce with the world, so that he or she is no longer an engaged participant. The empirical psychologist or psychophysicist puts the perceiver into a laboratory situation and assumes that the sensed quality that is revealed as a result is identical to the one presented – and purportedly hidden under subsequent accretions – when that perceiver is out in the world. An artificial product is read back into ordinary perception as one of its primitive elements, though there is no such element to be revealed in the lifeworld. It is forgotten that causal contributions and active perceivers are implicated in founding and founded relationships in which they influence each other reciprocally at all levels (*PP*, 5, 10–11, 13). Thus the empiricist commits what William James had called 'the psychologist's fallacy'. The end-product of a controlled situation is mistaken for a basic element of an ordinary situation within which it would stand in merely external relations.[4]

The proponent of empiricism may go on to reply that a revised and refined account is not committed to the idea of sensations of simple determinate qualities. What we encounter in our perceptual episodes are complexes of determinate qualities, and in good observational conditions we can and do apprehend these complexes without having recourse to highly controlled situations in laboratories. Certainly these qualities cannot cover the whole perceptual field, which is vague and fuzzy at its perimeter. At the edge there are indeterminate causal impingements incapable of being isolated and described. But this is not a problem, for our eyes are always pointed towards some particular sector of the visual field like searchlights. In good conditions they focus on and pick out a complex of qualities. Surrounding this figure to which we give attention is an imprecise fringe and beyond that the vague margin of the field. The word 'see' denotes success when one reports the vision of those determinate complexes making up empirical particulars. We can admit that perception is perspectival, but so far as the focal something is in clear view we will have a sensational complex that is free of indeterminacy or ambiguity, corresponding point by point with the outer stimuli. We have reached the thing itself and can – always in principle and sometimes in fact – work back to

---

[4] James 1981, 195.

the causal originals. Wherever there was confusion, it was solely confusion for us (*PP*, 4, 6).

Against this view, Merleau-Ponty notes that the clarity and distinctness of the presentation does not require an isomorphic constancy with the so-called originals. When small red and green dots are placed at certain intervals, for example, we see a uniform grey colour, as if the perceived surface were in fact uniform. And within an area of continuous colour under the same illumination, the different chromatic thresholds of rods and cones in the retina (and the blind spot) ought to make it one shade here, another there and achromatic in a third place, yet it also shows itself as uniform. Thus the sensible can no longer be described as the immediate effect of an external stimulus, and the cost of a constancy within a sensational complex (or an empirical perceptual constancy) is the absence of a constancy between that complex and the stimuli (*PP*, 8–9). This requires a revised conception of sensing:

> The sensory apparatus itself, as modern physiology imagines it, is no longer appropriate to the role of 'transmitter' that it was made to play by classical science .... [a]t the elementary level of sensibility, we catch sight of a collaboration between partial stimuli and between the sensorial system and the motor system that, through a variable physiological constellation, keeps the sensation constant, and thus rules out any definition of the nervous process as the simple transmission of a given message .... normal functioning must be understood as a process of integration in which the text of the external world is not copied, but constituted. And if we try to grasp 'sensation' from the perspective of its preparatory bodily phenomena, we do not discover a psychical individual, a function of certain known variables, but rather a formation already tied to an ensemble and already endowed with a sense. (*PP*, 9)

Advances in physiology and psychology have made the idea of an external world that is duplicated inside us redundant. And when we re-examine perception, we not only find constituted constancies in sensing but also advance selection. In the visual field most notably, certain qualities are always foregrounded, and when we focus on complete or partially occluded figures we do not at first pick them out indifferently. Their outlines and other features are selected and foregrounded according to the sub-egoic significances that they have for our lived and embodied awareness. Only some (and comparatively few) features will be picked out in the perception of a threatening figure because it will be configured urgently by the organism in order to facilitate its survival, whether or not a genuine threat is posed. It is a biological imperative that error always fall on the side of caution, for much less will be lost if a mistake has been made. When something is alluring in its appeal to a human interest, our sense organs are employed in a noticeably different way. Psychological, physiological and biological conditions collaborate, such that the peripheral stages of reception cannot be regarded as discrete. They are caught up in relations previously consigned to the central cortices alone (*PP*, 9–11, 195).

Other empiricists hold the qualified view that sustained and systematic attention brings us to *some* determinate qualities of the thing in itself. Closer examination will uncover elements that make up isomorphic constancies, without our having to believe that the ultimate elements are simple or that the constancies pertain to the entire sensational complex. We can work down from some features of a grossly perceived whole to precisely perceived parts, with these parts themselves comprising complex components of the totality. There are of course many appearances that will shift or decompose into other ones, and that evade everyday precision. In vision, the apparent size of a complex may vary at some distances, and a uniform colour will change according to magnification. But for the empiricist, these changes can still be explained. The influence of variables can be charted by the new sciences of light and colour and vision, and the core point is that we are not barred from arriving at other qualities that are objectively real and context-independent inside a sensed complex. These fall within the class of primary and properly measurable qualities, as described by early modern science and philosophy. The Müller-Lyer illusion brings out one such quality. When we pay close attention to its figures, we find the identity in length of the two parallel and horizontal lines (*PP*, 6, 8).

There is little doubt that such identities are to be found within figures. The problem for Merleau-Ponty is that in original and everyday perception the straight lines in the illusion are not seen as unequal, for they are nested within wider figures that are seen straight off as cramped on the one hand and sprawling on the others. In the field of lived perception, the overall figures have different senses that are not at all visualised in terms of measurement. The empiricist can reply that if one figure looks longer and is longer, we can still pay close attention to both in order to discern the equality in length of the horizontal lines. Once we distil out their equality we escape from the indeterminacy or ambiguity that is conveyed by terms such as 'cramped' and 'sprawling'. But this claim turns out to be a statement of the problem rather than its resolution. The precision and clarity involved in measurement has entailed a departure from originally lived perception and its description, replacing it with sustained theoretical inspection and dissection. It has necessarily involved a shift, not to a world of unbiased appearances delivering true realities, but instead to an abstract and artificial universe of mathematical ideality to which the two lines approximate more or less closely. We find that objective thought has again been brought into play, with the empiricist again falling into the psychologist's error. To project the abstracted element back into each configuration is to construe that element as a real and perceptually independent piece of the initial configuration, and hence as one of its basic building blocks (*PP*, 6–7, 8, 12).

It can be added that the Müller-Lyer illusion is not common to all human cultures and communities. Those people who have grown up in rural and non-western environments are much less susceptible to it. One hypothesis is that they do not spend most of their lives in our highly engineered or 'carpentered' environment of rectilinear and regular shapes, which leads them to zone in on such configurations in a more studied way. More than this, Merleau-Ponty seems to pass over the fact that those in industrialised societies frequently read their education in geometry (if not in measurement) into the things that they encounter. They do not so much shift systematically into an artificial and ideal universe as unconsciously project some of the features of the latter into their everyday perceptual episodes. John Drummond has contended that scientific standards of accuracy have been imported into our original understanding of the world and of worldly beings. This is why we do not speak of things as box-shaped or ball-shaped, referring to them instead as 'rectangular' and 'spherical'. We speak and write in this way because objective thought's portrayal of our world with its attendant – and highly valued – canon of exactness has become an important part of our cultural heritage, to the extent that it mediates our ordinary experience of certain figures by way of its theoretical judgements, which have come to operate as secondary passivities in our perceptual lives.[5]

2.3   Association and Memory

Gestalt theory is a refined empiricism that takes the figure–background structure as central, while construing the figure as a plurality of qualities comprising a block of space. We glance over and inspect it, so perception is no longer defined by the atomic impression, even if it is not appreciated

---

[5] Drummond 1983, 180, 199. Merleau-Ponty refers to the milieu we constitute through measurement, but makes little of this or of scientific concepts as secondary passivities. *PP*, 37.

that the thing in its inexhaustible aspects is never a bare block. The plurality of qualities is distinctive in the perceptual field in that it is configured into stable contours standing out from this background. The new empiricism then asks old questions. How do we take some visual qualities as making up a unity? How do they collectively gain an outer boundary to stand out from their background and possess significance? Following a traditional account, we have psychological mechanisms for associating contiguous and resemblant qualities, and these are allied to the projection of memories. In the past, I sensed a plurality of resemblant qualities beside each other, externally related by contiguity. With the onset of movement that involved a change of place, I noticed that some qualities stayed together, unlike those of the stationary background, which were left behind. This led me to associate the moving qualities, to bundle or group them together such that the ensuing complex made up one visual figure. When I subsequently encounter the same qualities standing still, the past association is remembered, the memory is projected on to these qualities, and in this manner the later grouping is recognised as the same figure or as a similar one (*PP*, 13, 15–17, 340).

Even as it moves away from objective thought, gestalt psychology retains this model. The form of grouping that is most natural involves the smallest interval, the factor of proximity. Like qualities tend to be grouped together, which is the factor of similarity, and qualities moving together manifest the factor of common fate. An apprehension of 'good form' is achieved when a grouping makes up a continuous or fully bounded figure, when a high proportion of the sensory data is registered, and when the qualities between different figures are less distinctive and more equivocal than those within the figures. Interior data are then 'pregnant' with the overall features of the figure. They are contributors to a closed pattern.[6] Merleau-Ponty notes that there are many groupings of sensed qualities that we never see in motion. We need only imagine those that present mountains and valleys and buildings. From visual inspection, it is not clear how the fixed groupings can be shown to be adherent, holding their qualities together to preserve their existing outer boundaries. This difficulty is compounded by the fact that a quality can be further from and less similar to a second quality within an overall grouping than it is to a further quality beyond the outer boundary of that grouping. We cannot be assured that an exterior quality will be less distinctive and more equivocal than the interior ones. There would seem to be nothing that can stop us perceiving at least parts of

[6] Wertheimer 1938, 74–5, 78–9, 82–3.

the sensible intervals between groups or figures as themselves parts of the figures (*PP*, 16–17).

The solution to the adherence, dissimilarity and distance problems lies in the exercise of one's powers of movement. When I move towards or to the side of a complex, I discover that some qualities – be they similar or dissimilar or more or less proximate – will detach themselves from what I took to be the overall figure, while others will not, no matter what standpoint I come to assume. But another problem cannot be disposed of so easily. Gestaltism perpetuates traditional empiricism in tacitly allowing that what we see may be made up of punctual, externally related qualities that have been associated through the factors of proximity and similarity. Let us assume that I am looking at qualities grouped together through these two factors, and that their association was easier because I remembered a past association and projected it onto this plurality. If the past association also depended on just these factors, we will be caught in a regress when we try to find criteria for recognising the commonality between the present complex or figure and the past one and its predecessor. If the individual similarity and bare spatial proximity of discrete qualities are the sole and decisive criteria for association, then the qualities might be associated differently each time, for they have the common characteristic of being building blocks that can be put together in ever-new ways. It is then hard to explain how the present assemblage of qualities could prevent a swarm of memories. Memory could call up every previous bundle or grouping of qualities that were individually similar to the qualities in the present grouping and collectively just as proximate, yet the *overall* figures could look dissimilar (*PP*, 16–7, 22–3).

For Merleau-Ponty, memory ultimately presupposes what it is meant to explain, and the projection of past associations onto present ones is an unfortunate metaphor hiding a deeper and achieved recognition (*PP*, 20–1). To the extent that it follows traditional empiricism, gestalt psychology of perception remains in thrall to objective thought. When it introduces the ideas of pattern and pregnancy, it provides an escape route, but its formulations do not exploit it. What should have been realised is that the proximity and similarity of punctual parts are not adequate for original and subsequent recognition. Punctuality has to give way to pattern and pregnancy as the decisive criteria. When I am seeing something, it does of course have a plurality of qualities, but they are not grouped in just any order. What is seen is a figure whose form is never a mere assemblage of externally related components. Rather, the figure is presented through a *specific* arrangement or configuration or structure. What is apprehended is an organised and integral whole, a particular pattern to which each quality makes its own contribution, being pregnant with the wider whole and therefore able to signify beyond itself, as we shall see. Because the qualities are already structured the figure has significance. What are associated temporally are a past structure and its successor. As indicative of a certain wider configuration, a present arrangement is a trigger for the memory of a certain earlier one, which reciprocally completes the present configuration, lifting it out of its background. Similarity pertains to patterns of wholes rather than to supposedly discrete parts, and when explicit and reportable identification takes place, a passive synthesis of pattern discernment has already done its work (*PP*, 19–20, 22–3).

The apprehension of a familiar object provides a suitable illustration. Imagine that I am walking along a beach and I see something sticking out above a sand dune, with its bottom largely occluded. There are features at the top of this something that are at first invisible, for they merge with the forest bordering on the dune. As I get closer, these features begin to stand out against the forest. If my unfolding perception seized on all of these punctually or individually, I would initially see what looks like a long wedge above the dune. Following on this and higher up, I would pick out what looks like a cross, and to the right of it a rectangle. But these are not what I perceive, for as I approach, I feel a tension in the situation. The features are coalescing and yet they look unfinished and unsettling; I feel the sort of uneasiness one feels in expecting a rain torrent from a storm cloud. As I get a little closer, the situation is suddenly resolved. I undergo an interpretative shift in which the shapes coalesce fully, and I realise I am seeing a ship that has run aground. It is experienced in one presentation that bridges all the disparities. Its partially occluded sides and superstructure are sticking out above the dune and its mast and funnel are sticking out against the forest. These details did not amount originally to good form, but they were enough to trigger the memory of other ships seen in unbroken aspects (at least above their waterlines). They let the past bring the present configuration to the fore because they were referring beyond themselves, being pregnant with the remembered pattern that their own arrangement served to reawaken (*PP*, 17–18).

After I perceive the ship as such, I may well discern some proximities and similarities amid the disparate details. The funnel is not far from the mast and is the same colour as the superstructure on closer inspection. But it is to be stressed that proximity and similarity were not the original and decisive criteria for recognition, rather the present patterning of data in a significant fashion. To perceive visually is to see an immanent sense bursting forth from a present constellation of givens without which no call to memory would have been possible, and for this reason to remember is not to bring before the conscious gaze a self-subsistent picture of the past. In not distinguishing passive and active syntheses, furthermore, empiricism forgets that there is always someone who sees, who has taken advantage of the prior association of patterned wholes and who explicitly recognises a certain thing, experiencing a harmony between what is evoked and what is presented. Even as it stands, the evidence of experience should have led to the conclusion that the relations of figure and background, thing and non-thing and the horizon of the past are structures of givenness for intentional awareness that are irreducible to the qualities appearing in and through them. Objects could never exist for us if they appeared through a mental chemistry of external and contingent associations. All knowledge becomes established through the horizons opened up by perception (*PP*, 23–4, 215, 334).

2.4   On Intersensory Perception

The foregoing discussions and examples relate to the seeing of things, and Merleau-Ponty maintains that horizonal structures of awareness are also to be found organising the other modalities of sense. In our being in the world each mode displays its own figure and background, even if it does not display an order of co-existences in the manner of vision. Hence we experience different forms of resistance, recognising our passive being-touched by wind or water, our actively or haptically coming to touch something, the light surface touch and the hard voluminous touch. In a piece of carved wood, we distinguish the smoothness of the worked surface from the coarseness of the grain that we also apprehend beneath it. With our ear, we distinguish the sound of something against the silence, or against the background of other noises. So too with the aroma of the rose, which pleases us against the more or less odourless air, or which delights us after the acrid smell of exhaust fumes. And all of these experiences signify beyond what is currently presented, which tells us once again that there are no bare givens. To touch or smell something is to predelineate the wider whole as attractive or repulsive. This is why we run our hands over what we have encountered, or quickly pull away from it, and likewise seek to get closer to or further from the source of a sound or a smell. Each encounter with this or that actuality is pointing forwards to a certain possibility (*PP*, 329–30, 343).

Reflection on modern empiricism shows that it has usually given priority to vision at the expense of the other senses. The privileging of vision goes back as least as far as Aristotle, who states that everyone desires to know, and that the mark of this is the esteem we accord to vision. In revealing the most differences, it is the highest of the senses.[7] Aristotle nonetheless recognises touch as the most important for life, and the unity of the senses with his idea of the *koinê aisthêsis* or common sense, a perceptual capacity by means of which the five specialised senses that he identifies are integrated.[8] Yet the modern empiricisms of first-generation objective thougzht are not so careful. In their pictures, as we have noted, separate receptors are held to convey pure and distinct sensory qualities that are brought together in the brain, and then only as the result of linkages that we gradually establish in our post-natal development. As Hass has observed, Locke provides an early and definitive expression of this view. Prior to their combination, our simple ideas of colour and coldness and hardness and so forth are produced by the mind, initially working on qualities that have entered by the senses simple and unmixed.[9] It is because they hold to such a theory, according to Merleau-Ponty, that modern empiricists have most often described sensations and their causal conditions like the fauna of a distant land. Even after their supposedly derivative combination with other modalities of sensory qualities, the visual 'data' in their description bear the traces of the theoretical emphasis on pure and simple givens. The items we are taken to perceive suggest a world of drifting and anchorless qualia that we have not geared into concretely, a 'portrait' world we perceive *at* without being involved *in*. The neglect of the wider body appears to leave us with a disengaged perceiver, a floating spirit endowed with eyes alone (*PP*, 214, 329–30, 393; *TS*, 241).

Empiricism is right to assert that each sense is specialised, and it is a truism that the structure of each one cannot be transposed onto the others. Empiricism also grants that there must be some way in which the organs of sense work together. If they could not communicate, we would end with a plurality of quasi-worlds, each the correlate of a specialised sensing self. There would be a purely visual world for a purely visual perceiver and a purely tactile world for a purely tactile perceiver and so on. A cognising subject would perch precariously on top of these disjointed worlds with their unique deliverances and unique selves, for its synthesis could not constitute a unity between the senses if none were found at the somatic level. Yet classical empiricism fails to realise that each sense in its

---

[7] Aristotle 1984a, 1552 (*Metaphysics* 980a20–25).
[8] Aristotle 1984b, 676, 691 (*On the Soul* 425a27, 434b10–12).
[9] Locke 1975, 119, quoted in Hass 2008, 28.

gestation is already organised so as to communicate with the other ones. We do not commence with discrete functions that must then be brought into harmony. Instead of being a sum of externally juxtaposed organs, the living and perceiving body is a synergetic system in which the different modalities are taken up and work together (*PP*, 224–5, 232–4, 242–3). On the new view as supported by developments in physiology, the unity between our different organs of sense and between these organs and our powers of movement is an original one. It is not 'produced gradually and through accumulation ... [r]ather this translation and this assemblage are completed once and for all in me' (*PP*, 151). The communal work shortly after birth is of course rudimentary and cannot yet facilitate the performative and recursive syntheses needed for cognitive activities. If new-born babies have no objects, however, their perceptual fields are not what James portrays as blooming and buzzing confusions (*SB*, 168, 176).[10] As Husserl realises, their biological drives find expression in their apprehensions of interest formations (*Interessengebilde*) that bring other modalities into play. Deliverances from one sense carry into the bodily pursuit of impending satisfaction from another, as when a baby turns her head towards her mother's breast on being spurred by olfactory information.[11]

The infant proceeds from interest formations to objects that she investigates with great curiosity, and her originally interconnected organs of sense and the segments of her body are drawn closer together in their actual employment. Their unity evolves by way of the things intended. This is another reason why laboratory conditions cannot isolate sensory qualities in and of themselves, for what the scientist uncovers are the deliverances of modalities already coloured by contributions from all of the others (*PP*, 151, 232–4, 241–2). Their functioning has been intermodal, or as Merleau-Ponty puts it, synaesthetic or intersensory (*PP*, 237–8). Some people exhibit pathological synaesthesia, in which they hear and taste colours and see sounds. They report that one modality *gives* an appearance from another with the same intensity and directness as if the latter had issued from the appropriate organ of sense. But ordinary intentional experience is synaesthetic in that each mode of direct perception appresents other modes of givenness. All the senses speak to each other before they are sundered apart and dissected by the objective thought that distorts empirical

---

[10] James 1981, 462.
[11] Manuscripts C 13 I, 6, 10b; A VI 34, 35a, 36, trans. Smith 2003, 152. See also *SB*, 176–7.

psychology, though the best illustrations can be drawn from a well-developed awareness:

> By opening up to the structure of the thing, the senses communicate among themselves. We see the rigidity and the fragility of the glass and, when it breaks with a crystal-clear sound, this sound is borne by the visible glass . . . The form of objects is not their geometrical shape: the form has a certain relation with their very nature and it speaks to all of our senses at the same time as it speaks to vision. The form of a fold in a fabric of linen or of cotton shows us the softness or the dryness of the fibre . . . In the movement of the branch from which a bird has just left, we read its flexibility and its elasticity, and this is how the branch of an apple tree and the branch of a birch are immediately distinguished. We see the weight of a block of cast iron that sinks into the sand, the fluidity of the water, and the viscosity of the syrup. Likewise, I hear the hardness and the unevenness of the cobblestones in the sound of a car, and we are right to speak of a 'soft', 'dull', or 'dry' sound. (*PP*, 238–9)

If we accept that most intentional objects in our perceptual episodes are predominantly thematised through a single modality, that particular sense still communicates with the other ones through a common and significant core. When I see the apple's roundness in my bag its feel is conveyed, and when I scrunch up my foot inside my shoe its look is conveyed. I am not encountering two different figures, the one tactile and the other visual, but two different ways of encountering the same figure, each appresenting and predelineating the other (*PP*, 150, 239). We are now in a better position to appreciate that a thing is an unsurpassable plenitude in which all its moments point to each other and to future experiences. Though a colour patch must be a certain size and have a certain surround of other colours in order to stand out in the first place, it would not be the same if it were not 'woolly red', if it were not the patch *of* a carpet that has a certain weight and feel and resistance to sound, and a certain place and role in the world of the shop and the home (*PP*, 5, 242, 326, 337).

It is worth stressing that Merleau-Ponty's remarks about the limitations of controlled observational conditions are not tantamount to a denial of what laboratory situations can tell us about causal contributions to experiences, at least when we are not engaged in demanding tasks and situations. Thus we can recognise that certain colours amplify certain responses to things, drawing on scientific investigations that have revealed their inter-modal contributions to ordinary perceptual episodes. Through the systematic observation of patients with injuries to the cerebellum or frontal cortex, it has been shown that colours have attractive or repulsive motor effects. In these cases our ordinary responses to things are accentuated. The specific colour of the figure or background alters the sweep and smoothness and accuracy of arm movements. Bright and intense or saturated colours – particularly red and yellow – generally favour inaccuracy and abduction, a shallower and slower sweep that turns from the stimulus towards the body. Blue and green generally favour accuracy and adduction, a wider, faster sweep that turns towards the stimulus and the world. Patients themselves state that red and yellow have a stinging and violent effect, and that blue and green induce peacefulness and repose. The affective significations of colours has long been understood by artists. Kandinski remarks that green makes no demands on us, Goethe that blue seems to yield to our gaze. Colours have a motor side internally related to their perceptual side, and again this is not a relationship of constancy. A green area produced by contrasting dots has the same motor effects and descriptive value as a homogeneously green surface (*PP*, 216–18).

The influence of colours on our affective existence is best appreciated in our periods of leisure. Having maintained that our experience seems to get close to the experience of simple sensory qualities when we are falling asleep or waking up, Merleau-Ponty goes on to state that there are some episodes in waking life where we feel something taking possession of us, and in these instances sensible experience is shown to be a form of communion, which shows us that traditional empiricism is not entirely abstractive. The figure–background structure of perception is ineliminable, yet there are certain daytime experiences in which it almost fades away, and which have helped to motivate the belief that the pure sensation of a pure quality is the building block of perception. If I lie down on the grass on a warm summer's day and look up at the clear blue sky, I may become so absorbed by the colour that I seem to float away or be lifted into it, such that 'it thinks itself within me' (*il se pense en moi*). The experience befalls me anonymously, and I do not see the blue in the same way that I work through mathematical proofs. The first expresses my sensitivity to colours, and the second the personal creation of a situation, stemming from my decision to be a mathematician. When absorbed by the blue of the sky, it is not so much that I perceive as that 'one perceives in me' (*on perçoit en moi*). An appeal has been made to one of my specialised modes of sensing, though it can be noted that the wider experience is not entirely impersonal or anonymous. I first had to lie down and shift around until I was comfortable, deliberately retreating from the world of active engagements, and then and only then could I feel my body beginning to merge into the blueness. The situation came from a sequence of activities, even if it began with a 'natural self', a specialised contributor to the intermodal whole that had sided with a sector of the world so the latter could motivate me to abandon myself to it. This is just one reason why I cannot say 'I' absolutely (*PP*, 216, 221–3, 234).

In the end we can view sensations as sensibles, as moments of perceived things in an existential environment. Because we are open to them affectively and because we gear into them intentionally when taking them up, the sensibles are never opposed to us in merely external relations. They are always suggesting something to us from somewhere. To a greater or lesser degree, every appearance is an invitation that can be acted upon or a refusal that can be retreated from in a rhythm of adduction or abduction (*PP*, 221–2, 242, 244). Yet the impingements of most sensibles in the phenomenal field are fated to be faint and confused. Most are scarcely perceived at all, for '[w]ithout the exploration of my gaze or my hand, and prior to my body synchronising with it, the sensible is nothing but a vague solicitation' (*PP*, 222). This marks the difference between things co-perceived and focally perceived, where the former fail to appeal to me in any reportable way. This being said, changes of posture and of direction may be solicited by the simplest of things standing out from their backgrounds. When walking down a sunken lane, I believed I saw a large flat stone that was really a patch of sunlight. Before discovering the illusion, I was already preparing to feel a smooth and solid surface beneath my foot. Through vision a flagstone was intended as there, and it had a wider significance for my body as easy to walk on, best facilitating my project of reaching a destination or of enjoying the birdsong by way of the lane. The original appearance issued a certain invitation that prompted a certain action (*PP*, 310, 330–1).

If sensing is structured and prospective, so are our reflexes in their own ways. Merleau-Ponty remarks that the physiology of his time is not merely abandoning the constancy hypothesis and the model of the thing as comprised of externally related parts, but is speaking of responses to situations rather than reactions to stimuli. Reflex movements show that our bodies apprehend so-called stimuli as moments of overall situations without any conscious intervention (*PP*, 11, 77, 81). When I scoop up a pile of dead leaves and feel sharpness, movement and warmth, I promptly put down the pile and step backwards before meant identification comes into play. My hands have encountered a prickly living something before I recognise a hedgehog's spines and contracting underside. When I am walking through a forest, I catch my shoe in a tree root. As soon as this happens the flexor muscles in my foot relax, and my body accentuates the relaxation to reduce momentum, obviate injury and help free the foot. On another occasion I miss my step coming down the side of a mountain. After initial relaxation, the flexor muscles contract in the leg (together with muscles higher in the body before my heel actually hits the ground. The organism is preparing to absorb the shock of the impact without collapsing (*SB*, 45).

A mechanistic physiologist might respond that elementary reflexes can be uncovered before and beneath these responses. We have only to recall the raising of one's leg when one's knee is tapped lightly with a hammer, or the punctual and localised excitation when one's skin is touched by a hair. But like the blue sky that I can only drift away into after lying down and making myself comfortable, these stimulations have resulted from sequences of movements culminating in the exposure of the receptor organ to certain external influences in a certain way. A circular rather than linear causality is in play, stimulus and prior behaviour co-causing the responses. And even then no causation can account for the ends sought by the physiologist and the trust placed in him or her by the patient. Furthermore, the constancy of the first reflexes (which is not repeated in succeeding ones) is only possible because these reactions are no longer woven into the general comportment of the organism. The simple reflex is an artificial product like the simple sensation, having been abstracted from situations in which the body responds as a whole. In the environment the various parts of one's body do not react discretely to discrete agents.[12] We cannot model them on laboratory reflexes, which resemble those that we would have walking in pitch darkness, without the organs functioning together as usual (*SB*, 13, 43–5; *PP*, 77, 81). The induced or 'pure' reflex is hardly ever found in the comportment of the human being, 'who has not merely a milieu but also a world' (*PP*, 89).

2.5   Physicalism and Some Beliefs

If we take descriptive phenomenology seriously, concluding that the horizons of perception are irreducible to those qualities that appear in

---

[12] This harks back to John Dewey's remarkable critique of the mechanistic conception of the reflex arc. A sound, for example, is not a mere stimulus, being taken up in an act of hearing by an existent whose prior psychophysical state conditions a reception that is already actively responsive. This is a sensorimotor coordination that formatively 'fixes the problem' in determining the sound's quality and that carries into an overt response (such as running away because the sound is heard as that of a dangerous animal). There is a complete circuit instead of an arc or the disjointed fragments of a circle. The circuit can be characterised as organic, since the overall motor response determines the stimulus just as much as the stimulus determines the movements. Stimulus and response are teleological distinctions of function, and their relation represents an integral organisation of means for reaching and maintaining a comprehensive end. See Dewey 1896.

and through them, we will soon realise that the empiricist remains unconvinced. For him or her, comments Merleau-Ponty, the horizons are nothing but superstructures to be broken down into the sensations whose derivative relations they express. Objective thought regards itself as detached and impartial, and is unaware of its own contribution to the phenomena. It is quite at home with theoretically pure entities in theoretical relations of constancy, and will never discover anything in description that amounts to a refutation. The physicist's atoms in the universe will always be more real than the historical and qualitative world, the psychic atoms more real than the perceived phenomena, and the physico-chemical processes more real than the organic forms. Without a conversion from the panoptical scientistic gaze, the theoretician will say that the descriptions cannot be understood, or that they are hopelessly vague and quite useless for properly scientific purposes (*PP*, 8, 24–5). Nothing positive emanates from the indeterminacy of phenomena, for anything appearing in this way is determinate in its real being. What is actually realised in things will someday be shown forth as such for complete scientific knowledge (*PP*, 7, 54, 498–9).

Today's empiricist would contend that second-generation objective thought has transcended explanation in terms of externally and mechanically related variables, and no longer posits isolated and unstructured sensations. Physicalism can still be pursued as a consistent and thoroughgoing programme of showing that everything above the physically founding level is fully translatable into this causal fundament by way of explanation. Every feature of perception and of consciousness ensues from or supervenes on its material substructure. On this line of thought, phenomenology will succumb to what Tom Baldwin calls the priority objection. We might grant that its descriptions reveal our pre-scientific experience of the world. These might even take methodological priority over the explanatory procedures of empiricism, since a proper description of everyday and engaged perception could contribute to a better causal account. If it is mistakenly held that a narrow or limit-case description of a phenomenon is adequate, we could end up with a causal account that is correlatively inadequate at the explanatory level. But if the founding priority of the description of pre-scientific experience is conceded, this is only temporary. When the founded stage of scientific investigation has done its work, we will have explained the complex causal processes beneath the experiences and their referents as first articulated in the descriptions. The latter are akin to ladders that can be thrown away once they have been climbed, since we will arrive at purely scientific accounts of how the processes carry on and determine everything else. The descriptive priority of phenomenology will be overtaken by the explanatory priority of natural science.[13]

Merleau-Ponty could retort that a better description of some pre-scientific experience is not of necessity final or conclusive. Phenomenology is an open-ended approach, and we cannot presume that we have got a description quite right the first time round (and that it points to all the causal conditions that need to be factored in). In speaking of a transcendental field, the phenomenologist recognises that 'reflection never has the entire world and the plurality of monads spread out and objectified before its gaze' (*PP*, 62). And as we shall see, phenomenological description to date has a specifically philosophical priority in silhouetting our motility and our awareness of it, what we imaginatively make of this awareness and our organisation of the perceived according to principles, all of which defy reduction to physical causation. In any event, the scientific determinations of existence cannot escape the lifeworld in which we first learned what a forest, a meadow or a river is (*PP*, lxxii, 59). This is the backdrop of Simon Glendinning's response to the objection. If the scientist cannot know just what she is investigating without a founding description faithful to first-hand experience, it is also the case that the investigation will continue to be *about* that particular thing. Equations pertaining to the course of a river and its bank erosion, for example, are intentionally directed to just that river, accepting their more general application. This is true even when one no longer appeals to the founding stage in using the theoretical apparatus, since it is applied beyond the features manifest at this stage to provide an explanation.[14] In her comportment, moreover, the scientist *remains* in the natural attitude all the while, for the world is still there for her throughout her enquiries. This is evidenced by the habitual precautions which she is taking at the riverbank in obtaining samples and will be evidenced by those taken in the laboratory when she is using solvents. All of which brings us to Husserl's insight that she is working within two attitudes. On closer examination, the scientific attitude is subordinate to the natural attitude of world belief, for she can only begin from the latter, stay within it pre-reflectively and conclude by having to turn her attentive gaze back to mundane matters (*TS*, 3–4; *Ids2*, 193).

The second-generation empiricist might object that physicalism is a theory of what is the case, and that we must ordinarily live outside the

---

[13] Baldwin 2004, 12, 20. Merleau-Ponty anticipates the priority objection without actually mentioning description. Cf. *SB*, 144–5.
[14] Glendinning 2007, 127–8.

attitude in which we clearly cognise what is the case does not make it any less the case.[15] But Merleau-Ponty could reply that some everyday beliefs within the natural attitude are not only eminently justified on their own terms, but count against physicalistic explanation when we parse them out in detail. When we observe the organic forms of animal life (not just those of specifically human comportment), we find that the structure of behaviour in the organism depends on the biological *significance* of each situation. This is not a physical or chemical variable (or second-generation condition) that is susceptible to mathematical determination, for it opens onto another and fundamental type of intelligibility (*PP*, 11). The point here – glanced on already in this chapter – is that organic behaviour never shows 'something like a first layer of reactions which would correspond to the physical and chemical properties of the world and to which an acquired significance would subsequently be attached' (*SB*, 130). The responses of an organism are only understandable and predictable if we think of them 'not as muscular contractions which unfold in the body, but as acts which are addressed to a certain milieu, present or virtual: the act of taking a bait, of walking towards a goal, of running away from danger' (*SB*, 151).

When we focus on specifically human comportment, moreover, description brings us into the lifeworld in which our genuinely natural attitude is personalistic. We are in this attitude doing business and living together, and it persists beneath the physicalist conception (*Ids2*, 10–11, 191–3, 196–9). Our scientist only seems to leave the lifeworld before returning to greet colleagues and friends and family. In Merleau-Ponty's rendering, it is 'the human space made up of those with whom I discuss or of those with whom I live, the place where I work or the place of my happiness' (*PP*, 25). In its business side, it has socio-cultural norms of esteem and reward, which the physicalist takes every bit as seriously as the literary critic and the historian (and the phenomenologist too). It is only by systematic abstraction that the meaningful objects constituted relationally can give way to the intrinsic being of material processes, and that they can populate a socio-cultural world at best derivative and at worst illusory (*PP*, 25–6). Hence Merleau-Ponty's contention that scientistic attitudes are naive and hypocritical, making use of the perspective of embodied and engaged awareness without mentioning it. They are naive in depending on but never silhouetting the lived experiences marginally present beneath all theorising. Insofar as their proponents are aware of cognitive dissonance, they are hypocritical in assigning a deficient status to the world that first formed around us and that began to exist for us. Many of

---

[15] My thanks to my second reviewer for setting out this objection.

its socio-cultural norms as explicitly affirmed in their practical evaluations and choices are relentlessly demoted in theoretical claims about its nature.[16] Yet even the 'physical' world supposes concepts with a practical warrant; we are correct to regard the more complex as founded on the more simple, where nature for us is not at first a sum of scientifically determinable processes. Rather, it is the crumbling cement beneath the monument and the tiring actor behind the character (*PP*, lxxii, 26).

This brings me back to the stubborn quality of many of our everyday beliefs in the macroscopic lifeworld, that of being eminently justified. We are rightly convinced that riverbanks and solvents are dangerous, that foodstuffs preserve our lives and that friends, paintings and music enhance them (*Ids2*, 10–11, 191–3, 196–9). In advance of our activities, we lean on core beliefs that none of us can avoid espousing, to the effect that certain persons and things facilitate certain outcomes and that the wider world exceeds its actuality to date. Every phenomenal field is again a transcendental field of possibilities for an engaged perceiver, one who constitutes and acts with a particular point of view and a limited power (*PP*, 61–2). To be in the world is to have the sense and background understanding of what can and cannot be done from field to field, and ordinarily one is oriented towards what can. In perceiving and imagining I intend and co-intend possibilities that are proximate or remote, that I can actualise myself, that others can actualise themselves and that we can actualise together. Phenomenology will do much to explicate our correlative and somatically founded senses of possibility and agency, though the intellectualism preceding it has affirmed freedom of intention and has not denied our personhood. Because its achieved world is nonetheless the scientific universe, it has little interest in the allure of things, and it has neglected the panoply of expressions peculiar to our living bodies. From its very beginnings, however, the transcendental approach perpetuating intellectualism has provided insights into perceptual constitution that are separable from this variant of objective thought.

---

[16] See Hass 2008, 44, 45–7, 50.

CHAPTER 3

Attention, Judgement and Other Work

3.1 Introduction

The empiricist has described sensations and their causal substrata without giving due regard to perception as we live it, and without recognising that the horizons of the subject open up the perceptual field as a sector of the wider world. Each of us perceives in the field from a certain perspective, and in dynamic perceptual fulfilment we experience a harmony between the intended and the given. Merleau-Ponty holds that the intellectualist alternative marks a major advance in bringing the active perceiver to philosophical awareness. It is realised that conscious acts are irreducible to the causes proffered in explanations, and that these must figure explicitly in the description of what is perceived. A state of consciousness is also the consciousness of a state, and to each element in the empiricist account of phenomena the phrase 'consciousness about' must be added. The awareness that is directed towards the world is simultaneously taken as a synthesising subject for that world, as a transcendental and constituting ego. Yet the character of this world undergoes no significant change. All that is denied is the contention that it can be experienced as a ready-made and independent actuality (*PP*, 23, 41, 215).

The critique of intellectualism is directed at objectivist presuppositions in cognitive psychology, Cartesian thought generally and the scientistic side of Kant's First Critique specifically. This is pronounced in the second edition, which is so greatly admired by Léon Brunschvicg, the foremost French idealist in Merleau-Ponty's time and, as Don Landes has argued, his chief and unnamed target.[1] Brunschvicg contends that when Kant found the reasons behind judgements in his study of human thought, philosophy assumed its definitive form. Through the analysis of the

---

[1] Landes contends that Merleau-Ponty's sustained critique of intellectualism is aimed at Brunschvicg first and foremost and at like-minded professors in the Sorbonne. Brunschvicg taught Merleau-Ponty at the *École Normale* from 1926 to 1930. Landes 2013, 47–8.

language that we use in expressing judgements, we can establish a distinctly philosophical science of the knowledge of knowledge, uncovering the laws of human thought without which there could be no objectivity and no natural science.[2] Knowledge in the Kantian sense is not something applied to existence from outside, to fully fledged objects lying before it. The world that is constituted by consciousness is nothing other than the world for us. A thing that would lie beyond our knowledge is by definition inaccessible and indeterminable, for it cannot come to be as this or that. On this view the structure of perception is found through reflection, which discovers the concepts that constitute a world for us and their rules of application in judgements. All perception is egoic, epistemic and object-directed and therefore describable and reportable. Whatever is cognised implicitly is capable of being made explicit, and the measure of being is not the vagueness of images but the clarity of the concept.[3]

In the first section of this chapter, I set out Merleau-Ponty's initial critique of intellectualism. Emphasising the role of judgement from the outset, it neglects the pre-conceptual factors that contribute to our apprehending senses and that motivate certain judgements. Not all these factors can come to be conceptualised in developed perception. In the same blow, intellectualism fails to do justice to the phenomena of perceptual attention and interest. It does not appreciate our attraction to things in the first place or the fact that concepts and judgements cannot be adequate to the things that solicit us. It passes over the singularity of things and of the perceiver in its commitment to an objective world for an impersonally transcendental subject. We see this in Kant's accounts of the quantified empirical manifold and the empirical subject, whose body is one more constituted object. Merleau-Ponty adverts to another side of Kant's thought that is not bound to the presumptions of objectivism, and in the final section, I run through the latter's ideas on synopsis, the productive imagination, bodily orientation and movement in space and interested perception.

3.2   Judgement and Motivation

For the intellectualist, the paradigmatic work of the perceiving subject is the act of judgement, already privileged in Descartes' Second Meditation. I see a piece of honeycomb wax, but once heat is applied it loses its smell, sweetness and hardness, and its original shape. What is left for sense experience gives me no knowledge of this particular existent I call wax.

---

[2] Brunschvicg 1897, 3, 25.   [3] Ibid., 2, 6, 36–8.

Only because I have judged that it has the properties of extension in length and breadth and depth do I know that it is still the same thing. Its nature is grasped by the mind or understanding, which on reflection must inform all perceptions, and most evidently those that are poor in data. Looking through the window in bad weather, I have to judge that I am perceiving shrouded people passing by, having no retinal images of anything behind the hats and coats (*PP*, 34–5). It is with my mind alone, claims Descartes, that I know these are real human beings rather than dummies moved by springs. Solely through the power of judgement can I go beyond what I saw with my eyes, which tells me that the analysis of sensible things brings me back to the knowledge of my own mind in its activity.[4]

Though Kant in his critical account of perceptual truth assigns a role to empirical associations founded on repeated experiences, it is stressed that the sheer fact of something following on from something else cannot prove the sequence to be necessary. Strict universality and objective validity depend on the conceptual categories of understanding allowing for experience (B 124–6). Concepts having empirical application through judgements provide contents of necessity and possibility for any world. One of them lets me assert that all bodies must be extended and that some may be heavy. If I say I feel an impression of heaviness in supporting a body, my claim is merely valid subjectively, but to state that the body is heavy is to assert the combination of the relevant presentations in the object itself. Whether or not I am supporting the body, objective validity is expressed. For Kant, the peculiarity of our understanding – presupposing the a priori unity of self-awareness and the awareness of outer things with certain concepts – is as little capable of further explanation as the functions of judgement. But the entire manifold or field of perceptual experience is determined by these functions as combined in one consciousness, and each thing in the field is reportable because the concepts working it over are discursive (A 68/B 93, 142–6). In this vein, Brunschvicg works towards an inventory of our judgements to show how they determine being for us.[5]

In Merleau-Ponty's eyes, intellectualism begins to manifest its shortcomings in its failure to give due consideration to the phenomenon of perceptual attention. In the empiricist scheme of things, attention is effectively a matter of one's sense organs being turned in a certain direction due to some cause, be it sudden and striking or a function of associations and projected memories. This is the searchlight model of focal and attentive perception. For the intellectualist, by contrast, attention must ensue in

---

[4] Descartes 1984b, 20–2.   [5] Brunschvicg 1897, 32–3, 36–8.

an orderly rather than haphazard succession of scenes, since through it we obtain the truth about the focal object. To clarify the object attentively is to draw out the intelligible structure it contains, which has been applied judicatively (*PP*, 29, 35–6).[6] The only intentionality discussed in the B edition Critique is that of acts, which is 'the intentionality of our judgements and of our voluntary decisions' (*PP*, lxxxii). Empiricism collapses the world into causal contents, and its bottom-up story of sensations is countered by a top-down story of imposed conceptual form. This is inferentially revealed through the procedure of analytic reflection:

> Reflective analysis thus becomes a purely regressive doctrine according to which every perception is a confused intellection and every determination a negation. It suppresses in this way all problems except for one: the problem of its own beginning … We will have but an abstract essence of consciousness so long as we have not followed the actual movement by which consciousness continually recovers possession of its own operations, condenses and focuses them in an identifiable object, gradually shifts from 'seeing' to 'knowing', and obtains the unity of its own life … In actual perception, taken in its nascent state and prior to all speech, the sensible sign and its signification are not even ideally separable. An object is an organism of colours, odours, sounds, and tactile appearances that symbolise and modify each other, and that harmonise with each other according to a real logic … [intellectualism] passes to a consciousness that would possess its law or its secret, and that as a result strips the development of experience of its contingency and the object of its perceptual style. (*PP*, 40–1)

For intellectualism, conscious and perceptual awareness either has a judicative and conceptual purchase on its object or it does not. Between the blurred figure and the intelligibly determined object, no intermediate stages enjoy attention. Because the focal object is actually determined and the background field latently determined, judgement is to be found everywhere. It is introduced as that which sensibility lacks to make perception possible (*PP*, 30, 34, 36). If I see two cardboard boxes in front of me full of the same materials without sensory impressions in my hands, I must judge that the larger one is heavier. Such an act is a position-taking or a taking of a stand, for it asserts something that would hold for every perceiver in the same situation. And if I am not making a judgement,

---

[6] In every act of attention, according to Kant, 'the understanding determines inner sense, in accordance with the combination which it thinks, to that inner intuition which corresponds to the manifold [of outer intuition] in the synthesis of the understanding. How much the mind is usually thereby affected, everyone will be able to perceive in himself.' B 156–7.

my perception must be drawing on earlier judgements that are now sedimented convictions.

But if we reflect on such an ordinary experience, according to Merleau-Ponty, we can draw a clear distinction between perceiving and judging. The larger box is at first a signification for my body, not for my understanding. On coming to see it I already anticipate its greater weight in my hands (*PP*, 36–7, 334). This is part of a larger thing's inner horizon, constituted as a sense through practical engagements before ever being posited as such. Though intellectualism takes conceptual cognition as all-pervasive, the phenomenon 'offers a signification that is inherent in the signs and of which the judgement is but the optional expression' (*PP*, 36–7). Yet this last claim is unconvincing, scarcely holding for developed perception after infancy. At this stage, we can admit significations for the body without dismissing later judicative work. In seeing the larger box and in anticipating its weight in my hands, I am not ignorant of the fact that greater effort will be required to lift it up *because* it is heavier. Should I have no thought of lifting the box, the conviction that larger objects are heavier than smaller ones may be dormant or offline, along with the relevant bodily anticipation. But this is not to deny that other acquired thoughts are contributing to the significance of my perception, and Merleau-Ponty subsequently adverts to the fund of sedimented knowledge that we draw on in our activities (*PP*, 62, 131–2). And if one is not always seeing as someone does when about to lift a box or a shopping bag, it is true that one often sees this way. The concepts as well as bodily expectations acquired in gaining some everyday as well as professional competencies mark the ways in which certain things appear afterwards (*PP*, 138–9, 197).

If conceptual cognition is always doing some work in a developed awareness, however, it is not all-pervasive as a consequence. If everything that we see is what we judge or have judged, remarks Merleau-Ponty, we will be unable to distinguish between true and false perceptions, since there will be no difference between seeing and believing that one sees. The judgement alone will be mistaken. We can only escape this difficulty if we admit that judgements are indexed onto signifying configurations and not bare sensations, and that just these judgements – either new or reactivated – rather than other ones have been motivated by the configurations, which in signifying have not appeared indifferently. When we examine Zöllner's illusion, by way of illustration, we find it presents the appearance of convergence by way of the shorter lines. According to one intellectualist account in cognitive psychology, the perceiver should pick out the longer lines on first view, noticing that they are really parallel. To pass over the primary elements of the appearance is at once to make the wrong judgement.[7] Illusory perception is also illusory intellection, and whenever one looks properly, the correct judgement will be made with the appropriate concepts, and one will then have achieved perceptual truth (*PP*, 36–8, 393).

This tells us that classical objectivism is stubbornly persistent. As with the Müller-Lyer illusion, it is supposed that there is a primary layer of impressions of parallel lines as if in the world, and a second-order operation that adds in 'auxiliary lines' and falsifies the appearance. Yet the notion of primary elements is only conjectural and is introduced to construct the illusion intellectually rather than to understand it, which demands a description of the phenomenon's peculiar patterning. In ordinary and original perception, we are directed to the whole of which the longer and shorter lines are moments, and hence to the apparent convergence. The overall configuration *resists* our looking at it in the way that the intellectualist assumes we should. It is not appreciated that an original relationship of signification has to be broken up in order to establish a new one, of which the correct judgement is the final report.[8] Prior to the external relationships established by objective thought, we can discover a perceptual syntax in perception, a system of sensible arrangements and patterns that makes up an overall empirical order. It motivates us to believe and judge in a particular manner and lets us access a stable environment for bodily articulation. While it misleads us about some elements of configurations before they come to be examined, this only holds for a minority of cases, and it must be in place for judicative determination to be possible (*PP*, 37–8).

Merleau-Ponty contends that the phenomenological conception of motivation is of necessity fluid and inexact, and has been formulated to account for the senses offered by phenomena. Motivations are not forces that determine us; instead they incline us towards certain behaviours and courses of action. The illusory flat stone in the sunken lane solicits me as easy to walk on, but not through physical causality. It motivates me in that it will seemingly facilitate my project of journeying or of hearing birdsong. When I decide to attend a funeral, the person's death has not objectively produced that decision, but has provided reasons for it. I will embark on this journey to pay my respects to the departed and comfort the family.

---

[7] Lagneau 1926, 134.

[8] It can again be objected that Merleau-Ponty has neglected the importation of an education in geometry and life in a carpentered environment into what we perceive.

Once the motivated phenomenon is brought about, these motivations will receive greater validation, for I will be happier for having acted on them. It should be added that the choice to attend also calls on empathic and sympathetic feelings. Hence it is not reducible to reasons, even if the feelings were mediated by social norms. In this context, it is notable that intellectualism lays the weight of human acts on rational motivation, which is most clearly opposed to physical causality. By the same token, it underplays everything that lies beyond these theoretically pure poles (*PP*, 51, 270, 310–11).

The thrust of intellectualism is to convert every motivation into a reason. Such rationalisations are especially evident in turning to Descartes' scenario of shrouded figures passing by outside my window. Since nothing of them is directly seen beneath their coverings, judgement must be performed (*PP*, 35). Yet it is not clear why the figures can reasonably be taken to be humans instead of automatons. There must be other factors in the perceptual presentations preceding my judgement, which is charged with the task of drawing a conclusion. The intellectualist will respond that I make use of sedimented judgements. The figures are dressed as I dress for the cold, and I have recognised the appropriate fit between their clothing and the weather conditions. I am employing my acquired knowledge of what hats and coats are for. I also know that the figures are leaning forward as I would lean to counter the force of the wind, so it is reasonable to conclude that these visual presentations are of real people.[9] But such an appeal to a multiplicity of intellectual operations cannot exclude other motivations behind the conclusion that I draw. The judgement that the passing figures are not automatons is just as much dependent on the fact that they are avoiding collisions with each other as people ordinarily do. The phenomenon of walkers taking account of each other may never have been objectified in a judgement, but it contributes to the sense underpinning my conclusion. Not everything that is tacit in a perceptual sense is a reason, and not everything tacit need be explicit (*PP*, 35). This also holds for practical estimations. If I look at a church steeple when everything apart from the sky is screened off, I may judge it is a certain distance from me. Should the screen be taken away, however, I see the houses and fields between myself and the steeple, and I then judge

---

[9] Descartes would add that seeing peoples' faces and hands does not warrant the judgement that they are rational minds, since the mind is hidden behind the body that it interacts with through the pineal gland. It is speech and again the perception of intelligent movements in different contexts that lets me conclude they are not automatons. Descartes 1984a, 139–40.

it is further away. This factor in earlier estimations has only been recognised fortuitously (*PP*, 39–40, 49–50).

Though intellectualists may concede that not everything in a perceptual sense motivating a conclusion can be made explicit in fact, they might insist that it can in principle, since everything is present as a term to be known. Imagine that I enter my friend's living room and immediately know that there is something wrong or out of place. My perception is pervaded by a mood of uneasiness, yet in the judgement I make I am unable to grasp why. Unbeknown to me, my friend has removed a picture that had always been in the room, not the big and imposing one over the mantelpiece, but the smaller one to the far side. The newly bare and freshly cleaned area of the wall is within my perceptual field, but is only perceived marginally. On earlier visits, I never brought that part of the room into my focal awareness, even when my eyes were roaming over the very place where the smaller picture was hung. The convinced intellectualist could argue that the absence of the picture would have been noticed had I paid attention to that part of the room on my previous visits. Accepting that I did not, I can at least in principle assemble my prior perceptions in memory and bring the originally marginal awareness into focus. But this is to assume that memories of perceptions are akin to detailed photographs that can be attended to such that each item is successively brought into thematic view. But there are no good reasons for granting that I can later bring to presence all the marginal factors giving the current perception its sense, either in fact or principle (*PP*, 335). What is an efficacious part of the perceptual syntax can be irretrievable, in this instance because of my past and prevailing interests in the large picture and face-to-face conversation.

3.3   Attention, Interest and Attraction

All this brings us back to the phenomenon of attention, which is selective by definition. A *phenomenology of perception* must recover the ways in which things gain our attention and hold it. Taken for granted by intellectualism are all the relations and operations leading up to cognitive syntheses, for its concern is with 'the idea of truth and the idea of being in which the constitutive work of consciousness culminates and is summed up' (*PP*, 41). There is no interest in elucidating perceptual attention as a passage from indistinctness to clarity prior to conceptual articulation, since clarification is a function of rational and spontaneous activity, the province of a developed consciousness with its act intentionalities. The wider field of inattentive yet potentially attentive and determinative perception must contain latent judgements, but such perception is half-asleep and only describable through negations. It is as yet devoid of objects to be grasped in their consistency by an alert awareness. Whatever is indeterminate drops out of this picture completely. To all intents it is no better than chaos, being insufficient for the describable determination of an object that is or was the work of judgement (*PP*, 29–30). In this top-down account of intelligible form, it is difficult to see how attention can be awakened or do significant work:

> How could one real object among all objects be able to arouse an act of attention, given that consciousness already possesses them all? What was lacking for empiricism was an internal connection between the object and the act it triggers. What intellectualism lacks is the contingency of the opportunities for thought. Consciousness is too poor in the first case and too rich in the second for any phenomenon to be able to solicit it. Empiricism does not see that we need to know what we are looking for, otherwise we would not go looking for it; intellectualism does not see that we need to be ignorant of what we are looking for, or again we would not go looking for it. They are in accord in that neither grasps consciousness in the act of learning, neither accounts for this "circumscribed ignorance," for this still "empty" though already determinate intention that is attention itself. Whether attention obtains what it seeks through an ever-renewed miracle or whether it possesses it in advance, in either case the constitution of the object is passed over in silence. (*PP*, 30–1)

To be descriptively faithful to the genesis and development of perception we need to look at how infants and children proceed, and at those aspects of their comportment that carry into adult life, albeit informed by subsequent epistemic work. If infants are initially driven or carried forward by their instincts, constituting elementary interest formations to facilitate the satisfaction of biological needs, they soon begin to show a distinctively perceptual interest beyond mere striving (and no longer attempt to put everything into their mouths straight away). Only by way of this interest can a proto-objective configuration exercise an allure leading to its objectification, such that the attentionally targeted thing is the motive and not the bare cause or bare reason of the perceptual event. Objectification begins with tactile phenomena, the child constituting a unity and identity in them that 'are not produced through a synthesis of recognition in the concept, they are established upon the unity and identity of the body as a synergetic whole' (*PP*, 330). To reduce things to manifestations of an intelligible core is to mask sensory contents pregnant with a sense and the organic relations of subject and world. As we grow up, the perceptual interest founds and becomes interwoven with a cognitive interest, initially practical and then more abstractly theoretical. Yet the passive synthesis leading to thematic perception always prefigures something as attractive or repulsive before it can be cognised as black or blue or circular or square (*EJ*, 197–8, 202–3; *SB*, 176; *PP*, 26–9, 33, 154, 334). What also persists from infancy is the endeavour to perceive the attractive object as clearly as possible. From early on, we gear ever more into the world as we seek a 'maximal grip' or 'optimal hold' on what we perceive, a better point of view and overall direction for seeing and dealing with it. Our postural attitudes display our orientation towards the greatest possible articulations of things, well before we pursue the privileged appearances or perceptual optima prescribed by our crafts or professions (*PP*, 261, 316, 332–3).[10]

The pursuit of an optimal hold is ongoing, and Taylor Carman expresses its value nicely when he remarks that the rightness and wrongness of our perceptual appearances are bound up intrinsically with the felt rightness and wrongness of our perceptual attitudes. There is a bodily normativity in which '[w]e have a *feel* for the kinds of balance and posture that afford us a correct and proper view of the world'.[11] We can discern such orientations in our very ways of seeing. Though empirical colour constancy is established in a manner that does not match the retinal distribution of rods and cones, one area of a coloured thing within a perceptual episode is usually a brighter and better-illuminated shade than another or others in the shadows. Prior to judgement the perceiver has the tacit awareness of one overall colour presented differently, attaining an appreciation of constancy in apprehending the relationship of light and shade. Yet he or she invariably attends to the brighter area of the visual figure on perceiving it because it is there that the latter reveals its features with the greatest clarity. Lighting

---

[10]   Merleau-Ponty remarks that for every visual object 'just as for each painting in an art gallery, there is an optimal distance from which it asks to be seen' (*PP*, 315–16). Before or beyond this interval its givenness will be impoverished in one way or another – we will lose either the overall figure if too close or its internal details if too far away. The distance between the object and myself is always 'a tension that oscillates around a norm' (*PP*, 316). Because perception is interested, however, the norm may owe more to the perceiver than the perceived. Some appearances emerging through attention are responses to questions I have asked myself (*PP*, 29). This touches on Husserl's insight that there are different perceptual optima for different interests (with their own criteria for proper fulfilment). Revisiting our familiar house, the optimal appearances for the builder are achieved in the main in examining its mortar and bricks close up, and for the buyer and seller in walking round it and through its rooms. Optimal appearances are different again for the architect and garden designer and painter. Our posture towards and distance from a flower will also vary according to whether we wish to sketch it or smell it or examine it botanically. The respective optima with their correlative bodily attitudes cannot be understood in abstraction from our practical, aesthetic and scientific concerns. *APS*, 61–2; *TS*, 97–9, 106–7.

[11]   Carman 2020, 104.

has motivated the perceptually interested and preferential gaze (*PP*, 235, 318–19, 323).

Early and interested viewings in infancy carry into more extensive actions favoured as the best and the easiest ways of reaching fulfilment. Attentional consciousness develops in and through these transition syntheses. Babies first use their hands to grab things, and having established the range and reach of their limbs by stretching and waving them, investigate the things at length and with great curiosity. They bring them closer and into the light, turn them around to see and feel their different aspects, and frequently shake them, bang them and throw them down to find out how they sound. As soon as they can sit up and crawl, they launch into far more extensive explorations of their milieus. The sensible articulations of things are revealed by factically interested existents, not by spectators with no concerns before or after theoretical cognition (*PP*, 29, 33, 316). If we describe the real as it appears to us, we find it burdened with anthropological predicates. Each perception is a communion, and we can only posit the thing 'at the end of a gaze or at the conclusion of a sensory exploration that invests it with humanity' (*PP*, 334).

As ever there is no question of ignoring biological or physiological conditions, and if we consider any one sense in its development, we find that attention increases in discrimination. In vision, young infants first distinguish basic monochrome shades from undifferentiated coloured ones. They then articulate coloured areas into 'warm' or 'cool' shades, and finally arrive at detailed colours. Once it is reached, every new articulation serves as an empirical condition of more detailed ones again. Of more obvious significance, however, are the aforementioned explorations in which infants overcome distances through grasping and locomotion. When we report that things draw them in closer, it should be added that the horizon of perceptual attention (the still empty though already determinate intention referred to by Merleau-Ponty) is not a mere co-intending of the hidden sides and back of a thing. It is also an anticipation of features within the aspect directly present to the perceiver that are too distant to be clearly articulated from the current standpoint. We are co-intending in this way when we walk up to a sign in order to read it. So is the baby who crawls towards a shiny something and who brings it up to eye level after clutching it. The thing solicits him or her to approach still closer to learn more about it, to discover more of the richness of its details (*APS*, 43; *PP*, 30–1, 32–3, 242).

The ongoing explorations are important in showing us that the thing already has a dynamic sense for the infant, for it has motivated both the

interest in and the expectation of new and novel fulfilments. It is apprehended as offering more than has been given through attention so far.
There is therefore an awareness in early life that what is currently perceived
has not been exhausted perceptually. Exploratory attention is for the most
part experienced as a progressive and satisfying passage from a broad and
loose determination of an object to one that is more refined and more
distinct. There is neither chaos at the beginning (since infants are motivated by alluring configurations) nor complete determination at the end
(since only some features are now more determined within an unsurpassable indeterminacy). We do not start with disjoined sensations nor end
with 'the return to itself of a thought that is already the master of its
objects'. Attention is instead 'the active constitution of a new object that
develops and thematises what was until then only offered as an indeterminate horizon' (*PP*, 33). It is the very broadness and looseness of features –
their element of indistinctness – that motivates continuing explorations
leading to novel articulations. Both empiricism and intellectualism see
indeterminacy in exclusively negative terms, as something to be elimin-
ated, whereas for Merleau-Ponty '[w]e must recognise the indeterminate as
a positive phenomenon' (*PP*, 7). Were the perceptual object the expression
of a universal positing power determining it absolutely, consciousness
would be destroyed 'since it congeals all of experience, as a seed crystal
introduced into a solution causes it suddenly to crystallize' (*PP*, 74).

The indeterminacy of a thing is not readily evident in developed
perception with its sedimented skills and judgements, and neither is its
singularity. Knowing how to get our bearings and deal with things in our
hurried working lives, we quickly use the door here and the table and
window over there. But when I have the time and the inclination to
attend closely to a thing, it ceases to be an allusion to a general type, and
I realise that it has a distinctive perceptual style, the apprehension of
which evokes something of the novelty of original perception. In zoning
in on a once-off arrangement of foliage or of growth rings, I am seeing
this feature of the tree or bench for the first time, even though I saw the
whole object before (*PP*, 41, 45–6). These uncommon episodes tell us
that adult perception usually passes over the empirical depth and richness of the perceived thing, and that the concepts we employ always do.
Yet the contours of natural objects are of no concern whatsoever to the
intellectualist. Their styles are inexact and therefore irrelevant, lying
beneath the purview of physico-theoretical concepts (*PP*, 40–1).
Descartes thinks this way in affirming the sameness of the piece of
wax. As materially extended in length and breadth and depth it can

assume an infinity of shapes and positions. These determinations are objective but indifferent, holding for each and every body. What is perceptually distinctive about wax and expected of it through its inner horizon is dismissed. For everyday perception, it will rapidly become soft when heated and assume a shade that suggests its softness. This will in turn suggest the muffled sound it would make if it were struck. These potentialities contribute to the sense of sameness of *this* peculiar something, even if the original smell, sweetness and shape have vanished without return, but Descartes never admits them as warrants for its permanence. These 'secondary' qualities have no bearing on the identities determined by science (*PP*, 34–5).

3.4   The Subject in Objective Thought

Passing over the singularity and richness of the perceived thing is one consequence of intellectualism's focus on precision, clarity and universality, and passing over the singular 'thisness' or *haecceity* of the embodied and situated perceiver is another. We are brought once again to the fundamental way in which analytic reflection concurs with empiricist explanation. Their only squabbles relate to the role and existence-status of the cognising subject, and whatever is unique to the perceiver as a consequence of his or her education and past actions and somatic situation is of no interest to either. For the intellectualist, embodied perception offers no positive factors to be accounted for, and the subject's *haecceity* is simply its own ignorance of itself (*PP*, 40). All the descriptions of hidden motivations in perception, of the development of attention prior to judgement and of sensible singularity are really allusions to unreflective experiences 'which in principle can never become utterances and which, like every psychology, are without truth when standing before the understanding' (*PP*, 51). In turning to the singularity of personal awareness, one only switches from physical to psychological peculiarities. The telos of intellectualism is to strip the subject as well as the things of all opacity, to divest it of its historical thickness and to reveal the transcendental and autonomously constituting subject that is everywhere and nowhere, without place or perspective (*PP*, lxxv, 39–40, 63). Such an approach passes over the earlier and somatic stages of constitution because its sole interest is in the highly derivative theoretical attitudes we come to adopt. In these, scientific or proto-scientific concepts are applied to appearances to determine objective validity for all times and places (*PP*, 40, 226–7). Instead of uncovering conditions of an object's actuality, the concern is with those that make it epistemically possible in a universe of absolutely determinate being (*PP*, 43, 62, 507).

From the very beginning, on Merleau-Ponty's interpretation, intellectualism has dreamt the determination of things as a fully realisable ideal. This dream is an article of faith in the Cartesian theology. An all-powerful divinity recreates the world from moment to moment and guarantees every truth about it. What I cannot know clearly and distinctly is known consummately in the divine mind. At the highest level all beings are total objects for an absolute intellection.[12] Thus we pass from the absolute objectivity of empiricism's determinate universe to the absolute subjectivity that lies behind it. After the religious belief is abandoned by critical philosophy, intellectualism attributes to the finite subject the power of recognising the absolute truths that scientific realism naively locates in a given nature (*PP*, 41, 205). The gap between cognitive determination and its completion is seen as ultimately insignificant. Reason in scientific investigation does not follow nature like a pupil, but like a judge compelling it to answer questions. When some are found to be satisfactory, the mind acts as a lawgiver, since it then introduces the intelligible order that we entitle nature (A 125–8/B xiii–xiv). In this endeavour, transcendental philosophers in the classical mould do not question 'the possibility of carrying out the complete making-explicit that they always assume is *completed somewhere*' (*PP*, 62). In the absolute acceptance of the ideas of truth and being in which the work of consciousness culminates, a God's eye view is presumed. Intellectualism takes an ideal telos as a real possibility and regards it as in some way extant. What exists for us in intention is realised in a system of true thoughts coordinating all phenomena, comprehending all perspectives and opening on to a pure object (*PP*, 41–2).

Merleau-Ponty anticipates an objection to these criticisms, to the effect that they are aimed at a caricature of intellectualism in which analytic reflection is enclosed in its results and consequently cancels out the whole phenomenon of human finitude. The regressive return to the conceptual and judicative articulation of things should be regarded instead as the first step in a movement to overcome empiricism. Intellectualism's approach can be modified to accommodate the other factors at work in perception. Yet the phenomenological elaboration of our perceptually engaged being in the world is a step which intellectualism can only accept at the price of undercutting itself. Its commitment to objective thought is definitive, making it what it is. When we examine this tradition from its inception

---

[12] Descartes 1984b, 33, 39, 43.

in Descartes and refinement in some of Kant's work through to the present day, we find that it has always and invariably been formulated as an epistemology for natural science rather than as a philosophy of perception (*PP*, 38–9, 41–2, 44). Brunschvicg asserts this quite unequivocally. One essential task of Kantian critique is to demonstrate the objectivity of practical reasoning. It finds its other justifications in establishing the external world as a reality for consciousness, the necessity of the truths of geometry, the possibility of physical and biological hypotheses and of the complete determination of empirical appearances through objectively valid judgements. As scientific concepts progress, the universe for their application advances in concert.[13] For Brunschvicg, the 'real' of everyday perception falls away from the object of knowledge when filtered through the subject's scientific idealisations. This has no disadvantages, for such perception is superficial, mutilated and extra-philosophical.[14]

Kant's intellectualism is not so thoroughgoing. Seeking to reveal the impetus behind scientific investigation, he posits transcendental ideas of pure reason, of unconditioned totalities or absolute unities in which all syntheses are completed. We have the ideas of the absolute unity of the thinking subject, of the absolute unity of the causal laws and series determining the world or nature, and of the absolute unity of all the conditions of the objects of thought in general or of God (B 379–80, 391). These ideas are not constitutive, for they do not make the world intelligible like the concepts of substance and causality. Instead, they pull us into the systematic investigation of the constituted world and constituting subject. In the theoretical field, states Kant, each notion has a regulative use that is excellent and unavoidable, for it directs the understanding towards a certain goal. Thus we work with the idea that we can find the fundamental elements of the physical realm and all the laws governing them (A 646–53/B 674–81). Attentive to our finitude, however, Kant asserts that we cannot reach this goal through scientific advance, since it lies outside possible experience. It is asymptotic, an infinite limit that we can only ever approximate (A 664/B 672, 692). The idea of a fully determined nature attracts the scientist forwards like a beacon, but without her having to posit a theory of everything that is awaiting its full concretisation in human consciousness.

Kant's explication of our finitude takes two routes. Most notoriously, he contends that our categories of experience and understanding apply to sensible entities or phenomena without ever reaching them as noumena.

---

[13] Brunschvicg 1897, 40, 174.   [14] Ibid., 233–7; Brunschvicg 1922, 446.

These things in themselves cannot be the objects of sensible intuition. If such things exist, they may be grasped intelligibly by some beings other than ourselves, but we do not even know if such knowledge is possible. The concept of a noumenon is employed negatively to mark the limits of our knowledge (B 307–11). But he also argues independently that rational or speculative cosmology and empirical science cannot determine all the laws and series determining the world (in the objectivist sense of the material universe) because they have no means of establishing whether it is limited in time and space, whether its components are simple and whether it presupposes a necessary being as its ultimate cause (B 454–88). Everything speaks for the conclusion that Kant does not presume a God's eye view either for us or in itself. The possibility of carrying out a complete making-explicit is not left unquestioned, nor the assumption that it is completed somewhere. This being said, better perceptions of things by non-human organs of sense are left open as empty possibilities (A 27–8/B 43–4).

Merleau-Ponty comes to allow for Kant's epistemic modesty, referring to the open and indefinite world for the situated perceiver indicated in the Transcendental Dialectic (if not in the Analytic). Yet he can still maintain that objective thought pervades the asymptotic approach to empirical reality, since all the discoveries to be made about a thing are anticipated as scientific ones. The thing is predelineated as an ideal unity for explanation (*PP*, 55, 317–18). This is quite overt in the account of the constituted phenomenal world in the B version of the First Critique. In the A edition it is asserted that a stable empirical order (or what Merleau-Ponty calls a perceptual syntax) has allowed for the application of concepts. We could have no empirical expectations for conceptualisation if we were confronted with a chaos in which manifolds of appearances change arbitrarily (A 100–1). Consistent with this, Kant suggests that things in the world need not be worked over by the cogitating self, at least in their initial appearances. He posits a threefold synthesis furnishing the object of epistemic perception, a synthesis of apprehension in intuition, of reproduction in imagination and of recognition in a concept. The synthesis of apprehension in empirical perception is a synopsis or viewing together, a composite and selective visualisation carving out an image or figure from within the empirical manifold as framed spatially. Successive appearances of that figure are unified by the reproductive imagination, and this is a condition of its being recognised explicitly as a certain particular and re-identified (A 97–9, 120–1).

In the second edition of the Critique, synopsis is absorbed into figurative synthesis. All empirical combination is embedded in an act of understanding that imposes concepts, and without which perception is not possible (B 42). Each thing in the world is cognised as a material substance standing in relations of mechanical causality with every other one, and the synthesis of apprehension draws out an outer figure by employing the category of quantity, necessarily conforming to it. The synthesis delivers a homogeneous, determinable region of space in the manifold of empirical intuition. Through the quantitative concepts of unity, plurality and totality, the thing is grasped as an extensive magnitude or measurable quantity of extension. Descartes would recognise it immediately, for it has enumerable parts outside parts (*partes extra partes*) in a continuum intuited as infinite and uniform. The latter only differs from the Cartesian space of indifferent positions with regard to its existence. It is no more than the form of outer intuition, the frame in which bodies appear as against a space comprised of bodies (B 129–30, 161–2, 203). One can well affirm that visual appearances in space are extensive magnitudes and can be cognised as such, but for Kant each thing is perceived *as* an extensive magnitude. Conceptually determined sensibility is an instrument for detecting the measurable in and of itself. Theoretical inspection in the scientific attitude supplants lived perception in the natural attitude (*PP*, 315). A transcendental subject constitutes the objective world of extended things and experiences it as do other transcendental subjects. Nature is arrived at through a single light in which all of them have an equal share:

> Beginning from the spectacle of a world, which is the spectacle of a nature open to a plurality of thinking subjects, critical philosophy seeks the condition that makes this unique world offered to many empirical myselves possible, and it finds this in a transcendental I in which they all participate without thereby dividing it, because it is not a Being but rather a [formal] Unity or a Value. This is why Kantian philosophy never asks the question of the knowledge of others: the transcendental I that it speaks of is as much the other's as it is mine; the analysis is immediately placed outside of myself, has merely to extract the general conditions that make a world possible for an I – whether it be myself or another – and never encounters the question of who is meditating? .... We must not merely settle into a reflective attitude or into an unassailable Cogito, but also reflect upon this reflection, understand the natural situation it is aware of replacing and that thereby belongs to its definition. (*PP*, 63)

If Kant has reconstructed the Cartesian subject so that it no longer has to be regarded as a separable soul-substance, it is nonetheless a universal constituting power, and perception in its appearance is effectively reduced to intellection (*PP*, 45). Self-experience in perception or self-affection is the appearance to the mind of its being affected by its own activity when it posits presentations through time or the form of inner sense (B 67–8, 153). It is then to be wondered how we can believe that we saw *with* our eyes, since self-perception is an inspection belonging to the mind. No reference is made to the experience of experience or the feeling of perceiving (*PP*, 215, 220). In this picture our sensing bodies and our psychological states are objectified through the same concepts applied to things. Whatever is relative to our situated and factical existence is inessential, for necessity cannot be derived from anything empirical (A 91–2/B 124). To the extent that he places the burden of constitution on the pure categories of understanding, Kant foregrounds the living body as the physically determined part of one's empirical subjectivity, and hence as something effectively constituted by and for consciousness. Thus I find my own body as an object that occupies a region of space from which I experience other regions. I also distinguish my existence as thinking being from other things outside me that include my body, without thereby learning whether I could exist as thinking being apart from human form (A 23/B 38, 409).

In this manner, Kant perpetuates the Cartesian picture of embodiment. As we saw in Chapter 1, this picture takes the body as a mechanical outside without an inside, and the mind as an ethereal inside without an outside that governs the automaton without inhabiting its movements and expressing itself through them (*PP*, 56). Such a mind is no less impersonal than its body. There is only an apparent antithesis, according to Merleau-Ponty, between 'the image of a constituted world, where I would exist merely as one object among others, and the idea of an absolute constituting consciousness' (*PP*, 43). To recognise our situatedness and avoid a dualism of purely mental and physical properties, the transcendental and empirical subjects have to be rethought. What we call mind and body are moments of an engaged and integrated existent. Furthermore, the line between the transcendental subject and the body is not that between the constituting and constituted (*PP*, 317, 450–3, 466, 544). Somatic syntheses pertain to this type of body with its peculiar organisation, giving us the world we have for our projects. The specifically human body is not a contingent fact, for without it our conceptual capacities could never develop, having no purchase on the environment. The material a prioris of the world of possibilities are found in the structure of the body, in its schematised movement and in the way it is experienced in moving. Once these conditions are revealed, it will be seen that the objectively constituted body is an impoverished image of the constituting body (*PP*, 173–4, 431, 455).

3.5 Imaginative and Somatic Work

Though intellectualism cannot forswear objective thought without under-cutting itself, it is nonetheless true that many of the advances within this tradition can be freed from the commitments defining it. Transcendental philosophy is exemplary in this respect, and Merleau-Ponty stresses its superiority to 'the intellectualism of the psychologists' that continues to posit a stratum of atomistic sense data beneath human cognition. The awareness that perception involves interpretation may help to clear the way for a true moment of insight, but a whole philosophy of causal explanation is implied whenever intellectualism accepts the naturalistic notion of a sensation (*PP*, 38–9, 47). Kant's synoptic synthesis of appre-hension as expounded in the A edition of the Critique is part of a strikingly different – and recognisably phenomenological – understand-ing of perception to be found in his writings. He grasps that we do not first see sensations, rather configurations. We apprehend figures synoptically prior to the explicit positing of diversity in conceptual syntheses, and in so doing we can imaginatively fill in their gaps when they are partially hidden (*PP*, 16, 17–18, 544).

Kant famously claims that imagination – the faculty of representing in intuition what is not itself present – is necessary for perception itself. Our transcendental syntheses must be accomplished through the productive imagination (A 120/B 151–2), an art 'hidden in the depths of the human soul' (A 141/B 180–1). Merleau-Ponty agrees; the productive and schema-tising imagination is needed for conscious anticipation and for the work of concepts and principles in developed perception. It allows us to anticipate events cognitively and must be in play when we prefigure possible courses of action (*PP*, 115, 181, 197–8). What we imagine cannot of course be observed or explored or handled, and we readily mark the distinction between direct perceptual presence and presence as phantasied (*PP*, lxxiv, lxxx, 338). Yet we rightly believe that some thought and imagined outcomes can be made real in the world, taking advantage of the recursive patterns and successions already accessed perceptually. This recursive order of 'affinity' is in Kant's view '[t]he ground of the possibility of the association of the manifold, so far as it lies in the object' (A 113). Such empirical order is also a necessary conformity of appearances to principles. All appearances associable in themselves are subject to rules for conceptual articulation

(A 121–3). For Merleau-Ponty, this is to point towards the distinction between the concept and perceptual life and the form already apprehended therein. The most basic organisation of the manifold is autochthonous, for synopses are passive syntheses foregrounding in certain ways those patterns in the phenomenal field that triggered them (*PP*, 11, 16–18, 53, 304). Form 'is the very appearance of the world, not its condition of possibility. It is the birth of a norm, not realized according to a norm ... not the projection of the interior into the exterior' (*PP*, 62). The affinity founding our initial expectations is 'the central phenomenon of perceptual life ... the constitution (without an ideal model) of a significant whole' (*PP*, 53).[15]

I referred above to schematisation, and in later chapters we shall see how the idea of a schema plays a crucial role in Merleau-Ponty's philosophy. The entire theory of the 'body schema' is implicitly a theory of perception (*PP*, 213). In its own distinctive way, it achieves a reconciliation of the general and the particular analogous to Kant's schematisations of pure and empirical concepts. Our schemas for empirical concepts predelineate empirical types in the latter's theory. The common schema of a figure in space is enriched by a more determined anticipation of appearances when the concept 'dog' comes to mind. The schema for dogs is not an image but a framework for the recognition of a figure (and presumably of its way of behaving) as that of the type of four-footed animal falling under the concept (A 141/B 180). The schema is not restricted to any one exemplar while being sufficiently determinate to stop me for the most part confusing a dog with a cat or a goat when the first enters my perceptual field. A schema for a pure concept of the understanding, by contrast, has to reconcile the concept's extreme generality with the empirical particularity of sensible intuitions for it to have its application. Such a schema functions as a rule-governed process in a judgement whereby the productive imagination applies the concept to the sensible intuition in its generation of an image. It is the formula by which imagination adds to the intuition in conformity with the concept, such that conceptual determination is effected through a certain ordering of time. The concept of causality is schematised in time as the objective or necessary succession of a cause by its effect. A sensible intuition is in this way cognised as objectively anterior to an imaginatively predelineated intuition. The generation of the image is

---

[15] Translation emended. Martin Dillon has shown that Merleau-Ponty sees Kant and Husserl as seeking a principle of autochthonous organisation preceding the immanence/transcendence bifurcation (Dillon 1987, 413–17). It is 'a spontaneous organization beyond the distinction between activity and passivity, of which the visible patterns of experience are the symbol ... an earthy and aboriginal sense, which constitutes itself by an organisation of the so-called elements'. *PrP*, 77.

triggered by the sensible intuition, and in filling it out or extending beyond it the imagined intuition remains anchored in it (B 176–81, 233–8). A glass bottle seen and heard rolling off a table awakens bad memories and an anticipation transcending merely empirical association, since perception and anticipation are implicated in an understanding structuring them by way of the schema of objective succession. My judgement entails a conceptualised image of the bottle breaking and only of necessity doing so after going over the table's edge, because only the fall will ensue in this brittle body impacting on a hard and unyielding surface.

Positing schemas for pure and empirical concepts, Kant is anticipating the theory of the intentional horizons of meaning pertaining to act intentionality. In the lifeworld the perception of the rolling bottle motivates me to rush to save it, or to wince at the impending crash and splintering if I am too late to do so. By contrast, the objectified empirical manifold in the First Critique is austere indeed, having been abstracted from practical and aesthetic interests and affectivity in general so as to isolate the proto-scientific universe for the physicist. But once we reflect on Kant's articulation of an even more austere domain in geometrical construction (one devoid of physical forces), we find the mark of an intrinsically embodied subject. Merleau-Ponty's view of the schemas and of such construction is heavily indebted to Pierre Lachièze-Rey, as Samantha Matherne has shown, and the reason for thematising it is to show that the geometer's deduction of properties of ideal space – the same uniform space posited in the Galilean and Newtonian approaches – presupposes his or her orientations and movements.[16] Kant observes that the motion in space of an object or motion as an act of the subject does not belong to geometry itself as a pure science, for it does not in any way determine its object. But without perceiving motion we could never have the concept of succession as a determination of time (as the form of inner intuition). And if we consider motion as the describing of a space, we realise that it involves the successive synthesis of the manifold of outer intuition through the productive imagination. In drawing a straight line or circle in geometrical construction one has to keep the previous parts of the figure in memory and anticipate how its completion should appear. In these senses motion belongs to geometry and to transcendental philosophy (B 155–6, 203–4, 299).

When we look closely at the constructive activity of the geometer, remarks Merleau-Ponty, we should conclude that he or she is a motor

---

[16] Matherne 2016, 203ff.

subject. Even in an imagined perceptual field, a triangle will be oriented according to up or down and left or right, and, as Kant himself states, a pure and ideal geometrical formation can only be understood when one traverses its sensible illustration (B 299). The ideal or formal relations and formal essence must be crystallised in a particular empirical thing with its concrete essence, whether drawn in sand or on paper. Such a subject has to trace out the lines with hand and stylus, and therefore project an oriented or directed gaze ahead of herself. She must also understand the figure as drawn *in* space (illustrative of an ideal formation in ideal space) and therefore grasp localisation in space prior to geometrical construction (*PP*, 405–6). To apprehend regions the subject must have already moved, and this 'motion that generates space' is distinct from the movement of things and from one's passively being moved. It is not a thought about space or 'the trajectory from some metaphysical point without a place in the world, but rather from a certain here to a certain there' (*PP*, 407). Only in active intentional movement, continues Merleau-Ponty, can one apprehend the world an open ensemble of things having places. This leads him assert that, for Kant, the moving body is not just an instrument or an object for a constituting consciousness, but an original intentionality required for the pre-conceptual constitution of any object.

As a report of Kant's view in the First Critique, this is far too generous, for empirical and specifically somatic necessity is ruled out of court, and the reference to a motion that generates space is attributable to Lachièze-Rey alone.[17] However, Kant's earlier and later writings do contain crucial insights into the constitutive contribution of one's body to having the world.[18] In his pre-critical period, he argues that the body is the fundamental ground of orientations in space. It is not a neutral instrument of perception, but an experiential structure that defies translation into an underlying and homogeneous continuum. If one looks at one's own body as well as those of others, one sees that all the limbs on one side of the body are matched part for part by those on the other side, and yet they are incongruent counterparts, since they cannot be enclosed in the same region as their opposites. No matter how much I twist and turn my right hand, I can never make it occupy the same space as the left hand with its peculiar shape and boundaries.[19] Space can be thought of as having three planes intersecting with each other at right angles, but only as they relate to my body as their ultimate ground can

---

[17] See Lachièze-Rey 1937, 30–4.
[18] For a remarkable study of how Kant anticipates phenomenological insights into the felt, skilled and oriented body, see Woelert 2007, 139–50.
[19] Kant 1992, 369–71, 396.

I come to conceive of directions or orientations in space. I stand vertically on a horizontal plane that allows for the orientations of above and below. One of the two vertical planes makes possible the distinction of my front and behind, and the other divides the body into right and left, which as we have seen are incongruent. The right–left distinction is what allows me to organise space into orientations. Even with an external marker or compass to pick out some direction, I could never identify the rising or the setting sun and find my way if the regions of east and west were not previously determined in relation to the subjective and irreducible ground of differentiation of *my* right and left.[20]

Here again, Kant shows his superiority to the intellectualism of the cognitive psychologists, for whom the body remains one more fact in the world (*PP*, 47, 215). He has realised that lived spatiality is composed of original orientations or directions, such that we never encounter a field of indifferent regions. To have the world is to have the sense of how to negotiate it, and without the anthropological relation not only right and left and front and behind but 'up' and 'down' and 'upon' and 'under' and 'next to' could have no reference and therefore no significance (*PP*, 103–4). Every orientation in space is intentional and projective, which is why figures serve as more than objects for understanding in their appearance, being indices of actual and possible engagements. One has only to be turned upside down (or to wear spectacles inverting the visual image) to experience a radical obstacle to ordinary understanding and to appreciate that perception is not an act guaranteed by this faculty and by healthy organs of sense. Orientation is not given through the head and feet as segments of a body whose functions just happen to be closest to or furthest from the ground. In this case they would furnish fields of things that are fortuitously up or down. Rather, it is given through head and feet as powers of articulating the things at intervals lengthened or shortened or closed up by way of movement. This is why references to right side up and upside down express already practical evaluations. An orientation is inseparable from the use one makes of one's organs and the correlative hold one has on things (*PP*, 47, 256–7, 262–4).

At the outset, according to Kant, the distinction of right and left is felt rather than intuited and is a natural necessity of bodily organisation. As Alfredo Ferrarin notes, he is affirming the very necessity he will deny in the First Critique.[21] In his post-critical work one's feeling of perceiving is reaffirmed and assigned even more significance. In the Third Critique,

---

[20] Ibid., 365–7, 369.   [21] Ibid., 368–9; Ferrarin 2006, 28.

perception is understood as an intrinsically felt operation going beyond self-affection as the mind's inspection of its own activity. Every empirical or sensuous presentation is taken to affect one's vitality or feeling of life, which is to say that it has affective significance for the percipient's body. Of itself the feeling contributes nothing to cognition, but it does result in consciousness relating the relevant presentation to its entire power of representation, and hence to the understanding and the productive imagination.[22] In the *Opus Postumum*, Kant goes on to contend that the perception of the empirical object is also the awareness of the moving forces of the subject as it is affecting itself in moving, albeit an awareness synthesised by the understanding. Only in moving can I appear to myself as sensitive and as embodied. Space itself can only appear as an object of possible perceptions through the material forces that are modifying the feeling of the self-affecting subject.[23] A founding role is accorded to the perceiver's movement and to the awareness of it, without which spatial objectification, imaginative representation and geometrical idealisation would be impossible.

Beyond its appeal to the feeling of life, the empirical thing has hardly been portrayed as something that someone might want to explore in any great detail. Once bodily satisfaction is achieved, so then may interest fade away. But when we read more of the Third Critique, it is made clear that sensible things exercise an allure that is distinct from biological needs and desires. Everyday human perception is an interested as well as somatically affective process in which things both gratify and please us.[24] And there is no stage of cognition higher again than aesthetic experience in which human interests would cease to count. In the apprehension of the beautiful, claims Kant, I experience a harmony of sensibility and understanding that is itself without a concept and that holds for myself and for others and between myself and others. The purposiveness or harmony experienced when the relevant object conforms to one's cognitive faculties involves a free play of understanding and imagination that is universally communicable in a judgement of taste. He adds that the consciously felt purposiveness and agreement of these faculties in their free play is requisite for cognition generally and is likewise communicable.[25] For Merleau-Ponty, one comes to discover and appreciate oneself as a nature that is spontaneously conforming to the law of understanding. The hidden art of

---

[22] Kant 2000, 90, 159.
[23] Kant 1938, 332, 364, 456. My thanks to Lilian Alweiss for pointing me to these paragraphs.
[24] Kant 2000, 176–8.   [25] Ibid., 99–103, 106.

imagination conditions the logical activities of an awareness that is never thoroughly theoretical or disinterested, either in itself or in its relation to others, so that the cognising subject 'is no longer the universal thinker of a system of rigorously connected objects' or the positing power imposing a bare law of understanding on the manifold (*PP*, lxxxi).

From the foregoing, we can conclude that the most insightful moves in transcendental philosophy are not tied to the presumptions of intellectualism with its projected panopticism in which all situatedness is surmounted. Kant has affirmed the irreducibly dynamic and constitutive functions of perceptual awareness, without restricting them to the epistemic act intentionalities of a transcendental subject and without divorcing them as a consequence from our specifically human embodiment and affectivity and interests. The phenomenological reading of Kant stresses that the synthetic function attributed to the understanding is shared across intentional life in its entirety. When the 'I think' becomes explicitly aware of a perception, the act is benefiting from work already completed (*PP*, 53, 247). Kant has in point of fact revealed and pursued a third way between the empiricism and scientific realism that absorbs consciousness into a universe of determined events and the seemingly antithetical intellectualism in which everything properly perceived or perceivable must be determined or determinable by way of scientific concepts. Phenomenology goes further again by foregrounding the work of pre-conceptual constitution and motivation, which is passed over by Brunschvicg and many cognitive psychologists. Motivation mediates the putatively mental for-itself and physical in-itself, and hence the hard dichotomy of reasons and causes.[26] For the perceiver, one phenomenon triggers another through the sense that it offers (even when that sense is allied to a discursive signification), and the world of the perceiver is that open and indefinite multiplicity where relations are reciprocally implicated (*PP*, 50–3, 73, 452–3). And if we are to do justice to our engaged and agential being in the world we need to uncover the constituting body as it is with us, as it is lived by us and as it predelineates milieus of possibilities. Its work goes on beyond causal processes and beneath the objectifying gaze of the epistemic subject.

---

[26] See Wrathall 2005, 111–28.

CHAPTER 4

Back to the Experience of the Body

4.1 Introduction

Following on his critiques of empiricism and intellectualism, Merleau-Ponty's turn to the experience of the body invokes the phenomenological reduction, the procedure of silhouetting and explicating the intentional threads that bind us indissolubly to the world. When I am climbing the steep hill to get exercise and enjoy the panoramic view from the top, or walking through the rooms of the house as a prospective buyer and renovator, it will be recalled that the whole experience requires bracketing. To be faithful to the phenomena, the entirety of the intentional living must be taken as a theme, which includes the attendant phenomenon of the body that is engaged in the one or other activity (*PP*, lxxxii). As we have seen, descriptive phenomenology has distinguished what we perceive and the way we perceive it, and in discovering that the genuinely transcendent thing can only be given inadequately we attain an essential insight (*Ids1*, 92). Eidetic phenomenology carries into a transcendental account when we ask *how* we perceive with our bodies, how we can intend things in a world that promises ever more experiences (*PP*, 94–5, 340–1).

In this chapter, I show that Merleau-Ponty not only works with Husserl's crucial distinction between the body as object and the body as lived, but agrees in large part with the latter's account of somatic constitution. This is an essential resource for his own contributions to the philosophy of embodiment. I begin by running through the Husserlian account of the body within the objectivist attitude, whose constitution as an empirical object is remarkably imperfect because of the impossibility of taking a distance from it. I then explicate Husserl's theory of my body as lived. As constantly being-touched in touching this body is constituted as a permanent presence with me, such that it is able to appear as mine. Following on Kant, my lived body is the ground or 'zero-point' of all orientations in space, and to show how it is apprehended as a here distinct from other locations there, Husserl explicates its kinaesthetic capacities for and experiences of movement. I have this same body as the organ of the will, with its capacities for movement having founded my 'I can' or sense of available agency. And my body's actual movements perpetuate my volitions, not being those of an implementation machine.

Though Merleau-Ponty explicitly concurs with Husserl's analyses, the latter's early and static account of the constitution of a three-dimensional and isotropic space passes over our lived spatiality, which is situational and anisotropic, always already privileging certain orientations in our practical engagements. Merleau-Ponty stresses that we only have this space in having the bodies that we do, and these bodies are also necessary conditions of geometrical idealisation, as Husserl comes to suggest. In our originally lived spatiality, moreover, we encounter familiar implements as ready-to-hand affordances for practical outcomes. In showing this, Merleau-Ponty draws on the ethology of Jakob von Uexküll and the existential analyses of Heidegger. I then return to the question of his phenomenological commitments, noting that he follows Heidegger in taking our existence as fundamentally projective. Against this backdrop he distinguishes the objective body or body as object from *le corps propre* or the body itself. This phrase refers to the phenomenal or lived body and the body schema that is central to his theory of embodiment. To reveal the work of the schema Merleau-Ponty will exploit pathological cases of bodily comportment.

4.2   One's Body as Object and as Lived

Husserl's account of embodiment hinges on the fundamental distinction that he draws between the objective body (*Körper*) and the body as lived or as living flesh (*Leib*). The first is the body of objective thought, studied from an external and third person scientific perspective as a physical or extended something characterised by relations of efficient causality. It is also one's body as explicitly thematised or objectified in everyday reflective episodes from the first-person perspective. The body as lived is the one I usually experience (i.e. when it is not obtrusive and when I am not thinking about it, for example in exploring the house or ascending the shallower slopes of the hill). It is lived as uniquely mine and as an attendant phenomenon that is present *with* me even when not present *to* me. The distinction speaks to two different facets of the body and ways of experiencing it. Yet if the somatically lived is irreducible to the bare physical body, the integrally founded and founding relationship between experiences and causal processes is not thereby denied. Ordinary language already refers to the interconnection, bearing the sense that *I am* this extended thing and that 'it' is mine. Thus each person says that 'I' eat and breathe and walk down the street or am pushed or pulled. I say that I am in pain and that 'it' hurts when I am cut, though not that something has been split by a wedge so that fluid trickles out. I report that I have cut *my* finger with a knife (*Ids2*, 35, 99–100, 168).

The everyday objectification of my body is inherently limited, for I cannot distance myself from it and take an external perspective on it any more than the body can distance itself from me myself. This already marks its difference from outer worldly things whose aspects are experienced from a multiplicity of standpoints, and which can and do disappear altogether from my perceptual field. I see the front of my torso and legs when I look down, and most of my side and the lower rear of my leg when I turn to look down. Yet these parts are not ordinarily in front of me or even at the margin of my visual field, let alone near its middle as my forearms and hands often are. My nose and upper eye sockets are at the margin, though the rest of my head is invisible. When taken as an object, the very body that is the means of my perception 'obstructs me in the perception of it itself and is a remarkably imperfectly constituted thing' (*Ids2*, 167). In concentrating on the lived body in the reduction, however, one foregrounds somatic structures that are ordinarily pre-objective to show how they are material a prioris of the explicit understanding of body and world. The phenomenology of somatic constitution unearths the constituting body behind the constituted one. In their work and as experienced unthematically, the somatic structures are transcendentally requisite for certain pre-conceptual senses and cannot be the preserves of humanity alone (*Ids2*, 6–7, 96–9).

The lived body is not a sum of externally related parts and is not experienced as such. And what is opposed to material nature is not a cogitating soul. Rather, it is the unity of body and soul, comprising a concrete psychophysical whole in which the one blends in with the other in the unitary stream of awareness (*Ids2*, 36, 146). Through the stream the body's presence with me is permanent. It is always marginally and sometimes attentively experienced in its undergoing of sensations, or in a more felicitous terminology in its undergoing of feelings. For Husserl, this essentially tactile presence extends to hearing and vision without having to do so, as witnessed by those who are deaf and blind. Even if sighted, I am not always seeing, and I can no more see myself in the activity of seeing than I can see the back of my head. The reflections of my eyes in a mirror can only appear like those of someone else. Certainly I always *feel* myself seeing, having localised experiences in my eyeballs as they swivel and bring an object into focus. The feeling is marginally present without being prominent when my eyes are unstrained, though I cannot imagine a being that does not *at all* feel itself in seeing or in moving more extensively. What is clear, however, is that the appearance of such a being's body would be drastically different to mine. It would be faced with a manifold of colour figures, but could never experience or monitor its efforts. Visual figures such as arms and hands might be moved by *fiat* of will, but would be mere shapes to be brought into or removed from visual presence, and by means of which other shapes can be made to appear or disappear. Such a perceiver could not attain a sense of ownership. It could never perceive its visual and motile body *as* its own (*Ids2*, 158).

As soon as we examine the tactile domain, we find that it involves a double sensation or experience. This we can explicate by considering the action of one hand touching the other. When I touch my left hand with my right, I feel something that is pliable and resistant and warm. These qualities of the left hand can quite correctly be objectified as properties of an extended something or *Körper*, but are only caught by way of the right and touching hand. In this hand there is a localised correspondence between what is felt and the feeling of it. Such localisation is a condition of determining the materiality of the touched hand, without the felt–feeling relationship amounting to an isomorphic constancy. And the left hand has its own localised experience of being-touched; it is at once object and living flesh impinged upon. Yet this relationship of touching and being-touched is interchangeable. I can alternate the roles so that the left hand becomes active and the right hand passive, and two-sidedness embraces the entire body. I have the tacit anticipation of what it feels like for any part of my body to be touched by another part and of what it feels like to do the touching. By means of the feeling in touch, the body is constituted as an exterior with a uniquely lived interior. In being felt on from the outside, it is simultaneously felt in from the inside, and this feeling from within is not precisely locatable under the skin like pieces of organic tissue (*Ids2*, 152–8).

Husserl goes on to observe that the relationship of active and passive touch does not have to involve my touching any part of my body. If I sweep one of my hands over a tabletop I experience it as flat and cold and smooth, properties again caught by way of the touching hand. Whenever I am feeling *anything* exterior, I am feeling it from within me. There are not two experiences in play, rather two moments of one overall experience. As

Husserl later puts it, they show a reflexivity peculiar to the body. Conscious reflexivity is the awareness of being aware, whereas bodily reflexivity is the feeling of feeling, of being touched when I am touching (*Ids2*, 153–5; *CM*, 97). It is the lived body's self-appearance or self-affection in perceiving things, and is arguably discernible in every experience of resistance (for instance from one's airways when breathing rapidly or from weight when waving one's arm). But one way or another, the experience of touching and being-touched is a material a priori of apprehending and explicitly recognising one of the things that I see from outside (however imperfectly) as uniquely mine. Through the feeling my visible body is itself constituted as an outside with an inside. In seeing my arm lying on the settee or waving so as to stress a point, I also have the localised feeling of it being at rest or of effort and articulation in moving it. Localisation in the visual field is correlated with tactile localisation, the externally seen limb with the internally felt flesh or *Leib*. By virtue of the somatic reflexivity of touch, I can progress to the idea that this unique body of mine 'has' or undergoes experiences, be they seen, unseen or unseeable (*Ids2*, 158–9, 160, 174). Stein comments that its peculiar reflexivity is best brought out in its absence, for instance when I wake up with a temporarily dead arm that was trapped under my torso. If I cannot move or feel it in any way, it will look strange in the fashion of a corpse, as no longer alive and not belonging to me.[1]

4.3   Body and Thing and Space

This lived body that is permanently with me in its being felt is also the fundamental ground of directions or orientations in space. Reaffirming Kant's thesis, Husserl remarks that all worldly beings appear right or left, above or below and near or far from the perceiver's perspective. For its subject the lived body has the distinction of being the unique 'zero-point' (*Nullpunkt*) of every orientation, the ineliminable and central standpoint from which the ego can come to intend and fulfil objects. In being a zero-point the body is constantly present with me as an 'absolute here', no matter where in the world I might be resting or where I might be approaching. We loosely describe an object within reach as being here, or even a wider locality, but this is always a relative position indexed onto what is absolute. In relation to this singular and uniquely experienced here, every other existent or place is sensuously and imaginatively apprehended as outside me, as a particular 'there' (*TS*, 109; *Ids2*, 61–2, 165–6). Yet the

---

[1] Stein 1989, 47–8.

senses of here and there with their apprehensions of orientations and distances are not primitive givens, but synthetic achievements. In his lectures on thing and space Husserl seeks to show how they are constituted, how we derive that composite sense of three-dimensional and unending space in which I am aware of occupying one place among others, a space capable of objectification and eventual theoretical idealisation in Euclidean geometry (*TS*, 130–3, 203).

The thesis that space is the form of our outer intuition is rejected; rather it is the form of bodily things themselves. However Kant's unexploited claim that material forces in bodily movement must modify the feeling of the self-affecting subject for space to become an object is accepted, with the crucial addendum that we must move in certain ways. Our sense of space with its sensible schema of the thing – or horizontal predelineation of its appearing as a thing in space – is an achievement that presupposes the deployment and experience of specific somatic capacities (*TS*, 37, 223, 257–8; *APS*, 212). Husserl seeks to account for our apprehension of a surround that is objectifiable as three-dimensional, infinite and isotropically uniform, having the same properties in all axes or directions. To show how the form is articulated through sensible syntheses, he again operates within the phenomenological *epochē* and reduction. We must thematise pre-scientific claims about spatial being in the natural attitude. The task is to return to these acquisitions without assuming their truth or falsity in advance. We suspend this question so as to unpack the significations in the claims. We must find their warrant in perceptual evidences and reveal how we can arrive at such founding evidences (*TS*, 118–20, 257).

The claim is that our sense of space comes to givenness through what Henry Charlton Bastian called 'kinaestheses'.[2] A kinaesthetic system is a perceiver's capacity or skill for a particular mode of self-movement, or active movement at will. Eye, head and leg kinaestheses comprise distinctive systems. In their operation the relevant systems are manifested in kinaesthetic experience. This is the ongoing awareness of self-moving, that is, the concurrent feeling of the activity. Kinaestheses inhabit all acts of perceiving, though their appearances are marginal. They do not present a thing or its qualities, and as deployed and felt unthematically they are not objectively present but co-present, so closely bound to seeing as to phenomenally blend into and be at one with it. Our kinaesthetic capacities enable certain visual experiences – and our expectations of the latter – in correlated and determinable ways. As active and as passively felt they are

---

[2] See Bastian 1882, 543, 591–611.

essential for revealing thing and space or constituting the sensible schema (*TS*, 134–8, 168, 237–8). Because my body is always present with me, I can distinguish kinaesthetic co-presence and absence and hence my moving or not moving, even if the marginal presence of developed kinaestheses obscures their contributions to spatial awareness (*TS*, 137–8, 241–4). Husserl's analysis is static, an ahistorical archaeology of their work. One kinaesthetic system and the visual horizon it constitutes is explicated at a time. Any consciousness having our space must have this system and experience it in its deployment (*TS*, 102, 118, 131–4).

Husserl begins with a scenario of a creature with a fixed body and head and single cyclopean eye that cannot swivel in the slightest. There would be no sense of perceiving in a field, since there would be nothing but a unifold or unilateral expanse with clear qualitative contrasts in the direct line of sight, whether a visual object or colour figure rested or moved. Once it started to move, it would immediately blur and quickly escape from sight. Husserl notes that the tracking of anything over time would be impossible. There could be no identification of a thing in and through its changing appearances because there could be no sliding transition of manifolds without the ability to traverse them visually. If a figure presented a qualitatively different aspect when brought back to clear view – for example a megaphone now presented from its side rather than front – it would appear as a different figure. Its re-identification would demand the restitution of the same frontal aspect, though a second megaphone looking identical could have been substituted for it (*TS*, 76, 92, 125, 131–2). Kevin Mulligan notes that if this creature had conceptual capacities, it would lack dynamic presentations. It would have no continuous transitions of aspects and performative identifications of unities to found judgments of identity.[3]

Let us now consider a simple motility, as if the creature were to gain and use the ability to swivel its eye. This furnishes a basic oculomotric field. Perceived within it and identified through its manifolds are colour figures or shapes that need not as yet convey substantial or causal properties. They can be above or below or left or right and change in individual and relative location and in size, shape and internal detail. They can appear, disappear and reappear, and be tracked near the periphery of the field without blurring, though optimal presentation is at the centre. The monocular field is not a surface in space, which makes no sense, and need not be a sheer two-dimensional manifold (*TS*, 139–41, 162, 269). It might have a depth value for a consciousness, though Husserl qualifies this carefully. It

---

[3] Mulligan 1995, 196.

would be devoid of contrasting and hence distinct values, since no means are available for determining them. Such depth would be pre-objective or pre-empirical, as against properly seen depth, which is always that of things (*TS*, 140, 146, 194).

Once its oculomotric powers are exercised a being can attain the awareness of perceiving in a field, for eye rotation reveals possibilities beyond the current manifold. More is brought to view looking right and up, for example, at the cost of losing what was left and down. The figures are particular possibilities of appearing by way of eye swivelling. Hence the horizon of a figure within a field is essentially indexed onto and constituted by what Husserl calls the system of oculomotric kinaestheses. Figure stasis is correlated with kinaesthetic constancy, and movement with felt kinaesthetic change. If a figure is spiralling across the sky, the relevant kinaesthetic sequence lies behind the sense of perceiving a unitary something. The unbroken seeing and feeling of seeing found the performative identification of a unity through changes of position and detail (*TS*, 141–2, 159). Let us now suppose the usual case of two eyes functioning together to effect binocular vision. In convergent vision it delivers the phenomenon of standing in relief and may reveal with the second eye what we as developed perceivers would call a further side of a figure. Binocularity facilitates the apprehension of distinctive depth-values, though we do not yet have the relief of things any more than their depth determinations (*TS*, 145–7, 194). We also lack the ability to distinguish movements of the body from those of its visual figures. Imagine that a head with an oculomotric system alone is carried right around a figure that it is viewing. The figure might subsequently rotate in such a way that the same sequence of visual aspects and feelings would elapse as those when the figure was static and the head being transported around it (*TS*, 148, 213).

We progress from here to the cephalomotric power of head rotation on several axes, and this system brings us into the cyclical manifold of turning. New oculomotric manifolds open up, and figure centering will demand different positioning. We gain up–down and right–left coordinates correlated with particular ways of moving and holding the head. At this stage, orientations of phenomena depend on our postures. Previously hidden aspects of a colour figure may be seen, widening it within narrow parameters. Head movement might modify a previous appearance of a dice, for example, bringing a new aspect into view that binocular vision was unable to reveal. Without these neck kinaestheses, a subsequent coming to appearance of that same aspect tells the perceiver that the figure is moving rather than its head (*TS*, 174–6, 196, 239). We enhance this capacity when we factor in the wider body leaning this way and that and rotating on its own axis, in which case an original field of unmoving appearances is recovered at the end of a full revolution (*TS*, 140, 192, 263, 267). These kinaesthetic systems can do substitutive duty; if the neck freezes in tracking something the torso can be turned sooner. The relations of kinaesthetic systems and vision are functional rather than one-to-one (*TS*, 144, 196, 244, 271).

The expectations and correlative perceptual senses constituted in the cyclical manifold are nonetheless limited. Expansion or contraction of a figure and gain or loss of internal detail cannot constitute the relativity grasped in developed perceptions of approaching and receding. Covering is also underdetermined, the phenomenon of a figure disappearing behind another and reappearing or its demolition and rebuilding not being informed by the distinction of 'beside' and 'upon'. Nor can it be grasped that sides and details of a figure may vanish and reappear due to its complete rotation or undulation (*TS*, 175, 201–5, 208–11). These shortcomings boil down to the inability of eye, head and trunk kinaestheses to found the full sense of three-dimensional space. While the collaborative senses of their fields and figures are vastly richer than the deliverances of a frozen eye and head and body, by themselves they would leave us with a total field that in its manifolds would be closed and unified in a spherical fashion, at least if we could see down and around as well as across and around (*TS*, 267–8, 271). Employing John Drummond's illustration, the field could not appear as more than a planetarium seen from inside alone.[4]

It will be surmised that the next step is to explicate our changes of place. We are not fixed in one location. Forwards and backwards kinaestheses and their vectors introduce what Husserl calls the linear manifold of approaching and receding. This enables appearances not potentially available in the cyclical manifold, and the sense that there are fields as well as objects completely beyond current experience while being available locomotively in the future. In the linear manifold, figure expansion and contraction and gain and loss are correlated with locomotive kinaestheses, as are their aspects and internal details. And in this visual field, some of the lateral changes are uniquely indexed onto kinaestheses. Imagine that we are walking down the middle of a long avenue lined with yew trees on either side. As members of each visual column, the trees appear, move outwards, expand and disappear, with more expected to appear if locomotion

---

[4] Drummond 1983, 189–90.

continues. In the course of our walk, one tree attracts our attention, and we swerve to approach it. What is encountered in both cases is non-uniform visual expansion. The outer figures about to pass by expand at a faster rate than the inner members of the columns, but the figure being directly approached expands more quickly again as one gets closer (*TS*, 177, 185–8, 197).

Differing rates of expansion and of contraction also manifest covering and revealing roles. If a certain figure is approached it increasingly hides other figures, and if one moves away and looks back, some of them reappear. Husserl contends that non-uniform expansion and contraction are essential to articulate our space of three-dimensions. Incorporated into kinaestheses, they show that the 'upon' relation of covering is separable from that of 'beside', and that visual figures and details in relief are not all *equally* removed from the perceiver. Kinaesthetically informed changes in their sizes during one's locomotive episodes are needed for the conscious grasp of relations transcending absolute depth, namely those of being nearer to or further from this permanently felt standpoint. What we call depth is not registered of itself alone. In the constituted empirical sense, it is relative, appearing through the percipient's apprehension of different intervals between the seen figures and its own zero-point position. The senses of 'here' and the near and far 'there' are co-constituted. Depth proper is an achievement founded on the correlation of locomotive kinaestheses with inconstant changes in visual magnitudes. Such awareness is *eo ipso* of different depth values between the figures (*TS*, 146, 197– 201, 239).

The relations of nearness and farness manifesting relative depth do not as yet have to be assimilated to precise determinations of space, that is to say to those marked out in terms of metres and kilometres and so forth. Conscious apprehension is not of necessity meant, conceptual and judicative articulation. The zero-point is not in front of oneself, and cannot as a consequence fall within the sphere of measurable presentation or calculative distance estimation (*TS*, 193). Like the things themselves, the intervals between them need not be perceived as extensive magnitudes. In this way, Husserl anticipates a thesis forwarded by Heidegger as well as Merleau-Ponty, that certain cognitive capacities characteristic of objective thought can be dormant. For the most part, we comport ourselves in a lived rather than objectified spatiality (*BT*, 139–40; *PP*, 272–3). A similar point has been argued by Christopher Peacocke. At a certain stage of life and in certain contexts, distance recognition does not have to be conceptualised. Phenomenal distances can be 'unit-free', in that quantities may be perceived empirically without being represented as measured or even as measurable through numerical quantity concepts.[5]

If the original yew tree retains our interest, we can see more of it again by walking around it. In completing an orbit we gain another cyclical manifold and end with the aspect that we began with. With the successive visual appearances informed by kinaestheses of orbiting, it is possible to apprehend a figure as closed and as enclosing an 'inside' with both its seen and unseen sides. And some figures can be orbited on all axes. Once this is grasped so too is the space surrounding them. As Husserl puts it, the omnisided closedness of the figure is at the same time its total separation from every other body. They are partitioned by means of what we describe as empty space, taken as the 'between' that can be imaginatively populated in this way or that. The senses of things and of space are equiprimordial; we gain a three-dimensional surround in apprehending fully bounded particulars at different removes with varied shapes and details (*TS*, 212–6, 220–3). Space also comes to be grasped as open to all possible orientations. In every phase of movement towards a thing, we can reverse our direction or strike out elsewhere, swerving to take another path. Once we gain the awareness of our *de jure* capacity to move in any direction without end, space becomes objectifiable as an infinite magnitude and as isotropic (*TS*, 99–100, 275). Our achieved schema of the thing in space is of a complete and closed corporeality over and in which sensuous qualities are extended, and which is always given in a location and an orientation (*TS*, 247, 257, 298–9).

4.4   The I Can and the Will

The body is the sensing, motile and dynamic bearer of the zero-point of orientation thanks to which the embodied ego has been able to intuit space and the whole world of the senses (*Ids2*, 36, 61). In developed perception with its fulfilments of empty intentions, it is a freely movable organ of experience, being used and unthematically experienced as an integrated totality of sense organs. So long as it is unhindered by pains and injuries, its free movement is immediate; there is no gap between an egoic intention to move and the actual movement that is made. My body is the sole existent I can move without mediation. Another body is always a there that is exterior to me, and to act on it I must close my distance from it (in the absence of tools or missiles or someone to act for me). Even the clothes

[5] Peacocke 1986, 1–18.

touching me need the mediation of my body to be moved. But if I cannot control anything remotely, neither am I remotely controlled. I may well be following a request or order, but the other is not directly governing my body. Husserl notes that my body is the only thing that I can move spontaneously as well as immediately, and for this reason it is apprehended as the organ of the will (*Willensorgan*). It is that in which and over which I hold sway, and is in the same blow the power or potentiality of effecting this or that outcome. I have power in the world on account of my power over my body. My body converts my decisions into actualities, and as such it constitutes my concrete freedom. Against spiritualism and certain strains of Platonism, it is that which enables rather than imprisons intentional life (*Ids2*, 159, 273; *CES*, 107–8, 217).

When I explicitly grasp one of my kinaesthetic powers, that is, my ability to move in a particular way, the relevant capacity is foregrounded as a positive potentiality, not as an empty ability (*Ids2*, 267). Thus I am aware that I can buy some last minute groceries if only I start running to reach the shop before it closes.[6] I am aware that I can avoid the garrulous bore at the party if only I avert my eyes and turn my head away before our glances meet. The *fiat* presupposes the *fieri*, the awareness of what is to be achieved, which entails the imaginative framing of a possible scenario. Should this possibility carry into actuality, it is ascribed to a free act of will. And because my body is the proximate potentiality for actualising what might be chosen, I presumptively *have* that body as at my disposal, not merely as belonging to me (*Ids2*, 99, 104, 297). Yet this raises a concern that Husserl has not escaped the Cartesian representation, decision and implementation model of action. On this model we may recall that the thinking and imagining mind has a physical body to furnish movement. As soon as I choose to pursue what I have imagined, the body carries the discrete decision into practice and realises the imaginative picture. On being exercised, the *fiat* of will gives way to the *facere* or making real.

Husserl addresses this concern. He begins by stressing that bodily movement is both logically and temporally prior to will in the sense of volition. Kinaesthetic capacities are in their origin indissociable from instinctual drives, as we see in the reaching and grasping activities of infants. Thus we can admit a primal will in the sense of a striving to satisfy biological imperatives. And this primitive striving is taken up and transformed in the acquisition and habitualisation of those capacities commonly said to comprise our second nature. Thus I move my hand

---

[6] See Taipale 2014, 43.

involuntarily (*unwillkürlich*) because it is in an uncomfortable position, while on another occasion I am suddenly seized by a desire to smoke, and instinctively reach for a cigar 'without further ado'. In both these instances the power shows up as an operative intentionality without any deliberate act (*Ids2*, 270–2; *EJ*, 84). As sedimented acquisitions, my kinaesthetic capacities contribute to the sphere of unconscious drives, associations, persevering tendencies and habitualities comprising my developed nature. This sphere of sensibility also permeates the life of consciousness or spirit, with its blind if not arbitrary operations marking the ongoing course of intentional life. Husserl contends that there are no volitions that I make *in vacuo*. The ego lives in the medium of its own history, and even its free acts have a nature behind them, though they do not by definition arise from merely natural lawfulness (*Ids2*, 289, 350).[7]

While kinaesthetic powers must be in place for involuntary movements, their contribution to voluntary ones or actions proper may be variegated more clearly. Each one lies behind (and for that matter inhabits) the *fiery*, the *fiat* and the *facere* as their mutual condition. The evidence for the kinaesthetic contribution to the first and the second lies in the particular ways that certain possibilities are imagined:

> In the physical sphere, all of my abilities are mediated by 'the operation of my lived body', by my lived bodily abilities and faculties. I know through experience that the parts of my lived body move in that special way which distinguishes them from all other things and motions of things (physical, mechanical motions); i.e., they have the character of subjective movement, of the 'I move'. And from the very outset this can be apprehended as something practically possible. Indeed, we have to say in general that only what has this subjective character admits a priori of such an apprehension. Originally, it is only here that the 'I will' emerges. Originally, it is here and only here that an imagined will can be affirmed and can become an actual willing.[8] (*Ids2*, 271)

When I form an image of a centaur, such a being is comprehended as logically possible (however remotely), but not as something that can sensuously appear or be brought to such appearance. It is not intended as capable of fulfilment beyond that of phantasy. When I imagine shifting my table to a nicer place in my kitchen, by contrast, I am at once anticipating the action and outcome as practically possible; it can be fulfilled spontaneously as well as dynamically. My kinaesthetic capacities have contributed essentially to the implicit sense and explicit meaning of the imagined

---

[7] See also Smith 2007, 11, 15–16.   [8] Translation emended.

situation (*Ids2*, 273–5). To predelineate with one's lived body as a positive potentiality – which again is different from an empty and undetermined ability – is to enjoy the *sense* of immediately available agency constitutive of the very situation. The sense seamlessly facilitates the weaving of the envisaged tapestry (i.e. the appearance of the kitchen if the table has been moved over there). In order to imagine a practical possibility or outcome, on this account, my bodily capacities must have founded the sense that 'I can' (*Ich Kann*) or 'I am able to' (*Ids2*, 267; *APS*, 51). If I am not currently in my kitchen, but imagining it from far away, the 'I can' is in the mode of the 'I could', as something I *could* do if I were there (*Ids2*, 277–9).

No physiological examination of the body as *Körper* can reveal how this sense of available agency is founded, and ordinarily it is not foregrounded. Seamlessly predelineating a practical possibility, the 'I can' is for the most part a pre-reflective or taken for granted awareness, the presumptive ability to do just this. The appropriate ways of moving were accomplished in the past and are enabling and inhabiting the imagined scenario (*Ids2*, 13, 272–3). Through the founded and founding 'I can', the ego may consider choosing a certain course of action and actually choose it. Husserl observes that only a practical possibility made explicit can be a theme of my will. I cannot will as an immediate outcome anything beyond my current competence, and it is only between practical possibilities that I can ever decide. The arcing forward into possibility of practical and somatically constituted intentionality is presupposed for the ego to have something towards which or against which it can exert itself in volitional terms (*Ids2*, 270; *APS*, 94). Thanks to the body's kinaesthetic capacities as taken up in the 'I can' or embodied sense of agency, the ego is always already motivated and oriented towards certain situations. It *must* live in the medium of its own somatic history with regard to the voluntary, since its freedom of intention is founded on – and continually depends on – its embodied freedom of action. The body is only the organ of the will under qualification, which is one more reason why the distinction between the pure ego and its acts – which are continuous with its bodily capacities – can be no more than abstract (*Ids2*, 105–6).

If a decision is not unmotivated, neither is it an abrupt and instantaneous *fiat* of will that gives way to physical execution, such that the former would disappear once the body as supposed implementation machine has been set in motion. We must of course speak of the event of decision and of rational as well as non-rational motivations if the very idea of freedom is to have meaning. Yet the act of will with its chosen outcome carries into the entire course of the relevant bodily movement, which is irreducible as a consequence to a physical event in the universe of objective thought as correlate of the outer and third-person attitude. Husserl is in broad agreement with Schopenhauer, for whom the act of will and the movement of the body are not two things objectively known which a bond of causality unites. They do not stand in such a relation, but are the same thing given in different ways, one as a representation for understanding and the other in immediate experience.[9] Once we focus on the acting body, claims Husserl, we can discern that the will is immanent in the movement sequence, inhabiting it and expressing itself through it in the observable striking and lifting and so forth. The acting body is animated through and through by the intentional act, perpetuating the act of will in effecting it in the world, which does not entail that one remain mindful of the decision or cognise one's body as goal-directed over the course of the activity. In the main, one is aware of the body through the tactile and kinaesthetic feelings and anticipations accompanying the relevant movements and constituting its presence with me (*Ids2*, 104–5; *CES*, 217–8).

One nonetheless remains on the scene as a psychophysically committed existent in bringing about what is aimed at in the willing. This is why the repudiation of a decision in the course of an action is experienced straight off as a re-orientation of one's whole being, embracing lived body and ego alike. The decision has ostensively ceased to be perpetuated in a doing (*CM*, 66–7). Where I continue to aim at what is willed but run into resistance, that experience is again undifferentiated initially, for it is that of the whole existent being slowed or frustrated. The hindrance or obstacle is experienced as such for the practically oriented self in its entirety (*Ids2*, 104, 270–1). Stein notes that in such experiences the causal conditioning of the will is clearest. When I am climbing a mountain but stop through tiredness, my volition does not win through and I become despondent. I only experience my will as efficacious should I overcome my tiredness and make it to the summit, in which case my mood is victorious – I have struggled and prevailed.[10] Yet consciousness and will were first conditioned by the possibility of climbing opened up by my kinaesthetic capacities. In practical behaviour, as Husserl remarks, one can even feel oneself conditioned by the call of a positive possibility (*Ids2*, 148, 197; *APS*, 43).

4.5   Inheritances and Affordances

In explicating *le corps objectif* and *le corps phénoménal*, Merleau-Ponty takes up Husserl's distinction between *Körper* and *Leib* and brings out even more of the latter's uniqueness. When I bracket the natural attitude and explicate

---

[9] Schopenhauer 1969, 100.   [10] Stein 1989, 54–6.

the experience of the body in the return enquiry or reduction, I realise that its permanence *with* me is a condition of grasping the permanence of objects in the world. My body as lived rather than as objectified is the very means of communicating with them. Its marginal presence – with its complementary characteristics of being at the edge of my visual field and not being focally or thematically present – is essentially and structurally necessary. Ordinarily it is neither visible nor tangible as *what* is seeing and touching, though it is co-experienced through these perceptions of things. External perception and the perception of one's own body vary together because they are two sides of a single act. But even when I thematise the bodily reflexivity of touching and being-touched required to recognise this body as mine, its ambiguity is ineliminable, a characteristic of the phenomenon to which Husserl does not advert. I have to switch from one moment to the other, giving only one my attention. I am always too late to catch the overall phenomenon. In action I cannot even successfully foreground either side of the experience. I may try to register my body explicitly from the outside over the course of an activity, as if it were an external thing being-touched. Alternatively, I may try to feel it explicitly from the inside. But any attempt to thematise one side of the body's reflexivity slows it down or throws it off course, making it slide towards inaction. The more I make the body explicitly present, the more the world towards which it is oriented recedes (*PP*, 92–5, 99, 191, 209–12, 336).

As Merleau-Ponty is well aware, few experiences make the world of action recede more than physical pain, and few show so well the ambiguity of bodily presence. If I say that my finger hurts because I have cut it with a knife, or that my foot hurts because I have walked on a nail, I do not mean that my finger or foot is a cause of the pain in the same way as the knife or nail, only differing in being closer in the causal chain leading up to this uniquely intimate experience or in being the last object in the external world before it begins. What I really mean is that the pain is constitutive of a 'pain space' that is voluminous or enormous without having a determinable shape and place like an external object. I will of course try to objectify a pain and its rough location to ease it and to pull away from its causal source, but language and external perception pass over the ambiguity of pain. Nothing attracts conscious objectification so strongly, and nothing resists its attempted determination so persistently. The lived experience is at once obtrusive and indeterminable (*PP*, 96, 220). Although Husserl has noted that I describe the painful body part as 'it' as well as 'mine', Merleau-Ponty is indicating another strangeness to which the former *does* advert. I may think that a pain is 'objectively' localised around the knife blade or nail tip, but experientially it bears no precise moment of location and extension. For Husserl, the pain is revealing a pre-empirical or pre-objective domain of experience that cannot be brought to clarity and distinctness (*TS*, 65).

Merleau-Ponty's proximity to Husserl is clearest on our embodied sense of available agency, the backdrop to his critique of the objectivist view of human action and to his own theory of the projective body schema. My decisions are never devoid of motives underpinned by my powers of movement, and when deliberating in full health I rarely need to think about these powers. The phenomenal or lived body is never an empty ability but a capacity for determinate action. Motility founds the original act intentionality of thought, imagination and will, for to consider doing something is to invoke the I can, my embodied sense of agency. But because my powers appear within the tacit unity of the I can, and because I use my body as a single organ, it is tempting to regard it an implementation machine or mere organ of the will. Objective thought forgets that the 'having' of the body in the awareness of immediately available agency is the outcome of a process of acquiring the appropriate powers, constituted as positive potentialities (*PP*, 139, 328, 330, 481). Obsessed with external relationships. it also forgets that the implementation of an act of will through movement is in the same blow its continuation. Walking and holding are expressions and perpetuations of living intentions (*PP*, 55–6, 330).

The distinction between being one's body and having that body is fleshed out elegantly by Gabriel Marcel, who remarks that a who (*qui*) as possessor of a what (*quid*) ordinarily stands in an external relation with the latter, even if its ownership by this or that person is socially and legally sanctioned. Strictly speaking, I can only have something whose existence is independent of me. Having-as-possession does not capture the having-for-oneself of one's body, in which there is an internal relation of the *qui* and *quid* without one collapsing into the other. Hence the idea of having the body as an instrument at my disposal misses its contribution to my identity, implying a lofty distance and mastery just as abstract as that of an awareness submerged in somatic drives and desires. Marcel helps Merleau-Ponty to qualify two everyday ways of referring to the body.[11]

---

[11] Marcel 1949, 155–66. Merleau-Ponty states that he takes *être* in the weak sense of a thing or logical subject of predication and *avoir* as the relation of the subject towards the terms into which it is projected (my having an idea or desire or fear). *Avoir* corresponds roughly to Marcel's *être* and *être* to

In the weak sense of *être* I am my body (*je suis mon corps*), since I am essentially embodied and this body is not someone else's. In another sense I have my body (*j'ai mon corps*) for my projects. As an enabling condition of my imagination and will, however, it inhabits my choices. I do not have it like my house or my hat, as simply owned and steered by me (*PP*, 151, 527, 529–30). And the choices having been made, it perpetuates them in the world in *ways* I need not formulate, as we shall see in a coming chapter.

Concurring with both Husserl and Kant, the lived body is the ground of all thing apprehensions and orientations. Without tracking, approaching and orbiting things and the awareness of bodily identity in the moving one could never have an intelligible thing in space; movement, its anticipation and its ongoing feeling first determine the sense of the thing. If the very words 'enclose' and 'between' are to have significance, they must borrow it from our somatic work. Without the presence of a psychophysical subject successively taking different standpoints, there could be no objective inside and outside (*PP*, 103–4, 209–10, 258). When one has apprehended the structure of depth, moreover, one has not received it passively but has accomplished it actively. Depth is the most existential of all dimensions, since it is always relative to the perceiver's unique perspective. In apprehending the milieu of the near and the far from here, one also apprehends one's situatedness here. Without this experience, the spatial world could not take on its sense before my eyes (*PP*, 266–9, 277, 430–1). The apprehension of relative depth prior to conceptualisation involves the awareness that the position of an object relative to a perceiver's standpoint cannot be reduced to its position within the perceiver's visual field.[12]

As a static procedure that uncovers the conditions of possibility of spatial experience for any consciousness, however, Husserl's early account passes over our human spatiality. Merleau-Ponty stresses that the latter is situational and anisotropic in that it privileges those orientations through which things are approached, taken up and used. Orientations are given through our bodies as positive powers of organising perceptual fields so as to act in them. Left or right, up or down and near or far are weighted practically in that body and thing and space are always polarised towards outcomes. The near or the far are also from the outset a better or worse hold on something, with the spatiality of bodily movement and 'external' space comprising a practical system (*PP*, 103–5, 262–5, 278). And without

his *avoir* (*PP*, 529–30). But as Landes adds, Merleau-Ponty *does* use *être* as Marcel does. See *PP*, 151, 527.

[12] Drummond 1983, 193. See also *PP*, 103–4.

having just these bodies to draw figures with, as we saw in the last chapter, we could never reach the ideal and isotropic space of geometrical synthesis (*PP*, 406–8). Husserl himself factors in our bodies in his late essay on the origin of geometry. Our ancestors foregrounded and took up certain things in their perceptual fields for practical purposes, notably those that were more or less sharp, straight and flat. They then discovered ways of making smoother the surfaces of the things to optimise their utility. When they combined these skills with the arithmetic that originated in the social need for just distribution, they were able to develop measuring techniques for surveying areas of land and for constructing buildings and pathways. Only on foot of these founding achievements could the theoretical and imaginative leap be made to the ideal isotropic space explicated in geometry (*CES*, 375–7).

Such an account integrates the somatic and the intellectual and is attentive to the wide variety of skills developed in the pre-scientific life-world, not least those of cutting and sharpening and polishing and moulding. Our bodies are essential for being involved in the world productively (and indeed for sheer enjoyment) as distinct from existing alongside things in a merely side-by-side fashion.[13] Yet Husserl still wishes to avoid anthropologism. The processes of refining surfaces that we traversed in factual history are taken to exemplify those that any conceivable awareness must traverse in any conceivable history. Stories that hang on specifically human movement are infected by species relativism, and even then the course that must be followed is a necessary but not sufficient condition of the theoretical leap into ideal and isotropic space (*CES*, 377–8). Husserl's account is nonetheless amenable to an existential interpretation. Merleau-Ponty can argue that there is no good reason to devalue the factical, since we have come to find eminent necessity in our specifically human bodies and in the kinds of motility that are peculiar to them (*PP*, 431, 455). He is not slow to clarify his own through-and-through view of somatic necessity:

> Existence has no fortuitous attributes and no content that does not contribute to giving it its form, it does not admit any pure facts in themselves, because it is the movement by which facts are taken up . . . all 'functions' in man – from sexuality and motricity through to intelligence – are rigorously unified. It is impossible to distinguish in the total being of man a bodily organisation that one could treat as a contingent fact and other predicates that necessarily belong to him. Everything is necessary in man, and, for

---

[13] As my second reviewer has noted, Levinas is right against Heidegger in emphasising the importance of enjoyment. Our bodies are for play as much as for work. See Levinas 1969, 110–21.

example, it is not through a simple coincidence that the reasonable being is also the one who stands upright or who has opposable thumbs – the same manner of existing is expressed in both of these cases (*PP*, 173–4).

The import of the closing words has been brought out adroitly by Paul Crowther. The upright posture lets us survey things near and far in a glance, and comprehend the internal complexity of distant wholes without always having to resolve them into parts. It must thus be understood in conjunction with opposable fingers and thumbs. Our hands let us take things apart and put them together and anticipate doing so when things are out of reach. The integral unity of our cognitive function is founded on our simultaneous apprehensions of complex wholes and component parts we can analyse and recompose. Our bodily skills foreshadow our explicit intellectual achievements, produced in a reciprocal relationship with language.[14]

When Merleau-Ponty turns to the *unthematic* way in which familiar things appear in our developed human spatiality, he takes up insights from Heidegger and from Uexküll, whose importance has been flagged by Katherine Morris.[15] The basic premise underlying Uexküll's work is that organisms and their worlds from insects through to humans must be understood through biology as ethology, the study of their lives in their environments and not in the laboratory. Harking back overtly to Kant, appearances for a specific organism are structured by that very organism.[16] It is a 'subject' in so far as it actively appropriates specific aspects of its surroundings, selectively cutting out its own milieu to attain the ends of its species. What we call its environment (*Umwelt*) is formed invariably from the interrelations of its perceptual world (*Merkwelt*) and its effect world (*Wirkwelt*), the latter comprising everything that it effects or produces by means of its activities.[17]

Uexküll initially uses the metaphor of a bubble to characterise the environing world of each organism, but also talks of the threads that it weaves out to qualities of things. Its web overlaps with those of other organisms in symbiotic relations, though its world is closed in being the only one it can have and in being inaccessible to the others (though it must be mediately accessible to us if we can say anything about it). Within each world each thing appears in different spatialities and places. Used by different organisms in their own ways, it has qualities for each alone.[18] Seeing the flowers in the meadow, a young woman gently grasps and

---

[14] Crowther 2015, 270–1. [15] Morris 2012, 141–4. [16] Uexküll 1926, xv–v.
[17] Uexküll 2010, 42, 53. [18] Ibid., 43, 53, 69–70, 126–32.

plucks them by their stems, transforming them into a decoration for her lover. An ant runs along a single stem, using its surface pattern to reach edible leaves and aphids and transforming it into a path. With her mouth a grazing cow tears up the stems and flowers alike, transforming the whole plant into agreeable food. An environment's appearances are bound to the ways that an organism can take them up. It searches out for aspects of things facilitating situations of sustenance and safety – and indeed of romantic attachment – and responds no less actively to hindrances and predators. All this being the case, its environing things are not raw stimuli but signs or carriers of significance for wider possibilities to be actualised or avoided. They have a sense pointing beyond what is directly presented, in each instance towards some outcome. And that the use features of the tree or flower are not intrinsic to that thing but essentially relational makes them no less real. A stem might only be a pathway for an ant, but this takes nothing from the genuine opportunity it manifests.[19]

In our own environing world, we notice the 'sitting' of the chair, the 'drinking' of the cup, the 'climbing' of the ladder and even the 'walking' of the floor. We perceive in the objects the acts to be performed with them as assuredly as their shape or colour. Once we learn how to use something, its perceptible features assume a functional shading or 'effect tone', to the extent of becoming vehicles for its usage signification. The effect tone can extinguish those perceptual features foregrounding the thing as if it were a relationless and self-standing object.[20] Human implements are unique in being produced through extensive and explicit planning and in being employed in diverse ways. Thus a chair may be used as a weapon, gaining a hitting tone as well as a sitting one.[21] Throughout this narrative, Uexküll is setting out what J. J. Gibson has entitled an 'affordance' of an environment, something it offers to an animal or human and furnishes for good or ill. Whatever affords an action and its outcome for a particular organism cuts across the dichotomy of the subjective and the objective and reveals its inadequacy.[22] Uexküll goes on to remark that an organism plays its own

---

[19] Ibid., 96, 140–5, 186.

[20] Ibid., pp. 49, 94–7, 125, 141. When he attends to our dealings with finished implements like cups and knives in our lived space, Husserl already notes that we gain an immediate command of them when we refine our movements. See Manuscripts A 6, 10, 11b; D 10/21, 31, 42, 43; D 13-I, 8–10, trans. Jacobs 2014, 95–6. New horizons of association and evaluation are opened up through manual activities, and we then perceive the things for immediate use and benefit, such as the cup for drinking and the violin for playing (*Ids2*, 193, 197–9; *EJ*, 50). Jacobs is right that the manuscripts anticipate Merleau-Ponty's account. But they do not bring out *unthematic* readiness-to-hand, or bring out our readiness-of-hand and schematic organisation of posture and milieu.

[21] Uexküll 2010, 92–5, 97, 199–200.   [22] Gibson 1979, 127–9.

unique melody in its actions, and a simultaneous duet with the things of its environment or percept-effect world. Human voices melt into one another in a composition composed for both. By analogy the duet that the organism plays with its environment comprises a melodic and harmonious unity.[23]

Heidegger's human existent or Dasein is unique in that its own Being is an issue for it. It has a world it stands out from rather than being immersed in. For all that it is fundamentally 'there', always engaged in and towards the world in being projectively in the future and only ever 'here' as the zero-point of orientations (*BT*, 67–8, 182). Radicalising the conception of intentionality as an arcing forward into possibility, Heidegger sees Dasein as the being transcending itself – it is more than it is in the factual present. In projecting a commonplace future that it takes as more of the same, it is inauthentic, having fallen short of itself. But in projecting and pursuing a future that is self-transformative, it is authentic and loyal to its own potentialities, having gathered itself towards what it is to be in the face of its finitude (*BT*, 185–7, 369–82). In both of these modes, it encounters the things in its environment as equipment for its concerns. Things are 'ready-to-hand' for Dasein, who apprehends the hammer in the hammering or the pen in the writing. Neither is thematised as an isolated object in space, for what is intended is the end of the task and not the means. In working with the hammer or pen, our practical perception is 'circumspective', for we are seeing through and around it towards what it affords, taking its utility utterly for granted (swallowed up in the *telos* like its hidden aspects or sides). For Heidegger, the practical and circumspective apprehension of things in terms of readiness-to-hand (itself unthematised) precedes the disengaged inspection or abstractly theoretical perception of them as present-at-hand (*BT*, 95–101).

Our implements are rarely perceived as extensive magnitudes with such and such a weight and volume and so forth. If the hammer is laid down because it gets heavy, it immediately becomes obtrusive, being objectified as 'unready-to-hand'. But even then it is an object too difficult to wield before being a steel head of so many pounds or kilograms. If the pen skids out of my grasp, it is slippery before being a badly manufactured cylinder of phenolic plastic. In such 'breakdown' situations, our attention most often shifts to the further consequences of what has happened, our inability to fix the leak in the roof or to record the lecture, with these proximate ends bringing to mind even more

[23] Uexküll 2010, 170–2.

fundamental possibilities of Dasein's existence, in these instances of health or education (*BT*, 102–6, 114–19). As with smaller implements, so with larger ones; these too are organised anisotropically according to our concerns. Buildings with fixed orientations were planned for the utility (and often beauty) that they still display. We prefer the house taking advantage of the evening sunlight and the open prospect to the one that has become surrounded by fir trees. Distances are also evaluated in terms of human utility. The house that we favour is not near or far with regard to its geometrical coordinates, but in the ease or difficulty of reaching it. The long and winding road that is easily traversed is in its practical apprehension nearer to the dwelling than the 'straight' path across rough ground and brambles, which is only closer as the crow can fly (*BT*, 135–47).

4.6   More on Merleau-Ponty's Approach

The mere presence of a living being, remarks Merleau-Ponty, 'transforms the physical world, makes "food" appear over here and a "hiding place" over there, and gives to "stimuli" a sense that they did not have' (*PP*, 195). The adult human encounters an environing world that is largely if not exclusively composed of affordances that are ready-to-hand for short and long-term purposes. My tools are caught up in my tasks rather than standing before me (*PP*, 108–9, 335, 439). Uexküll and Heidegger have explicated the way we encounter things practically, something Husserl would scarcely find difficult to accommodate. Yet Uexküll does not say much about our lived and motile bodies, and in *Being and Time* readiness-*of*-hand gets very little attention. It is Husserl who embarks on a phenomenology of lived embodiment that Heidegger leaves out of account (*BT*, 143), and it is Husserl's work on somatic constitution that is built on, albeit framed by Heidegger's claim that our existence is projectively beyond itself. For Merleau-Ponty, all the directions that we ourselves take in life are instantiations of an 'intentional arc' or 'funda-mental function' of projection orienting us towards the possible (*PP*, 137, 160, 196–7), and this brings in the productive imagination as a picturing of proximate and distant futures.[24] To be human is to be actualising some

---

[24] Matherne notes that Merleau-Ponty gets the term 'intentional arc' (*intentionale Bogen*) from studies on schizophrenia by Kurt Beringer and Franz Fischer. Beringer sees it as an underlying function of projection in which we think about what is present in relation to the possible, and Fischer sees it as involved in our organisation of space and time. Projection plays a pivotal role in Heidegger's account of understanding, and in Merleau-Ponty's Heideggerian framework perception, motility,

possibilities and entertaining other ones, all informed by one's somatic and cognitive capacities and cultural and moral outlook. Possibilities are weighted affectively and some valorised, in that I desire them and believe I should pursue them. I may imagine a life needing years to attain, yet reckon with it by way of my capacities and because I consider these capable of development:

> [T]he life of consciousness – epistemic life, the life of desire, or perceptual life – is underpinned by an 'intentional arc' that projects around us our past, our future, our human milieu, our physical situation, our ideological situation, and our moral situation, or rather, that ensures that we are situated within all of these relationships. The intentional arc creates the unity of the senses, the unity of the senses with intelligence, and the unity of sensitivity and motility. [25] (*PP*, 137)

A projected outcome can only be realised by that existent who is a 'being toward the thing through the intermediary of the body' (*PP*, 140). Hence the arc can hardly create the unity of the senses and of sensitivity and motility. It would be better to say that it is founded on this unity in the child's first 'I cans', before ever it founds the wider and indeed adult unity just invoked. The power of imaginatively placing oneself in a situation (of reckoning with it) is inseparable from the extant or anticipated power of making it real or of forestalling it (*PP*, 112, 137). The arc in each of its instantiations is the holistic projection of a certain potentiality and is itself amplified when one is committed to a self-transformative project. Without our working towards new ways of being – and improving on old ones – our capacities could not knit together more closely and comprehensively. They could not develop into springboards for still more demanding tasks. And whether the projected is more or less transformative or more or less familiar, it must be of some outcome in the world that entails an already being involved in it and a working through it. The movement of transcendence in this or that endeavour is always a project *of* the world (*PP*, 454).

At this juncture, the projective body can be brought to the fore. In reading Husserl's universalism through an existential lens, Merleau-Ponty has agreed that we must have the bodies we do and *experience* them as we do. Our somatic structures as lived and immanently experienced are material a prioris of the pre-conceptual senses of things, senses that survive

---

imaginative representation and intelligence are all brought together through the arc. Matherne 2014, 137–42, *BT*, 183–6, 418 and *PP*, 137, 160, 454.
[25] Translation slightly emended.

their conceptualisation. These forms of conscious if pre-reflective awareness cannot be bound up with their factual conditions as if to their causes
(*PP*, 269), though there are other and passively synthesising forms of
awareness that transcend efficient causality without being consciously
accessible in any manner. All of these enable and inhabit the active
syntheses of an epistemic subject separating itself from its objects (*PP*, 53,
241, 251–2, 474). This brings us to one of the most important moves in
Merleau-Ponty's big book, namely, his explication of a form of perceptual
experience that is not marginal or pre-reflective and that is inexplicable in
objective thought. To give it its place, the distinction between the objective
and the phenomenal body is nested in a still wider one between the former
and 'the body itself' or 'one's own body' (*le corps propre*). This phrase in its
full extension includes the non-phenomenal body schema (*schéma corporel*), the projective organisation of one's posture and advance appropriation of the environment for one's projects (*PP*, 100–3, 155, 252, 548). The
body schema in its motor intentional schematising functions sub-
consciously (sub-reflectively rather than pre-reflectively) and can be
inferred from our everyday engaged comportment as bracketed and faithfully described. Husserl may even be glimpsing its work when he adverts to
an effective, living or operative intentionality (*fungierende Intentionalität*)
presupposed in everything that I discover about things. In its operation '[it]
carries me along; it predelineates; it determines me practically in my whole
procedure, including the procedure of my natural thinking', though he
cautions that it may be undisclosed and utterly beyond my cognitive
grasp.[26]

Beneath act or thematic intentionality, according to Merleau-Ponty, we
can unearth the intentionality that first constitutes the pre-predicative
unity of life and world, and that once discovered 'appears in our desires,
our evaluations, and our landscape more clearly than it does in objective
knowledge' (*PP*, lxxxii). At work before every thesis and judgement, we
should in Kant's terminology regard this peculiar form of intentional
projection as an essential part of that 'art hidden in the depths of the
human soul' in relation to which every active *Sinngebung* is derived and
secondary. Like every art, it is only known through its results, and Merleau-
Ponty's reference to its appearance within a landscape has a literal signification (*PP*, lxxxii, 265, 453). The embodied subject in its commerce with
the world depends on motor intentional predelineations of action possibilities in its perceptual fields. Operative and passive syntheses projectively

---

[26] Husserl 1969, 234–5, translation slightly emended.

structure these possibilities behind my cognitions and representations (and behind my body's presence with me). Giving every 'I can' that I take up its traction, they support and colour my explicit act intentionalities, making them efficacious in the world by anonymously articulating it in advance *for* them. Through my days I depend on a sub-conscious and sub-representational system of action projection, on a body schema that itself comes to be coloured by my acts. Without it there would be no socio-cultural world and no science with its posited universe. We need the body as 'a universal arrangement, a schema of all perceptual developments and of all intersensory correspondences beyond the segment of the world that we are actually perceiving' (*PP*, 341).[27]

To foreground intentional experiences and enquire back into their constitution, Husserl makes use of illusions in everyday life and imaginary scenarios of beings lacking our powers, such as fixed heads with fixed cyclopean eyes. Heidegger sticks with situations where our practical comportment breaks down to foreground the way we encounter equipment and our shorter and longer term purposes. Both illusory and breakdown situations are employed by Merleau-Ponty to reveal the anonymous work of the body, and he makes extensive use of pathological cases of comportment in which people's living bodies no longer work in their normal fashion. While he pays little attention to the fact that bodily 'normality' is not a fixed and unambiguous notion, varying according to age and health and other factors, his approach makes clear enough sense.[28] What can loosely be called the normal functioning of the lived body as an intentional system of action towards outcomes is too close and familiar to each of us, to the extent of being largely hidden. We are not explicitly aware of many of our bodies' performances and are not aware of other ones at all. As Russell Keat has helpfully observed, Merleau-Ponty employs pathological cases as heuristic devices for shocking us into the awareness of our normal comportment, for starkly throwing into relief what is taken for granted, being too intimately with us and for us to be ordinarily discernible.[29] Although the natural attitude of unhesitant and usually successful action is witnessed in my lived body and those of others, its organisation can best be brought to light when contrasted with those bodies in which such action has been altered, that is, perpetuated in mutated form and often slowed down. Such cases effectively bracket and silhouette the normal performances so we can

---

[27] See also *PP*, 453.

[28] Husserl is far more sensitive than Merleau-Ponty to the shifting and context-sensitive characteristics of normality. For an impressive explication of his conceptions, see Taipale 2014, 121–68.

[29] Hammond, Howarth and Keat 1991, 181.

get them right descriptively, identify their concrete essences and enquire back into their hidden and sub-reflective conditions (*PP*, lxxvii, 105, 133).

Pathological cases should not be reduced to baldly heuristic devices, since their help in explicating what is normal in human comportment reciprocally casts light on their own character beyond their first appearances. But even if we take all this on board, Matherne warns against what she calls the 'motor-centric' interpretation of Merleau-Ponty's use of pathologies, in which he merely uses these cases to highlight our bodily way of dealing with the world that occurs without intervening thoughts or reflections. If his approach is genuinely anti-objectivist and anti-Cartesian, he should more properly be interpreted as seeking to show why pathologies manifest themselves holistically, that is, why motor, perceptual, cognitive and linguistic impairments go hand in hand. Though intellectual disorders cannot and should not be divorced from the body, the motor-centric interpretation tends to neglect their function in pathologies.[30] Matherne's warning is well made, though it must be qualified for some of the cases that Merleau-Ponty examines. In some strange attempts to move the intervening thoughts are not so much impaired as misled, and misled because of the phenomenal rather than physical body. This we shall see with the condition of the use-phantom limb, which is employed in his initial explication of the postural and projective body schema.

[30] Matherne 2014, 137–8, 143.

The Body Schema and Our Skills

5.1 Introduction

For Merleau-Ponty, one's own body is in the world as the heart is in the organism, giving it life and forming a symbiotic system with it. The reference to the heart is eminently appropriate, for the organ circulates oxygenated blood and nutrients throughout the body, preserving the life of each and every part. In a similar fashion, my body with its capacities nourishes the visual spectacle in front of me, keeping it alive as a field of proximate and distant possibilities. Things in the world call out to me as attractive and as useful because I can approach to admire them and employ them towards outcomes. And because I can only apprehend the unity and the features of worldly things through the mediation of my body, the theory of the body schema is implicitly a theory of perception (*PP*, 209, 213). As it stands, the idea of the schema is ambiguous, for it is at once underdetermined and fertile, like all those ideas that make their appearance at turning points in science and philosophy. At the outset, 'they are employed in a sense that is not yet their full sense, and their immanent development is what breaks up previous methods' (*PP*, 101).

The development of the idea provides a guide as to how Merleau-Ponty takes it up.[1] The body schema was initially regarded as an associative sketch or model of one's posture that develops gradually. It is an overall representation of the body by means of which one can locate its parts. This was replaced by a better account in which the postural awareness is non-representational, and in which each current posture is related to its predecessor. Thanks to a sub-conscious body schema, one has a pre-reflective and proprioceptive awareness of posture that does not involve an image or an object. But this second story is insufficient in its turn, for one's changing posture is projectively organised to move in the service of one's goals. My

---

[1] For a helpful account of this history, see Tiemersma 1982, 246–55.

schematised body spatiality turns out to be an oriented spatiality of situation instead of indifferent position. If my body is a function that privileges certain figures and directions against indifferent backgrounds, this is because it is polarised by its tasks, existing towards their completion (*PP*, 101–3). The body's spatiality of situation needs to be brought to light as the third and always implied term in the figure-background structure. We shall see that its spatiality is 'the deployment of its being as a body, and the way in which it is actualised as a body' (*PP*, 150).

I begin this chapter by running through the early theories of the body schema and indicating in broad strokes how Merleau-Ponty understands it. Our outcome oriented movements manifest an internal unity, being embraced by the schema as the organisation behind one's overall awareness of posture. But only in the descriptions of our actions can we find what the schema facilitates, helped by existential analyses of patients who exhibit anosognosia or use-phantom limbs. To gain an adequate understanding of these conditions is to bring out the way our bodies are experienced in our being towards the world. For our outcome-oriented movements to be both immediate and unobtrusive, our bodies must be habitualised. Their work depends on the acquisition and sedimentation of practical capacities. These comprise an anonymous repertoire of immediately available skills and correlatively immediate affordances. In the deployments of the skills through the body schema, our limbs are not focally or representationally present, and the comportment of anosognosics and amputees brings this out. Furthermore, the boundaries of the schema are not those of the physical body. In action, the schema may leave parts of the physical body out of account, and when implements become immediate affordances it extends beyond the limits of that body. Without this schema, we could not gain a theoretical distance from our perceptual fields or reckon practically with the possible. All this makes up the first phase of explicating how we gear into the world, before Merleau-Ponty focusses on the projective character of the body schema.

5.2   Schema, Image and Strange Limbs

The purposive movements of a fit and healthy agent display an intersensory and sensorimotor coordination. To account for the awareness of where one's parts are to be found in moving, some physiologists and psychologists posited a postural 'sketch' or 'model', a summative representation of one's repeated impressions of this or that movement. In childhood, these famil-iar and remembered impressions or images are associated and culminate in a 'centre of images'. This is a conscious representation of one's overall body by means of which its different parts are surveyed as they come into play; through it the parts are tracked in their movement.[2] In a highly influential study published in 1912, Henry Head and Gordon Holmes set out an alternative theory of a sub-consciously founded awareness of posture. On their view, the 'body schema' does not work from or involve an image or a representation of one's body, even though one may accompany it. The schema is constantly registering fresh and already grouped sensations from each new posture or movement, bringing the latter into relation with its predecessor with this feedback to constitute an ever-evolving awareness of overall posture. Changes in posture can only enter consciousness and be recognised when the relation is complete. Every change comes to awareness 'already charged with its relations to something that has gone before, just as on a taximeter the distance is presented to us as already transformed into shillings and pence'.[3] Head and Holmes also posit a schema of body surface through which one can localise any area being touched. With these schemata, we can project our awareness of posture and movement beyond the edge of the body to the end of an implement held in the hand like a spoon or a stick.[4]

For Merleau-Ponty, this theory rightly abandons the view of the schema as an associative and representational awareness of posture. In cases of allochiria, where patients experience in one hand a stimulus applied to the other, they can simultaneously describe its form and location in the corresponding area of the untouched hand. An already structured feeling has been transferred across, entering consciousness in a manner that is inexplicable through familiar and previously associated impressions. And in many simpler instances of whole-body movement, one can immediately replicate another person's changing posture without any precedents to draw upon. Such imitative courses of movement comprise novel sensori-motor unities and novel experiences of postural changes, so no summative representation of familiar impressions could serve as a model for tracking one's moving parts. It is rather that the schematised awareness of posture is evolving holistically, and that it is immanently embracing all of the parts (*PP*, 100–2, 140–2). Through the schema, I 'know' the position of each of my limbs, and here Merleau-Ponty is referring to what Charles Sherrington first called 'proprioception', the perception of one's own.[5] This is the body's global appreciation and my pre-reflective appreciation of

---

[2] Head 1893, 189; Pick 1922, 312–18.   [3] Head and Holmes 1912, 187.   [4] Ibid., 187–8.
[5] Sherrington 1907, 475–9.

the location of each of its parts in relation to the whole, and hence in relation to the other parts. When I rest my arm on the table in front of me, it would be wrong to say that it is *next* to the ashtray in the way that the latter is next to the telephone. In terms of awareness, my body parts 'are not laid out side by side, but rather envelop each other' (*PP*, 100). Proprioception is preserved when parts of my body are tactually prominent as they usually are. When I stand in front of my desk and lean on it with my hands, the rest of my body is aligned experientially with my hands and arms. Its entire stance is given with them, embracing torso, legs and feet in one spatiality of situation. As ordinarily felt in its resting or shifting location, a body part is not an object; the marginal feeling of it is continuous with the overall postural awareness that is pre-reflective and pre-objective. Such a global and undivided awareness amounts to 'a "form" in Gestalt psychology's sense of the word' (*PP*, 102).

This peculiar formulation is indebted to Klaus Conrad, though it still falls short of the phenomenon, since the awareness includes an experience of orientation right through my movements.[6] Conrad states that the body schema is dynamic, and Merleau-Ponty adds that I apprehend my body 'as a posture towards a certain task, actual or possible', or as a posture pointing towards a particular outcome (*PP*, 102). It is experienced this way because the sub-reflective body schema behind the global and pre-reflective awareness of posture is itself organising my posture, integrating and coordinating the parts of my body according to their value for my projects. This is to adapt an idea that he gets from Paul Schilder, who contends that the schema's work is projective, since it organises or coordinates the evolution of one's posture in the pursuit of this or that goal. When I think of doing something and resolve to do this right away, the body schema carries the intention into actual movement. It lays down an advance plan of the process or a 'motor projection' (*Bewegungsentwurf*). Motor projection is the seed of the movement that contains the ultimate end within its plan, so that in action the thought intention manifests itself through it.[7] In Schilder's theory, the plan commences as an undeveloped psychic knowledge, as a mere thought. As soon as this is delivered over to the schema, it is converted into the beginning of motor activity. The schematic plan of movement then develops through to completion in continuous contact with the experience of moving.[8] Schilder's motor plan is a representation for guiding movement, whereas Merleau-Ponty's account anticipates recent ones in which the schema draws on the vestibular and visual systems

---

[6] Conrad 1933, 365, 367.   [7] Schilder 1923, 64–5, 86.   [8] Schilder 1950, 51, 69–70.

and other sources to maintain balance and orientation, doing this without picturing anything.[9] In his own theory, it is an operative and context-sensitive mode of intentionality, in that its organisation of posture towards an outcome is at once an appropriation of and accommodation to the wider environment. When he comes to justify these claims through phenomenological analyses, he will also reject any conception of a 'mere thought' as a discrete and unconditioned plan of movement.

Shaun Gallagher observes that Schilder's ideas have been the source of much confusion about the body schema.[10] For the latter, it is a modulation of 'the body image' or 'the picture of our own body which we form in our mind'. The schema organises postural development as a projection of this 'tri-dimensional image' that everyone possesses.[11] Though Merleau-Ponty is careful not to confuse the two, the confusion has been compounded by Colin Smith's original mistranslation of *schéma corporel* as body image. We need to stress that the schema playing a dynamic role in governing posture and movement is a sub-conscious and non-pictorial system. When our motor capacities are activated, they ordinarily work without conscious monitoring, which does not exclude the marginal awareness of evolving posture.[12] The body image, by contrast, is the whole system of objectifying perceptions, attitudes and beliefs concerning one's body. It includes all cognitions about and imaginative representations of the body, and its conscious monitoring in the minority of occasions when this is needed. The schema and image inform each other (notably in learning skills), but their distinctiveness should not be forgotten.[13] In the main, the body image is one's body as objectified in the lifeworld rather than the scientific

---

[9] Merleau-Ponty does not make the relationship between postural awareness and postural organisation clear. A more adequate account will distinguish sub-reflective proprioceptive *information* and pre-reflective proprioceptive *awareness*. The first is essential to the body's schema's organisation of posture, needing continual updating of individual and relative position through vestibular, muscular and exteroceptive feedback. Gallagher 2005a, 29, 46–8, 68.

[10] Ibid., 19.

[11] Schilder 1950, 11, 51–2. Merleau-Ponty holds that Hugo Liepmann takes a better route when he invokes a sensorimotor capacity integrating the optical and kinaesthetic, structuring each action as a determined unity. But Liepmann then posits a prior representation and 'movement formula' (*Bewegungsformel*) of intermediate goals and of the final goal. This is converted into movement because it triggers a certain sequence of kinaesthetic memories or automatic reflexes that were acquired once and for all (Liepmann 1905, 40–7, 55–9). As soon as praxis is characterised in this manner, according to Merleau-Ponty, we are condemned to an exclusive account of any deficiencies in motility, blaming either ideational preparation or automatic reflexes. The awareness of movement is confined to representation, and the body 'executes the movement by reproducing it according to the representation that consciousness adopts and according to a movement formula that it receives from it . . . The problem is only resolved if we cease distinguishing between the body as a mechanism in itself and consciousness as a being for itself.' *PP*, 523–5.

[12] Gallagher 2005a, 20, 68.   [13] Ibid., 24, 26–9.

universe, coloured by the way one represents it as appearing to oneself and to others. It is one's habitually objective body, or one's body as objectified with all the weight of sedimented imaginings and evaluations.

Merleau-Ponty examines cases of injury to show that the body schema's sub-conscious and non-representational functioning is inseparable from our being towards the world, and at first to reveal the peculiar presence of our arms and legs within it. Here he devotes most of his attention to the pathologies of use-phantom limbs and anosognosia because of what they silhouette. His main source is Jean Lhermitte, a neuropsychiatrist who examined a large number of patients exhibiting these conditions. Lhermitte perpetuates the confusion of the schema with the image, but recognises the dynamic and holistic character of the former.[14] In the more common cases of phantoms, an amputated limb is felt as painful, as a whole, and as continuous with the remainder of the body. Most recent amputees attempt to use their missing limbs, having them as felt-phantoms and use-phantoms. Yet a significant minority of patients retain these phantom limbs for many years, usually without any pain. They try to use them and experience them in their seeming use. Many such cases are documented, including a handless man who feels himself holding a knife and fork and another one who moves at first to play the piano. The experiences have the highest degree of vivacity for the patients.[15] More recently, Vilayanur Ramachandran has reported similar cases, including an amputee holding a cup on a table. He is very upset when the doctor seemingly wrenches it from his grasp.[16]

Of especial interest is a man who lost his leg seventeen years ago, but who tries over and again to walk from a standing position, presumably forgetting his crutch and not being discouraged by repeated falls (*PP*, 83). As reported by Lhermitte, the standing patient often swings his phantom forward and down to the ground, expecting to meet the latter and having the initial illusion of so doing. Also reported is a reclining patient amputated from the thigh who often swivels himself off his bed and tries to stand up, again assuming he can rely on his missing leg.[17] Mechanistic models are unable to explain the experience of having the whole movable limb, and the new physiology has moved beyond them. But even a reformed explanation confined to third-person processes cannot tell us why the missing limb still counts for the person. A purely causal approach will take the

---

[14] Lhermitte 1998, 86, 156, 163.   [15] Ibid., 57–9, 85–7.
[16] Ramachandran and Blakeslee 1998, 42–3.   [17] Lhermitte 1998, 66.

initially untroubled attempt to move as an objective process indistinguishable from a reflex. Consciousness may observe it, but is in no way engaged with it (*PP*, 78–81). Nor can empiricism explain why a situation resembling the one in which a limb was destroyed can give rise to a phantom in a patient who did not experience it hitherto. Such experiences usually lead to frozen phantoms, locked in the felt positions of the real limbs when they were lost. An intellectualist theory proffered by cognitive psychologists seem better suited to such cases. A certain situation triggers a memory that is so intensely affective as to be traumatic. Erupting out of the unconscious, it ensues in an imaginative representation of the limb. The theory can be modified for use-phantom cases. A situation triggers a memory that is just as intense but not traumatic. An overwhelmingly positive memory of limb use is brought to awareness and reinforced heavily by a decision to reject the reality of the current situation. We should understand use-phantoms in terms of wish fulfilments, for the patients are representing as actually present what they intensely desire to be present. With some patients, the phantom gradually shrinks into the stump and disappears, and the claim is that they have come to accept mutilation.[18] With others, the phantom persists, and their experiences are taken as showing their ongoing refusal to accept their loss. They are thinking and representing what they do because they are willingly remaining in denial (*PP*, 79–80).

The intellectualist approach appears particularly appropriate when we look at cases of anosognosia as well as asomatognosia. In the latter cases, patients deny that paralysed limbs are theirs, completely disowning them. Stein is depicting this very condition when she contends that a limb which is both paralysed and insensitive will no longer appear as mine in any fashion. It will be present as an alien thing that I cannot shake off, in the fashion of a foreign physical object that has become stuck to me.[19] With anosognosia, by contrast, limbs which are paralysed but still sensitive are completely ignored by patients in their activities. While they retain a sense of limb ownership and can describe the feel of their arms, they behave as if there is no impairment. When asked to offer the paralysed hand to shake, for example, they promptly offer the other one. For the intellectualist, they are representing the upsetting presence of a paralysed limb as an absence, as against the use-phantom patients who are representing an absence as a presence.[20] Once the efferent and afferent or command and feedback nerves between stump and brain are severed, however, the phantom

---

[18] Ibid., 72–3, 99–100; Schilder 1950, 67–8.   [19] Stein 1989, 47–8.
[20] Lhermitte 1998, 61; Riddoch 1941, 197–8; Schilder 1950, 63–4, 67–8.

disappears, so physiological conditions cannot be ignored (*PP*, 78–9, 82). Merleau-Ponty is incorrect here, for sometimes the result of this extreme procedure is a phantom that either replaces or accompanies the first. More recent research points to the roles of the somatosensory cortex and neural networks in generating phantoms. But if he gets the details wrong, he is right to hold that the condition is always physiologically founded.[21]

Because we need an all-inclusive account of the phenomenon of the use-phantom limb, a hybrid explanation that combines physiological and psychological conditions looks promising. To be compelling, however, both sets of conditions must be combined to form an articulate whole, integrally co-determining the phenomenon. The difficulty is that any endeavour to combine an empiricist third-person process (or bare physical reflex 'in itself') with an affective and ideational *cogitatio* (or wish fulfilling thought and imaginative representation 'for itself') is working with terms that are fundamentally heteronomous. These abstract creations of object-ive thought reproduce the Cartesian model of a mind that is unextended and a body that is not, with the former governing or having the illusion of governing the latter (*PP*, 79–80). In the Sixth Meditation, Descartes realises that his theory clashes with his experiences of pain and injury. He does not seem to be in his body as a pilot in a ship, since he is affected in his entirety. Mind and body seem to intermingle rather than standing in an external union. But if the somatic feelings run against the theory, they never unseat the picture of an ego directing the body from on high.[22]

5.3   Integrally Available Hands and Legs

To better understand both the pathologies and ordinary movement, our starting point must be a phenomenological description that is attentive in Heideggerian fashion to our being in the world as being engaged. In embodied thought and deed, we are actively oriented towards the possible. Throughout the day, I understand my world and live my body through the projects to which I am committed, projects first elicited by others and things and later on by my motivated choices. What the comportment of the anosognosics and amputees reveal is an 'I' who is first and foremost oriented towards outcomes, and who 'continues to tend towards its world despite deficiencies and amputations and that to this extent does not *de jure* recognise them' (*PP*, 83). As we shall see, the acting patients are not

[21] See Ramachandran and Hirstein 1998, 1603–30.
[22] Descartes 1984a, 139–41; Descartes 1984b, 56; Descartes 1984c, 339–48. See also Smith 2007, 12, 22.

banishing or preserving images of their limbs, contrary to the intellectualist reading of anosognosia as the false representation of an absence and of the use-phantom as the false representation of a presence. While the first condition does not involve a total ignorance or repudiation of the paralysed limb, its genesis can be elucidated by my experience of a close friend's recent death. I am marginally conscious of the bereavement, but I do not properly comprehend it until I think of asking him something. Only then does his passing from the world hit me sharply and sadly. As a consequence, I begin to avoid those situations where his death will become obvious, pushing the memory into the background. In an analogous way, the anosognosic begins to leave the paralysed limb out of account so that the impairment will not intrude consciously. She gradually learns to negotiate practical situations, reconfiguring as far as possible the world enjoyed prior to paralysis. This is done by developing new action strategies with the other arm and by coming to avoid situations where no new strategies will suffice. The patient can credibly deny the deficiency on learning how to bypass it. When it ceases to be an obstacle to her projects the still sensitive limb becomes virtually absent (*PP*, 82–3).

Someone with a use-phantom has it as virtually present, since it counts for him or her as distinct from being left out of account. When Lhermitte's standing patient tries to walk, he describes the strange motility of his phantom as identical to that of his real leg before he lost it. He launches himself straight into the action, and after apparently swinging his leg and meeting the ground with his heel, feels his toes as his foot rolls on the ground. Unfortunately he cannot enjoy any actual support and falls over. Lhermitte notes that everything in the patient's comportment matches his own first-hand description of his phantom. In its form and situation and movement, the phenomenon is similar all in all to the leg that was once there.[23] This is already suggesting that anosognosic absence and use-phantom presence cannot and should not be understood in terms of mere wish fulfilment or fiat of will (*PP*, 83). Only after having dropped or recalibrated earlier projects in her being towards the world can the anosognosic have her paralysis as virtually absent, and only through the phantom's peculiar mode of presence can the amputee presumptively have it for his or her projects, whether that use-phantom is of a lost leg or arm:

> To have a phantom limb is to remain open to all of the actions of which the arm alone is capable and to stay within the practical field that one had prior

[23] Lhermitte 1998, 66.

to the mutilation. The body is the vehicle of being in the world, and for a living being, having a body means being united with a definite milieu, merging with certain projects, and being perpetually engaged therein. In the evidentness of this complete world in which manipulable objects still figure, in the impulse of movement that goes towards it and where the project of writing or of playing the piano still figures, the patient finds the certainty of his bodily integrity. But at the very moment that the world hides his deficiency from him, the world cannot but help reveal it to him ... [a]t the same moment that my usual world gives rise to habitual intentions in me, I can no longer unite with it in actuality if I have lost a limb. Manipulable objects, precisely insofar as they appear as manipulable, appeal to a hand that I no longer have (*PP*, 84).[24]

Because certain things appear usable – the pen for writing and piano for playing – they are still motivating attempts to use them. In a similar manner, we can envisage the standing patient trying to walk to the kitchen to make a pot of coffee, or the reclining patient swinging himself off his bed to work on the rigging of his model sailing ship, which he has spotted on the table across his bedroom. These individuals are tending projectively towards their original worlds and assuming that their floors are walkable for getting from here to there. Because such patients are missing a leg, however, the surprise and pain of falling should militate against the attempts to walk far more than wish fulfilment militates in favour of them. Other factors must be in play for the things to appear so readily reachable. There must be 'regions of silence' within the totality of each sufferer's body as there are in one's own (*PP*, 84).

The patients are showing that the body marginally with me is also a habitual body that has a whole history of acquisitions behind it, most of which it still has and holds. Initially able to wave limbs and grab, my body came to acquire and exhibit other 'body habits' or skills, first of lifting and turning things around, then of sitting up and using beakers and spoons, and later again of opening doors, doing up buttons and tying shoelaces. Each skill was both founded and founding, a condition of gaining further and even more complex ones. My set of skills enriches my affective and imaginative life and founds my fiats of will. As it widens, it orients me towards the world in novel ways. The habitual or skilled body constitutes the horizon of capacities for future actions, and by the same token the horizon for certain outer configurations. It lets environing things invite us into situations or facilitate existing projects (*PP*, 115, 140). In Husserlian terminology, I am solicited to co-intend things as means for

---

[24] Translation slightly emended.

ends. My sedimented skills are the kinaesthetic capacities founding the 'I can' and appropriating everything requisite when available agency becomes actual agency. For Merleau-Ponty, the habitual body is my repertoire of readily available motor skills, or skills available immediately and unthinkingly. In its development, it enlarges the world of practical possibilities appearing within and pointing beyond my perceptual field of the moment. The latter becomes a manifold of opportunities, of things and pathways to be taken up towards the genuinely and for the most part proximately realisable (*PP*, 84, 103). Putting it another way, the gaining of skills enlarges the transcendental field, though only so many possibilities will be salient at any one time, namely those pursued in my current project or imagined in a future one. Following Dreyfus, it is better to speak of skills rather than kinaestheses or body habits to foreground the outcome-oriented character of our movements.[25]

Once I acquire the skill of using something, its significance bears chiefly on my body. Ordinarily it comes before my eyes *for* my hands or my feet, as we see when a craftswoman is working at her bench. Her hands and fingers are centre-points of the intentional threads linking her to the things she is employing (*PP*, 108, 145, 439). She has approached and taken them up in a certain manner, zoning in on particular features to achieve the desired outcome. Thus the thing is not given neutrally for the body as an intersection of physical causalities or as a representational unity. Rather, 'it is inwardly taken up by us, reconstituted and lived by us insofar as it is linked to a world whose fundamental structures we carry with ourselves' (*PP*, 341). The habitual or skilled body constitutes an internal relation between the agent and the articulation of the thing. The infant in the high-chair already grabs the two handles of the beaker to bring it up to her mouth. When she learns how to make noises with her activity board, she picks out in each glance the twisting of the wheel for clacking, the pulling of the lever for ringing or the pushing of the button for squeaking. She is practically articulating the entire board into parts before thematically taking them *as* wholes and parts. After the skills are acquired, the board cannot look as it originally did. For adults, things also appear differently without the appropriate skills. The novice clothes designer cannot zoom in on the way a dress is hanging badly and know how to alter it any more than he can pick out the artificial horizon in an airliner's control console. This is because his perceptions are not informed by the performative and meant appreciation of function. We do of course recognise things straight off as dresses or

---

[25] See Dreyfus 2002, 367–83.

consoles, but their technical features are no more readily available to everyone than check valves in the house of objective thought.

Skills are observed in action, through the postural attitudes people assume in appropriating things. Thus we see the poise of the craftswoman in her chair, working with tools taken from the same bench she is now leaning on. To go behind such achievements, we need a detailed account of the act of learning, and though Merleau-Ponty does not supply it, we can elaborate on some of his remarks.[26] The very young infant does not perceive things at distances as ready-to-hand or even as utensils. They will be strange and mysterious, as if fallen from the sky like meteorites from another planet. Only by perceiving a thing employed in a certain situation can the child apprehend it as a tool when no one is using it and imitatively use it (*PP*, 370, 425). And in the learning of more advanced and difficult skills, we cannot and should not write out cognitive contributions. A child watching an adult filling a sink is informed that she too will someday turn the tap or faucet to run the water, and is assured that she will. The tap appears as 'manipulable eventually'. With help, the child is shown how to hold and turn it, using both her hands with the help of the adult to compensate for her comparative lack of strength. At this stage, the child extensively objectifies her hands and imaginatively represents a successful action. Then she learns to turn the tap herself, albeit with some difficulty. For her, it has become 'manipulable for me'. When her technique improves, along with her strength, she comes to turn the tap with ease, and it is then encountered as 'manipulable in itself'. It is no longer just an affordance, but one that is immediate or ready-to-hand (*PP*, 84–5, 89).

Dreyfus has provided a much more detailed story in which one moves from being a novice to an advanced beginner, and from there to someone who achieves competence, proficiency and even expertise, the last stage being the one we associate with athletes and sportspeople generally.[27] We know from Uexküll and Heidegger that when something is an immediate affordance, it does not appear as a self-standing object, being used unthematically or circumspectively. The sink tap unobtrusively solicits and facilitates actions in a variety of situations, for quenching one's thirst, cooling one's face or washing the dishes. It functions as a solicitation or as a moment of a prior project because it readily affords drinking,

---

[26] Merleau-Ponty's preference for a genetic phenomenology never carries into a detailed account of skill acquisition. His typical characterisation (*PP*, 141, 260) is of a consummately *adult* body that has passed through its apprenticeships. Sheets-Johnstone 2011, 201, 210–11. On the body image and body schema in motor learning, see Tanaka 2021, 69–84.

[27] Dreyfus 2002, 368–72.

refreshing or washing. But it is not only the tap that has become unobtrusive – so has the body employing it. The skilled tap-turner launches straight into her task without needing to objectify her hands or think about her technique in any way. With the thorough acquisition of the skill, a region of silence is marked out in the body, for the capacity and its realisations are taken completely for granted. In forgetting about the body at her disposal, the latter has become 'anonymous' and 'almost impersonal' (*PP*, 84, 86). Hence there is an upsetting experience of impairment if a habitual expectation is suddenly frustrated from a sharp pain in her wrist or cramp in her leg. The body and correlative thing needed to realise a goal are revealed radically differently because they have been split apart. Such somatic breakdown reveals one's unreadiness-*of*-hand or unreadiness-*of*-leg as much as it does the newly unturnable tap or unwalkable floor. Every perceived affordance has been an immediate or mediate solicitation to action, but not every solicitation is an affordance. But it must have been a habitual affordance if it can still count as a solicitation – there must once have been readiness-of-hand providing genuine readiness-to-hand. No affordances are out there autonomously, since they must be the correlates of one's somatic capacities. The presumption that something is manipulable in itself misses the internal relationship of body and world.

Merleau-Ponty's next move is to show that every skilled performance that is immediate and unobtrusive is a deployment of the body schema. The comportment of Lhermitte's standing patient brings this out. His remaining nerves and wider brain are keeping what is physically absent in the field of practical existence. They are sustaining his leg's phenomenal space and his habitual body's history to fill in that space, his history of skilled engagements with the world. The nerves and brain make the phantom count for the patient because in sustaining it they simultaneously sustain the sensorimotor circuits through which he tries to reach things. A condition of either a solicitation or a thought project carrying straight into action is the ability of one's body to immediately engage with the appropriate means when one perceives the first or thinks the second, even if the engagement cannot be brought right through to successful completion. Without this most minimal of abilities to begin – founding the 'I can' or one's confidence in starting and finishing – an entire region of projection withers away and dies. Thus in each of his attempts to walk the patient proceeds straight off, without any delay or hesitation in the manner of an uninjured person. But just as essential to this is the anonymous *way* that his use-phantom counts for him. It counts in harmony with the rest of his body, which means that his body schema is still doing its original work.

The patient never checks whether his leg is really there before starting to move, and the reason is that the use-phantom is already experienced as there, in the very way that the missing leg once was. It is not merely felt, but felt in the right place in a schematised awareness and schematising organisation of posture embracing it. Felt and placed as the real limb used to be, the phantom is present for all intents and purposes without attracting any attention whatsoever. It is not experienced of itself because it is an integral moment of the patient's phenomenal body, which remains pre-reflectively present with him as immediately and integrally available, as an undivided whole that is utterly at his disposal (*PP*, 83–4, 88–9). If the phantom were not being experienced in this fashion, the patient would not be presuming over and again that he is able to walk. This gives us a more satisfactory understanding of why he is not refusing the loss of his leg as the intellectualist story would have it, and why on every occasion that he attempts unaided locomotion his deficiency is being hidden from him until he falls.

Positing an imaginative representation of the limb that floats across awareness and settles on the stump, intellectualism has distorted observation and description through its theoretical bias. This approach gets things wrong in a number of ways. It does not just forget that the use-phantom must be causally founded, but that it is not a representation or image in the first instance. An image or imaginative representation could only replace the original awareness of the leg if the latter's presence had been that of an object. Because the theory gets the original experience wrong, it posits the wrong kind of phantom. On an alternative and phenomenological account, one's skilled leg or arm is not an object or a focal power of action. As with the use-phantom, its presence is marginal, non-representational and integral. Ordinarily my leg is with me as an ambulatory power, not as something located eighty centimetres beneath my head. My hand is with me as a power of grasping and lifting and manipulating and so forth. The first in moving downwards perpetuates my moving forwards, and the second in rising upwards what I desire to take hold of (*PP*, 87–8, 147). One has no more to objectify the limbs through the flow of an action than one has to search for them in order to begin, whether the action commences and proceeds in this way or that, for example in reaching out for an old landline unit:

> If I am seated at my desk and want to pick up the telephone, the movement of my hand toward the object, the straightening of my torso, and the contraction of my leg muscles envelop each other; I desire a certain result and the tasks divide themselves up among the segments in question, and the possible combinations of movements are given in advance as equivalent: I could

remain leaning back in my chair provided that I extend my arm further, I could lean forward, or I could even partly stand up. All of these movements are available to us through their common signification. This is why, in the very first attempts at grasping, children do not look at their hand, but at the object. The different segments of the body are only known through their functional value and their coordination is not learned. (*PP*, 150)

When an action unfolds in which the body is implicated more or less extensively, its unobtrusive character presupposes the integration of the latter's parts by the body schema as I commence and complete my work, whether over a shorter period (say in picking up the telephone) or a longer one (say in getting out of bed and going downstairs and into the kitchen to make coffee). One subordinate task will silently give way to another in the service of their common and ultimate end. Hence I am not explicitly aware of having stopped walking when I reach the kitchen worktop, lift the kettle, put it under the tap and boil the water for the coffee pot. Prior to and over the whole course of the action, the limbs are moments of a body that is an indivisible power of moving towards the outcome. My organs appear equivalently within the unity of the 'I can' and in their actual operation, since the body is deployed as a single organ (*PP*, 328, 330–1). Like the standing and reclining patients before things go wrong for them, there are marginal expectations of feeling everything in the right place when I touch the ground for walking, and after this when I use the kettle and tap. The marginal feelings in the present and the fulfilments of the anticipated ones maintain my body's presence with me rather than to me because they are buttressed by the regions of silence of its skilled and schematised parts.

5.4 What the Schema Incorporates

The coordination between the different segments of the body which is not learned is nonetheless refined and reshaped extensively when one acquires a new skill and proceeds from bare competence to proficiency, say in gaining the ability to turn a tap with one hand rather than two. In the progression from infancy through to maturity, the acquisition of a body habit involves 'the reworking and renewal of the body schema' (*PP*, 143). Once the skill is fully acquired, 'our previous movements are integrated into a new motor entity', and 'the first visual givens are integrated into a new sensorial entity' (*PP*, 155). Because the body schema actively integrates the segments of the body according to their value for one's projects, however, those that have lost their value will fade out from it wherever possible. The anosognosic has come to rework the schema so that the paralysed area of the physical body no longer counts within it (*PP*, 102). We find 'an affective presence and extension', according to Merleau-Ponty, 'of which objective spatiality is neither the sufficient condition, as is shown in anosognosia, nor even the necessary condition, as is shown by the phantom limb' (*PP*, 150). The schematic postural organisation behind the schematised awareness need not always embrace the entire physical body, and as well as leaving out areas within the body it extends beyond its boundaries. Ordinarily the schema expands when we take up certain implements in the service of a task, and it contracts when we put them down again. Those actions that I habitually engage in incorporate their habitual instruments, and even our clothes come to be embraced by the schema. As abstracted from their socio-cultural significance, they function as artificial fur protecting us from the cold (*SB*, 174; *PP*, 93).

The prompt expansion and contraction of the body schema in everyday life is the outcome of a process, and Merleau-Ponty takes up an example first proffered by Head and Holmes.[28] A woman begins to wear a feather in her hat, and she may or may not calculate that it is seventeen centimetres long and three centimetres wide. But there is no doubt that she has an objective if rough knowledge of its length, of its angle in relation to the hat, and of the fact that it is something that will kink and break all too easily. So it is necessary for her to forestall this eventuality by reflecting on her choice of posture and route. Yet she rapidly learns to keep a safe distance between the feather and whatever might break it, sensing where the feather is like one senses where one's hand is. If she is subsequently driving through traffic and wishes to take a short cut through an alley, she sees that her car can pass through it without comparing the width of the laneway to the wings and bumper or fender. The hat and automobile are no longer things whose objective size and volume have to be remembered as she journeys about (*PP*, 144). Once their use becomes habitual, her body schema dilates to incorporate them, extending to the feather tip or fender edges. An even better example of incorporation is the blind man's white stick. This extends the scope of his touch both ahead and sideways as he swings it, providing a substitute for sight as a vigilance sense that apprehends threats and opportunities at a distance. With practice, it has become intimate to him in his outdoor life. The stick resembles his arm in that its length or weight or rigidity is not an explicit middle term. It is so familiar as to be no longer an object, and his attention is devoted to the position and character

---

[28] Head and Holmes 1912, 188.

of the things he touches through it (*PP*, 144, 153–4). In the then contemporary literature, George Riddoch reports a case in which a patient was fitted with a prosthetic leg that came to coincide with his phantom, and with which he could differentiate objects he was treading on, such as buttons or matchsticks.[29] With the extraordinary advances in biomedical engineering and nerve and electronic interfaces, it is to be expected that such experiences will become much more widespread.

When I come to unthinkingly incorporate things and achieve outcomes, what I have gained in each case is a somatic or 'praktognosic' understanding (*PP*, 141). This term was formulated by A. A. Grünbaum to signify a competency that is a practical knowing in its actual deployment.[30] As used by Grünbaum and Merleau-Ponty, it anticipates Gilbert Ryle's more familiar reference to a 'knowing how' as distinct from a 'knowing that'.[31] Each mode of knowing is marked by the other, for a higher stage acquisition deployed sub-consciously had to be learnt consciously, and in the act of learning one was drawing on and transforming skills first used pre-cognitively and by extension sub-reflectively (*PP*, 144, 146). To meet the objection that the skills are nothing but conditioned reflexes, irrespective of what they incorporate, Merleau-Ponty points to the teaching of a skill and its ensuing adaptability to new situations. When we observe the way novices are tutored, we find that the learning process is systematic. It does not weld together individual movements and stimuli. The novice dancer or footballer imitates an entire movement, however badly, and the instructor then shows him or her how to refine it, proceeding from whole to parts (*PP*, 143–4). In teaching a dance or a tackling strategy, shorter but still complex movements within longer performances are run through to the end, and are distinguishable from simple exercises of stretching and limbering up. And when we consider the sheer speed with which we incorporate instruments and master those with the same functions but different layouts, we find further evidence going against the reflex theory. Musicians already demonstrate flexible competencies as they achieve and modulate affective outcomes. This is why an experienced organist can immediately execute kinetic melodies corresponding to scores never played before, without fixed motor memories. The same organist can also play an organ that he has not encountered previously within an hour and up to his usual standard. The new instrument has key groupings and stops whose arrangements do not match up with the one he is familiar with. The short preparation time shows an intelligent and undivided response,

---

[29] Riddoch 1941, 198–200. [30] Grünbaum 1930, 386. [31] Ryle 1949, 28–50.

a comprehensive reapplication of a skill to a situation with same overall signification but without the same immediately available features (*SB*, 120–1; *PP*, 146–7).

The idea of conditioning can be retained so long as reflexes are understood as part of a systematic response in which changes are global in view of an end. Yet the mechanistic conception of the conditioned reflex has been stubbornly persistent. In this light, Merleau-Ponty criticises Bergson for characterising a motor habit or skill as 'the fossilised residue of a spiritual activity', something that in the progression from reflectively governed attempts at learning towards full proficiency has turned into a mechanism.[32] Consciousness and volition have gradually disappeared, giving way to unconsciousness and automatism. Yet the acquisition of a skill and its sedimentation does not freeze it into repetition without alteration, since the organist has shown that the skill contributes to a bodily know-how that is capable of modification and reapplication, a topic to be revisited in the next chapter. The sedimented is not an 'inert mass' that locks us into certain ways of acting (*PP*, 131–2, 143–4, 526). Mark Sinclair has maintained with good reason that this does not fully address Bergson's claim, for a body habit can involve the inclination to repeat an action that goes beyond the mere facility of doing it. Fossilisation should be recast in terms of spontaneous tendencies not fully under conscious control (e.g. when I unthinkingly select my old key to open my door after having changed the lock). The action is not automatic and self-moving, for it does not occur without the end in view, yet I am being carried forward in a way that I would not choose were I paying attention to my key selection.[33] On other occasions (which are happily rare), I suddenly discover myself following an old itinerary after an episode of daydreaming, though my chosen destination is elsewhere. On the upside, the new route ran at first with the old one, so the habitual body has not been anarchically sending me in the wrong direction from the beginning. Personal experience also tells many of us that we can end up just where we wanted to be when we began to move, without recalling the reason for getting there. In all such cases, consciousness has fallen short.

Sinclair notes that Merleau-Ponty is just as exercised by Bergson's reference to a 'spiritual activity', which veers into intellectualism.[34] Here a body habit is learned like a school lesson, by way of intellectual decomposition and recomposition. I only perfect a new one by repeating each

---

[32] Bergson 1992, 231–2.   [33] Sinclair 2011, 46–7, 49.   [34] Ibid., 45.

phase I have pictured.[35] On this narrative, our organist would reflectively draw up a representational map of his body's position and of the new keys and stops, and modify the former to match up with the latter. When he actually comes to play, he would put this two-sided blueprint or formula into effect, with his body being its passive recipient. But it is just this story of cognitive and imaginative surveying from above that falls short of his comportment. As he sees the organ for the first time, his skilled and embodied awareness apprehends what is seen as an 'I can after some time', but without any associated thematisation of his body. Matching up is only found within his actual movements, as we find when we look at his procedure to see what is happening. Prior to his first rehearsal, he sits down in the seat and shifts around until he is comfortable. Then he works the pedals up and down with his feet and pulls the stops in and out with his hands. In doing all this, he is getting the feel and the measure of the instrument with his body, or coming to incorporate within his schema the relevant directions and dimensions. He is settling into the organ like one settles into a house (*PP*, 146). No matter how well imagined and memorised a formula for learning might be, it is one's body that must catch and comprehend the correct movements (*PP*, 144).

The skills of organists and typists provide particularly noteworthy examples of praktognosic knowledge. It often happens that the experienced practitioners are quite incapable of designating on the keyboard the individual keys corresponding to this or that note or letter. They will of course know some of them, but the knowledge for conscious reactivation seems limited (*SB*, 120–1). There is no reason to suppose that it is sedimented in the depths of awareness as a memory embracing all keys and stops. Yet all of them are available under the practitioners' fingers and thumbs. There is a total awareness of the keyboard that emerges within – and only within – the actual practice of playing or typing, 'a knowledge bred of familiarity that does not provide us with a position in objective space' (*PP*, 145). Once the subject takes her place in front of an instrument or machine, a motor space stretches out beneath her hands in which she will play or type what she has read. There is 'a certain physiognomy of visual "wholes" that calls forth a certain style of motor responses', such that each visual structure in the end carries its own motor essence, or the concrete essence carrying it straight into action (*PP*, 145).

In a different but nonetheless genuine sense each of us incorporates places, for wherever I live and work must have a privileged status vis-à-vis

---

[35] Bergson 1991, 79–80.

its negotiation. I can well conceive of my apartment as if viewed from above, successively imagining what I myself or someone else would see as I draw its floor plan on a piece of paper (*PP*, 209). Before anyone is able to do this, however, they must hold a system of lived significations around themselves 'whose correspondences, relations and participations do not need to be made explicit in order to be utilised' (*PP*, 131). I must also have the dimensions of the apartment in embodied and motile memory, holding its principal distances and directions in my hands and legs. To walk towards the bathroom involves passing the bedroom to the right, and to look out the living room window involves having the fireplace to one's left. All this is invoked in drawing out the plan, even if the developing illustration on paper is needed to reactivate the memories in more detail and to place them with more accuracy. Yet there is one affordance that cannot be incorporated in any substantive manner, namely the earth beneath me. I am effectively in permanent contact with it, even in hanging off things, and it must be replicated in ships, aeroplanes and spacecraft when I am not jumping or falling. Though modern scientific theory with its technically enhanced observations tells me that it orbits the sun in a moving galaxy in an expanding universe, this is not the way it is actually lived. The motion and rest of things and my own movement are experienced as relative to something that does not move or rest. I do not encounter the earth as a body at rest, since there is nothing further in experience that it rests on, and it is not encountered as a body in motion, since it does not empirically arrive at or depart from some place (*PP*, 453). It is my primordial support and the basis of movement and place that does not itself have a 'where'.[36]

5.5   Distanciation and Reckoning with the Possible

The transition from the manipulable for me to the presumptively manipulable in itself is also understood by Merleau-Ponty in psychoanalytic terms. Because the reflective procedures used for learning give way to anonymous availability when proficiency is attained, each skill should be regarded as an 'organic repression' of conscious awareness.[37] Constituted with its regions of silence, one's own body is to all effects an 'innate complex' at the disposal of one's explicit goals. Psychoanalysis has already shown that

---

[36] See 'Foundational Investigations of the Phenomenological Origin of the Spatiality of Nature', trans. Fred Kersten in Husserl 1981, 222–33. See also *Sns*, 180.

[37] Merleau-Ponty here adapts Freud's conception of organic repression. The diminution of the olfactory sense and corresponding growth of shame about body odour is associated with the assumption of the upright posture. See Freud 1985, 288–89.

a certain complex can come from a traumatic event that was abnormally repressed into the unconscious. A person embarks on a certain project, but lacks the strength to overcome an obstacle on the one hand or to abandon the enterprise on the other. As a result, he or she ceaselessly repeats the same doomed attempt. What was once a personal and datable event lives on in hidden form and continues to shape experience.[38] The body schema functions analogously, since envisaged outcomes and things motivate us through the skills underpinning them, some gaining a preferential status for future comportment. What embodied consciousness will take advantage of has facilitated its orientations in advance (*PP*, 85–6).

This existential version of organic repression recalls insights from Nietzsche no less than Freud. In *The Genealogy of Morals*, it is asserted that forgetting is as an active and positive faculty of repression. By virtue of it, what we experience and absorb enters our awareness 'as little as the thousandfold process involved in physical nourishment'. Active forgetfulness closes the doors and windows of consciousness so that they will be undisturbed. Its work is to make room for new things, in particular 'for the nobler functions and functionaries, for regulation, foresight, premeditation'. We should conceive of such forgetfulness as a kind of doorkeeper, a preserver of psychic order, etiquette and repose. The person in whom this positive faculty is damaged or destroyed resembles a dyspeptic, unable to 'have done' with anything.[39] Although Nietzsche is only referred to in passing by Merleau-Ponty (*PP*, lxxi), his idea of active forgetfulness resonates through much of the following:

> If man is not to be enclosed within the envelope of the syncretic environment in which the animal lives as if in a state of ecstasy, if he is to be conscious of a world as the common reason of all milieus and as the theatre of all behaviours, then a distance between himself and what solicits his action must be established . . . each momentary situation must for him cease to be the totality of being, and each particular response must cease to occupy his entire practical field. Furthermore, the elaboration of these responses must, rather than taking place at the centre of his existence, happen on the periphery and, finally, the responses themselves must no longer require, each time, a unique position-taking and must rather be sketched out once and for all in their generality. Thus, by renouncing a part of his spontaneity, by engaging in the world through stable organs and pre-established circuits, man can acquire the mental and practical space that will free him, in principle, from his environment and thereby allow him to *see* it (*PP*, 89).[40]

---

[38] Freud 1984, 288–91.   [39] Nietzsche 1967, 57–8.   [40] Translation slightly emended.

Needless to say, the reference to renunciation is figurative – in perfecting a skill one does not think of or decide to surrender anything. One wishes instead for some sense of achievement. The kernel of Merleau-Ponty's account is that the educated body schema is itself the doorkeeper for consciousness. With its active and sub-reflective remembering it is the enabler and preserver of psychic order, etiquette and repose. There is an organic repression *by* the posturally integrated and skilled body *of* the body that was thematically present to me in the act of learning. Ordinarily my awareness is not swallowed up or submerged by my current tasks because I have the capacity to cope with them rapidly, fluidly and unthinkingly. I can cognitively and imaginatively plan and create on foot of bodily acquisitions because the familiar tasks of the present and near future do not intrude on my attentional awareness. The anonymously schematic exercise of each skill is part of its concrete essence and is a material a priori of cognitive distanciation. It allows my consciousness to free itself from its environment so I can inspect the latter at a distance, and do so in theoretical attitudes with communicable criteria for observation and evaluation.[41] Be it more practically or abstractly theoretical, each *Sinngebung* of act intentionality is indebted to the body schema with its operative intentionality.

We have seen that ignorance of our constitutive accomplishments facilitates the belief in finished objects that are the source of their own significance. Objective thought lives off what is hidden underneath it, though it is a recurring aspect of our cognitive articulations of states of affairs – such theoretical consciousness is a habitual orientation towards an intentional pole or towards a world. So long as we can situate the coming to awareness of an objective world back into the order of humanly lived existence, in Merleau-Ponty's view, we need find no contradiction between this consciousness and bodily conditioning through skill development. That it provides itself with a habitual body 'is an internal necessity for the most integrated existence' (*PP*, 89–90). Which is not to deny the wider factors on which the epistemic subject remains dependent. Language is needed, and as noted before, the conception of a community of reasonable spirits is only persuasive in places where vital and economic equilibrium has been established locally and for a certain length of time. Rationality has had the chance to develop and even become commonplace (*PP*, 57). One's body schema will nonetheless remain opaque to the rational gaze. Not being learnt, the most elementary of skills exercised after birth did not

---

[41] Here I draw on Mooney 2017, 64–6.

require the thematisation of the body. The schema was already organising our original opening onto a perceptual field in which nothing was conceptually or reflectively attended to or posited, in which there was as yet no subject or object (*PP*, 241–3, 251). Without it, our earliest act intentionalities could not have got off the ground, for they could not have intended any possibilities without any expectations of fulfilment. Through the schema, we intended the manipulable and first carried our seeing of the analysable and the recomposable into imitative practice. It expressed our first significations by giving them a worldly place (*PP*, 147). Even in developed life, one cannot enumerate how its operations have contributed to one's sphere of motivations. They already functioned sub-consciously and have been overwritten by those acquisitions that are themselves feeding secretly into the present. The anonymity of the body schema 'is inseparably both freedom and servitude', and in the same vein '[w]hat allows us to centre our existence is also what prevents us from centering it completely' (*PP*, 87).

Merleau-Ponty stresses that the skilled agent who draws on the hidden past need not be a professional researcher. He or she can manifest foresight and premeditation as much as immediate somatic proficiency, apprehending threats and opportunities well in advance of the neophyte. In the relevant area of endeavour, that person enjoys a sedimented panorama of cognitions 'with its accentuated regions and its confused regions' by which particular signs are read off from the perceptual field of the moment (*PP*, 131–2). Extensive advantage will be taken of acquired concepts and judgements without the original syntheses in which they were acquired having to be repeated in the present situation. Scheler gives the instance of an experienced sailor who readies his boat for a storm without being able to report which specific change – of cloud formation or of temperature – first served as a warning. Developing insights from Uexküll, Scheler maintains that my environment or milieu of the moment embraces 'everything with whose *existence* or *absence*, with whose being so or other than so, I practically "*reckon*"'.[42] Merleau-Ponty agrees (*PP*, 335), while recognising that the work of imagination goes beyond the anticipation of scenarios having better or worse consequences in terms of sheer utility. Through waking life, 'the normal person *reckons with* the possible, which thus acquires a sort of actuality without leaving behind its place as a possibility' (*PP*, 112). In lived existence, we psychosomatically

---

[42] Scheler 1973, 140.

'understand' in phantasy not only some definite milieu, but beyond this an infinity of possible milieus (*PP*, 341).

Our power to reckon with the possible has been expounded by Komarine Romdenh-Romluc, who notes that, on Merleau-Ponty's view, we ordinarily perceive more opportunities for action than those pertaining to what we are currently doing. We can picture Lucy as an experienced kickboxing instructor who is demonstrating a defensive move to her students. In the absence of a real assailant, she is 'interacting' with an imaginary one. She can be taken as acting with regard to a merely possible situation. But because her demonstration involves the exercise of her fighting skill, she is accessing that skill by way of imagination. This is a two-way relation, for if the agent can imbue a possible scenario represented in thought with motor significance, this is only because the skills are already in place for her to access. Put another way, she must be capable of accessing those skills that she *could* use to act in that situation if it were real.[43] This is also true when thinking of scenarios where one will not be demonstrating anything (at least beyond enjoyment and affection), for instance when imagining dancing with a loved one. The power to reckon with the possible allows me to break out of the actual into genuinely realisable situations.

Romdenh-Romluc's account is sure-footed and insightful so far as it goes, and of interest for another reason. On reading it, one can better discern the overlap between the Husserlian awareness of available agency and the Merleau-Pontian reckoning with the possible. I can move this table straight in front of me to a nicer place in my kitchen, and I could dance with my partner if we were to attend a party together. The 'I can' and the 'I could' with the other are essential to the action scenarios. Our somatically founded imagination extends to possibilities that are less as well as more proximate with regard to their dynamic fulfilment, and in the usual course of events there is no question as to our capacity to realise them when on the scene or as soon as we are on the scene, accidents and interruptions apart. Once I am willingly there for dancing and the other also, our beginning right away is not an issue for us. For each person, the skilled body must be available as an undivided power of action, with all its parts integrally placed so as to be present for all intents and purposes. The body schema envelops one's body and things beyond it, sometimes in union with a skilled partner. And in organising one's posture towards an outcome, it keeps up its silent work all the way to fulfilment. In phenomenological terms, it is the advance and ongoing organisation that remains to be explicated. Another

---

[43] Romdenh-Romluc 2011, 91–2, 93, 97–8.

pathological case will help to bring out the joint schematising of body and environment as we move to realise the diverse goals characterising our engaged being in the world. The task is to uncover 'these strange relations woven between the parts of the landscape, or from the landscape to me as an embodied subject' (*PP*, 53).

CHAPTER 6

Motor Intentionality and Our Landscapes

6.1 Introduction

Though the body's spatiality envelops its parts, Merleau-Ponty stresses that its unobtrusive character is equally dependent on its movements inter-meshing with the world as they unfold, forming a practical system with things in evolving orientations. The body must take an appropriate direction to constitute 'the darkness in the theatre required for the clarity of the performance' (*PP*, 103). When I move to realise a goal, my body is not with me as its neutral executor, for it is following on and shaped by an imma-nent plan. In pursuing a prior project or in responding to an invitation, I depend on a schematising intentionality that works with and beyond my visual articulations of the phenomenal field. In this field, certain orienta-tions and figures are privileged against indifferent backgrounds. If my privileging body is polarised by its tasks, existing towards their completion, then it is in focussing on the course of its movements that its spatiality of situation is to be uncovered. We must work back to the body schema's advance organisation of my posture and correlative prefiguration of par-ticular sectors of my current milieu (*PP*, 103, 105).

At first it is difficult to discern this intentional organisation, since it is hidden behind the objective world it helps to constitute (*PP*, 523). Merleau-Ponty contends that a unique case of morbid or pathological motility will be of signal help in uncovering its anonymous and projective work, that of the injured war veteran Schneider. He suffers from psycho-logical blindness, intellectual inflexibility and context-sensitive deficits in postural awareness. Yet his reflexes as unthinking responses to situations appear to be normal, as do his concrete or habitual movements. He is also well capable of executing what I call concrete-like and context-familiar movements, or mimes involving the entire body. He begins to run into trouble when trying to execute context-strange mimes in which imitative movements are ordinarily abbreviated. His troubles are exacerbated when he is asked to perform simple abstract movements of tracing out figures. Typically he can only complete them after a number of attempts that require his having to objectify his body. For Merleau-Ponty, Schneider's range of comportment has been curtailed because his motor intentionality falls short of the last type of movement. Motor intentionality is needed for the thought of movement to carry seamlessly into actual movement.

I commence this chapter by setting out Schneider's difficulties as reported by his physicians and running through their attempts to explain them causally. Merleau-Ponty notes that their early and exclusive explanations already show the shortcomings of objective thought in its classical form. An alternative and intellectualist story endeavours to understand his problems in terms of conscious and imaginative deficits. The patient has problems with abstract movements and context-strange mimes because his representational power of projection is diminished, bringing him close a thing that functions automatically. As ever the intellectualist story marks an advance on the empiricist one, though it is unduly abstractive. It overplays his imaginative shortcomings and misses the absence of a motor intentional plan to schematically and non-representationally organise body and milieu towards an outcome, to constitute an action solution and a route to realisation. And if we must appeal to the productive imagination and motor intentionality for immediate mimes and abstract movements, I argue that many novel movements – including practical ones – demand a more specific appeal to motor intentional transpositions of skills. In conclusion, I maintain that Merleau-Ponty passes over the role of engaged reflection in the flow of action, though his account can be reconstructed to accommodate it.

6.2 The Schneider Case and Explanation

In front-line army service in 1915, Johann Schneider was hit by mine splinters or shrapnel that penetrated his skull and occipital lobe, damaging his primary visual cortex. Though he suffered from several defects, there is insufficient evidence – and still no agreement – as to the precise character and extent of his deficiencies. He was treated over several years by the noted neurologist and psychiatrist Kurt Goldstein and the psychologist Adhémar Gelb. In the case studies, Schneider can track things and focus on them with no difficulty when actually at work, though he is classified as psychically or psychologically blind. He seems to have exhibited what is now called associative visual agnosia, the selective impairment of the ability to recognise visual objects.[1] If he sees certain things outside their habitual contexts of use, he can only perceive their separate qualities, and must build them into objects inferentially, laboriously traversing a sequence of steps.[2] When shown a fountain pen, he sees something that is black and blue and long and straight with a shiny patch at one end. After examining the shiny clip, he concludes that it is for writing, and must be a pencil or pen. Nor can he build up complex spatial figures from simpler ones. If presented with four isosceles triangles and asked to make up one square with them, he responds that he can only make two. He has to be presented with a square made up of the four to understand what is meant (*PP*, 105, 132–3).

Schneider can quite correctly subsume things under logical principles and abstract categories, but only do so explicitly and methodically. Without painstaking analyses, he cannot grasp analogies such as 'fur is to the cat what feathers are to the bird', or 'light is to the lamp what heat is to the stove'. Language in its metaphorical use is also senseless at first – he must be shown what is meant by the 'the foot of the chair' or 'the head of the nail'. He never speaks to express a possible situation, and false statements are meaningless to him, such as 'the sky is black' when uttered in the daylight (*PP*, 129–30, 202). In fact he rarely speaks unless spoken to, and then his replies are formulaic, requiring advance preparation. On those occasions that he does ask questions, these are also formulaic and stereotypical. After he is told a story and asked to recount it, furthermore, he cannot accentuate its essential points, repeating it indifferently rather than understanding it as a melodic whole with its own highs and lows (*PP*, 136, 202). What is displayed is not a lack of overall intelligence, rather of speed and spontaneity. He suffers from intellectual inflexibility in his thinking, and this is shown in his comportment. He is serious and meticulous, never singing or whistling or displaying any levity and only going out on a specific errand. When passing Goldstein's house, he fails to recognise it because he had not journeyed with the intention of going there. Another region of his milieu cannot form a possible situation because one task monopolises his focus (*PP*, 136–7).

The patient has no problems with what the doctors call concrete movements. These are the skilled and habitual movements we make in our practical tasks. With some difficulty, he learnt to make wallets, but

---

[1] Associative visual agnosia is distinct from apperceptive visual agnosia, in which a person has difficulties with the recognition of visual objects across the board (with their shapes and other features and therefore with what they are). For a comprehensive account of the different types of visual agnosia attributed to Schneider, see Jensen 2009, 373–4.
[2] Goldstein 1923, 143, 155–6.

after this he proceeds quite well in cutting the pieces of leather and sewing them together. The scissors and needle and other materials are ready-to-hand for him as immediate affordances, and his output is about three-quarters that of an ordinary worker. He can perform other concrete movements of grasping with his eyes shut, such as taking matches out of his pocket and lighting his desk lantern. Just as easily, he can find his handkerchief and clear his nose. All these actions can be performed on request, and when a mosquito bites him he immediately slaps the area that has been stung. His reflexes are as prompt as his concrete movements (*PP*, 105–6, 108). Schneider begins to run into problems when asked to imitate concrete actions in unfamiliar places and in unfamiliar postures, that is, to perform part-concrete-like and context-strange movements. If asked to mimic combing his hair, he has to mime combing and looking into a mirror, as if in a bedroom or bathroom. If asked to salute at his workbench, he has to stand up, adopt a respectful military posture and carefully raise his hand to make the salute, as if to an officer on a parade ground. If asked to mime hammering, he must mimic holding a nail to a wall. He has to imaginatively locate himself in scenarios demanding completely concrete-like and context-familiar movements, matching up his entire body with the concrete originals. In these mimes, there is a delay in moving and no economy of movement, though the movements flow smoothly enough. If he is interrupted in the process of imitation and brought out of the imaginative situation, his dexterity completely disappears, and he has to start all over again, from the beginning (*PP*, 107). When making all such concrete-like movements to order, in Goldstein's words, the patient places himself 'in the affective situation as a whole, and it is from this that the movement flows, as in real life.'[3]

Outside habitual contexts of action or action imitation, Schneider's postural awareness is defective. If he is asked whether his arm is horizontal, he has to visually check its position in relation to his torso, and his torso in relation to the vertical. If asked whether he is lying down or standing, he can only find out from the pressure of the mattress under his back or the ground under his feet. If part of his body is touched gently and he is asked to point to it, he has to shake his whole body to find the general area, and then twitch his skin to find the more precise point of contact.[4] In this he resembles patients with cerebellar injuries – though his own cerebellum is undamaged, his pointing lacks the immediacy of his grasping (*PP*, 106, 109). If he is asked to perform simple abstract movements, he runs into

[3] Ibid., 175–6.   [4] Gelb and Goldstein 1920, 206–13.

serious difficulties. These are not purposive or habitual, following from no practical models. He is at first dumbfounded on hearing the requests, but tries to respond to them after some time. When asked to raise one arm to the horizontal, he has to find that arm visually and track it up the same way. After a number of attempts, he succeeds. If his eyes are closed, he has to fall back on his sense of feeling and touch. He shakes his body to find the arm, and having found it, swings it up several times to establish a kinaesthetic and directional background for the movement. And when asked to trace a square or a circle in mid-air with his arm, he again has to locate it with his eyes, or if his eyes are again closed, through feeling and touch. He then brings his arm up to a certain level and moves it out, as if to find a wall in the dark. He is much happier, however, when he can use his eyes. All these attempts follow an invariant formula. He must first locate the limb, then make rough movements to establish a seen or felt route for realising the request, and finally refine the movements until the figure is completed. Occasionally and fortuitously, he lurches into an attempt and gets everything right the first time. When this happens, he immediately stops (*PP*, 105, 112–13).[5]

Sean Kelly has drawn attention to the fact that Schneider's difficulties are not unique, having recurred in similar form in the recent 'D.F.' case, that of a woman who has survived carbon monoxide poisoning.[6] Scans and measurements of her brain and her movements have shown that her injuries are comparatively clear-cut. In studying her behaviour, the neuroscientists David Milner and Melvyn Goodale have noted that her abilities to recognise or discriminate between visual patterns and their size, location and orientation are severely impaired. She exhibits comprehensive or apperceptive visual agnosia. But within a matter of weeks of her injury, she was well able to reach and grasp things for practical purposes, as well as catching balls and sticks and negotiating obstacles in her path. Unlike her disengaged perceptual reports at a distance, her concrete actions are often quite successful.[7] Milner and Goodale have argued that the two broad neural pathways for vision – the ventral and the dorsal – contribute essentially to 'what' information about things and their qualities and 'how' information about dealing with them. D.F.'s ventral stream is damaged, though it does not function in isolation from the dorsal. Her problems are very much a consequence of depleted inter-stream communication.[8] Obviously Gelb and Goldstein did not have

---

[5] Ibid., 213–22.   [6] Kelly 2002, 378–81.   [7] Milner and Goodale 1995, 126–8.

[8] Ibid., 132–4, 202–3. Milner has stressed that the initial selection of an action and use of a relevant tool requires some awareness of what is to be acted on. On the best evidence to date, the 'how' awareness is not confined to the dorsal stream (even if chiefly dependent on it), since ventral information about

our contemporary technologies of neural imaging and speed and accuracy tracking at their disposal, and the issue is not with a causal explanation of the Schneider case. It is with whether Merleau-Ponty draws defensible philosophical conclusions from the documentation available.

The initial attempts to diagnose the case empirically are nonetheless of interest to him in bringing out the shortcomings of first-generation objective thought. One hypothesis invoked psychological blindness to explain Schneider's difficulties. When engaged in concrete movement, his sight does not slow him down, for what he sees is embedded in a habitual milieu of action. In constructing abstract movements, his visual sense is deficient, but he still prefers to use his eyes because sight is causally fundamental. It might be objected that the blind from birth easily perform abstract movements, but their responses to requests could be quasi-simultaneous, the results of practice. The claim that psychological blindness is the root deficiency was never refuted (*PP*, 118–19). A second hypothesis attributed Schneider's difficulties to a tactile disorder. Another patient 'S' seems free of visual defects; he readily identifies things in different contexts and can knock on a door and turn its handle without any difficulty. But once the door is hidden, S cannot imitate the actions of knocking and turning. Even when it is in view but out of reach, mimicry is impossible for him, and he is utterly incapable of abstract movements. Visual deficiency is not plausible in this case, which suggests that what is lacking is a sense of virtual touch. In our normal bodies, awakened memories of approaching and touching induce tactile anticipations well before we reach the relevant things. Lacking such memories and anticipations, S is confined to the immediately reachable (*PP*, 119–20, 519).

If Schneider's disorder is of this nature it cannot be as severe, his sense of virtual touch being deficient but not destroyed. He can mimic combing or hammering when the relevant implements are at a distance and even absent. He can construct abstract movements with his eyes closed by building a kinaesthetic background and eventually complete them, surpassing S. On this explanation, he is faster when using his sight – itself deficient – to compensate for his deficient tactile anticipation (as if of a wall when his eyes are closed). This second hypothesis was not refuted either. S appears to have undamaged sight but cannot mimic any movements whatsoever, so the loss of tactile anticipation seems to blame. Nor can this hypothesis be proved. The sense of virtual touch in the blind from birth is

what something is for allows us to fine-tune our employment of it. D.F. can pick up an implement, but not always grasp it in a manner appropriate to its use. See Milner 2017, 1300–3, 1305.

unmarked by sight, but they may not execute novel abstract movements as the sighted do. A sense of virtual touch could be insufficient on its own (*PP*, 119–20). It turns out that no experiment is decisive and no explanation final. But only in older empiricisms is it assumed that an inductive generalisation can be decisively verified. A reformed method only requires the most probable explanation. On examining many cases, the variable missing most frequently could reasonably be taken as the cause (*PP*, 118, 120–1).

Yet the persisting assumption is that there *are* variables to be identified and determined separately, allowing for an exclusive interpretation in terms of visual or tactile damage. Though this procedure works in the region of the physical universe, it is not applicable to the patient's behaviour. One cannot reach a determination of his vision or sense of virtual touch independently of each other, and hence of the supposed cause of an immediate performance. Goldstein quickly realised that the tactile and visual procedures are coloured by each other, so we cannot know how much each one is contributing to an abstract movement over its course.[9] This is not a failure of causal explanation, but of the search for causes in external and mechanical relationships (*PP*, 120–1). The first-generation physiologist might respond that the contribution of any one sense can still be determined. We can isolate its original work because the colouring it gave to the others will fade away with time. The contribution of that sense can be identified by comparing behaviour in which it is present with behaviour well after its loss. But if the remaining senses change in response to the damage or destruction of one, this does not involve a return to some primordial purity. They developed integrally with that sense and have now compensated for its damage or destruction, which means that its original contribution cannot be read off from them on either count. And if there never was an original contribution, the pathological cannot serve as a model for the normal, since the development of these other senses was different from the very start (*PP*, 121–2).

6.3   Intellectualism and Motor Intentionality

An alternative approach seeks to understand Schneider's shortcomings rather than to explain them. There must be an underlying reason for his symptoms, the loss of an intellectual and representational power that inhabits vision and touch but which has been passed over by empiricism.

---

[9] Gelb and Goldstein 1920, 227 ff.

Goldstein takes this route when he claims that the patient cannot effort-lessly inhabit the 'categorial attitude' in which we immediately understand and organise perceived objects, qualities and states of affairs according to ideas and principles. We do not have to laboriously subsume empirical particularity into intellectual generality. On this view, cognitive rather than physical deficits are inhibiting the performance of abstract move-ments, already evidenced by the patient's inability to point spontaneously to parts of his body on request. Whereas grasping is a concrete and habitual activity, the act of pointing supposes that one can isolate a specific area of one's body, objectifying it in thought and at one remove as a necessary prelude to the action.[10] Schneider is no longer a subject who can properly face an objective world that transcends the practical milieu in which he is immersed (*PP*, 122–3). A complementary story is set out by Ernst Cassirer, the Neo-Kantian whose emphasis on act intentionality is sometimes intel-lectualist (*PP*, 126–8). For the latter, our power of imaginative representa-tion is necessary to discern 'symbolic forms' in our perceptions of things. To apprehend a thing representationally is to take it as symbolically 'pregnant' with one or more form, as bearing a 'vector of meaning'. In its apprehension a sensuous presentation in the here and now carries a reference to at least one possibility lying beyond the here and now.[11]

Only the productive imagination can let us envisage a symbolic form to be taken up or reckoned with. This is Kant's faculty of representing something without its actual presence in sensuous intuition, the faculty essential to perception itself. When I see the wine glasses in the cupboard, I lift one up and bring it into the light to admire, and think of carefully dusting and polishing all of them to shine more brightly for a homecoming celebration. I then search for my smartphone because the shining glass has reminded me of my decanter and my friend who gave it to me, prompting me to arrange a meeting with him. The perception has been symbolically pregnant with multiple references to possibilities. Such is the backdrop to Cassirer's reading of the case, helped by his conversations with the patient and physicians.[12] Schneider's productive imagination cannot have disap-peared, for perception would then be impossible. But it has undergone a drastic change, and is now functioning 'within narrower limits, in smaller and more restricted circles'.[13] Without a solid foundation in what is sensuously present to him, the patient finds himself directionless. His

---

[10] Goldstein 1931, 456–7, 459–60.
[11] Cassirer 1957, 114, 202, 222. For a detailed outline of his account, see Matherne 2014, 127–33. I draw on the latter in my exposition.
[12] Cassirer 1957, 134, 239, 271.   [13] Ibid., 222.

inability to express possible situations and understand statements clashing with the sensuously present show that he cannot venture onto the ocean of thought beyond the actual.[14] Outside habitual action, he is lacking 'the spiritual view into the distance, the vision of what is not before his eyes, of the merely possible'.[15]

On these lines of interpretation, the patient's injuries have brought him close to the kind of existence that would proceed automatically. This would be a self-contained being in itself as opposed to the normal being for itself that arcs forward into the possible. Schneider and the ordinary person are seen as having the same concrete milieu with the same habitual movements, the only difference being that the former cannot escape it. What he has lost almost entirely is the conscious and imaginative power of projection. For Merleau-Ponty, these construals are helpful if partial, neglecting his other shortcomings. Certainly he cannot make use of his body by way of his imagination like the ordinary person who extracts it from a concrete situation to deliver a salute sitting down or the actor who takes on a radically different persona. Without trouble, each of them can 'detach their real body from its living situation to make in order to make it breathe, speak, and, if need be, cry in the imaginary' (*PP*, 107). It should be noted, however, that the patient *can* extract himself to some extent from his practical milieu, albeit with difficulty. In order to mime combing his hair or giving a salute, he must already understand and imagine what it looks like and feels like to fulfil the request. He *is* a subject who can project an objective world without actually being in the bathroom or on the parade ground, even if that world is not ours. His imitative movements are unabbreviated as whole body mimes, being concrete-like and context-familiar. In these procedures, he must make extensive use of his memory and reproductive imagination.

Though all are agreed that the productive imagination has priority for pointing and for abstract movement, Merleau-Ponty maintains that intellectualism overplays its diminution. Schneider is dumbfounded on hearing requests to move abstractly, but they are not meaningless to him, since he eventually tries to meet them and ultimately succeeds. More than this, he must be imaginatively representing what it looks like to trace a square or a circle in mid-air. Otherwise he would not stop moving when he gets the movement right, and on rare occasions the first time round. Knowing and picturing the request with its peculiar success conditions, he understands perfectly well whether he has satisfied it or fallen short of it (*PP*, 112–13).

---

[14] Ibid., 254, 257.   [15] Ibid., 277.

This shows us that the productive imagination is a necessary but not a sufficient condition of performing the movements immediately. Typically Schneider has to construct an ideal formula for the abstract movement, an imaginative model of how best to proceed so as to realise the already imagined goal. Part of his procedure seems to be modelled on our ordinary way of reaching out to find a wall in the dark, and may even comprise a concrete-like and context-familiar mime (if he became accustomed to underground bunkers during bombardments). He then implements this formula for the movement, though a gap opens up between the thinking and picturing and the doing. As he proceeds he continually objectifies his body, as we see when he searches for his arm, locates it and performs rough movements to establish a route that he gradually refines. His problem would seem to lie in his inability to objectify the limb immediately and to align it immediately with his ideal formula. This stops him from copying the movement off from the imagined procedure in the one blow.

Merleau-Ponty holds that such an interpretation is fundamentally mistaken, for it rests on the assumption that our normal movements are of a kind with Schneider's, differing only in their degrees of objectification and in their speed, fluidity and accuracy. Because he is compensating for functions that are damaged or destroyed, his procedure is itself pathological. Behaviour after injury is like childhood, for it is a complete form or configuration of existence with its own concrete essence (*PP*, 110, 112–13, 127). This is recognised by Goldstein, who notes that all normal movement takes place against a background, and that with the patient movement and background are no longer moments of a single whole.[16] When I represent a requested action that is an immediate possibility for me, according to Merleau-Ponty, I do not have to check for a fit between my body and some formula for the action in order to execute it. Nor do I have to envision a formula of how to move in the first instance:

> He [Schneider] is lacking neither motility nor thought, and we must acknowledge, between movement as a third person process and thought as a representation of movement, an anticipation or a grasp of the result assured by the body itself as a motor power, a 'motor project' (*Bewegungsentwurf*), or a 'motor intentionality' without which the instructions would remain empty. Sometimes the patient thinks of the ideal formula of the movement; at other times he throws his body into blind attempts; however, for the normal person every movement is indissolubly

---

[16] Goldstein 1923, 163, 178.

movement and consciousness of movement. This can be expressed by saying that, for the normal person, every movement has a *background*, and that the movement and its background are 'moments of a single whole'. The background of the movement is not a representation associated or linked externally to the movement itself; it is immanent in the movement, it animates it and guides it along at each moment. For the subject, kinetic initiation is, like perception, an original manner of relating to an object. [17]
(*PP*, 113)

The requests conveyed to the patient have an intellectual significance for him without having a motor one. They are not initially apprehended in terms of the 'I can'. At first Schneider hears strange sounding letters that demand translation into the range of mediate possibilities that he has left. Only after some time does he realise he can fulfil them by way of a formula, which of its essence requires bodily objectification (*PP*, 113, 139). For the normal person who agrees to perform a simple abstract movement, by contrast, how it will be executed is not an issue, requiring no consideration or objectification whatsoever. The request is apprehended as an immediate possibility because the straight-off fulfilment of the goal will be taken care of through a motor intentional plan. What will guide the movement is an action solution and route to realisation that the body schema has already prefigured sub-consciously and non-representationally. The observable changes in the person's posture will have been projectively organised from the outset (*PP*, 102–3, 140–1).

Whereas concrete movement is centripetal, following on well-worn projects and solicited by what is familiar within the perceptual field, abstract movement is centrifugal, exhibiting creativity in not adhering to habit or customary milieu. Unlike Schneider's phenomenal field, that of the ordinary person is plastic. It can be spontaneously organised into a new orientation by way of an imagined action that is an immediate possibility. Should the action be embarked upon immediately, the field becomes the actual landscape in which it unfolds (*PP*, 114, 133). With all such imagined actions the pre-reflective awareness of available agency is sub-reflectively warranted by potential motor intentional prefigurations for their realisation. Without the latter our powers of projecting into and reckoning with the possible would congeal into laborious planning, and our milieus would correlatively congeal into obstinately familiar pathways. With them our imagined actions can be taken up as projects that 'polarise the world, causing a thousand signs to appear there, as if by magic, that guide action,

---

[17] Translation emended.

as signs in a museum guide a visitor' (*PP*, 115). Ordinarily we have several 'holds' on our bodies. They are readily available for fictional and phantasied situations existing before us as though real (*PP*, 111). The situations have their being in the imaginary, and most will never be taken up or pursued. Embodied awareness represents many possible worlds, and 'sketching out these landscapes and abandoning them indivisibly demonstrates its vitality' (*PP*, 132).

When a possibility *is* pursued, what I call an action solution is the plotting out of specific deployments of head and torso and the various limbs to achieve the desired outcome. In working with vision, this motor intentional plan is at once a route to realisation; it prefigures these postural developments to traverse the phenomenal field towards the outcome. The milieu and its things for use or avoidance are polarised within vectors and lines of force that constitute an anisotropic spatiality of situation as against an objective spatiality of absolute and indifferent position (*PP*, 102–3, 115). My friend achieves all this in setting off on his bicycle. The machine is incorporated into his schema when he puts it to use, and in gaining speed he keeps it close to the sidewalk to avoid cars. After some seconds, he looks back and gives me a jaunty wave, maintaining his balance and distance from neighbouring vehicles. Without representing or objectifying body or machine or sidewalk, he is combining practical movements with those expressing cheerfulness and exuberance. A player in a game of football does more again in his dynamically shifting environment. The touch-lines of the pitch, the penalty area and the movements of opponents have their places as immanent terms of an evolving orientation with which the player is at one in seeing and taking up an opportunity to score (*SB*, 168–9). The game is a fast-moving illustration of motor intentional gearing into the world, though our simpler and prosaic actions through the day do their own duty.

Remembering a helpful critical commentary in the course of my writing, I reach up for this particular book, which is leaning at the end of the stack on the shelf above my laptop computer. As the use-phantom cases have shown, I do not have to find my limb before initiating the action. Just as importantly, I do not have to plot out the route or trajectory that my arm is taking from the keyboard towards my target. I am not trying to follow any kind of formula because my eyes and attention are focussed wholly on the book. In my moving of my arm, its final position is immanently anticipated, such that 'I have no need of directing it toward the goal of the movement, in a sense it touches the goal from the very beginning and it throws itself toward it' (*PP*, 97). Nor is there any need for me to plot out the way that my approaching hand is opening so as to take hold of the book, adapting itself to the latter's shape and size before it has actually reached it. My hand is preparing to move around the thing to be touched 'by anticipating the stimuli and by itself sketching out the form that I am about to perceive' (*PP*, 78). There is a pre-comprehension of what is to be achieved in the moving limb, an outcome orientation manifested in and through it. The operation of raising and shaping and grasping proceeds directly and shows the continuity of explicit intention and action, of the thought of finding the helpful paragraphs and its actual execution. All these movements are realising the motor intentional plan that runs ahead of them as 'something like a seed of movement that only grows later through its objective trajectory' (*PP*, 96). Having taken hold of the book, I bring it down, turn it around and cradle its spine. With my other hand, I open it and flick through its pages. On finding the desired information I go back to my writing and then put the book back up on the shelf. Seized by thirst a few minutes later, I reach for my water bottle. Again, there is no need to plot an appropriate route, or the way that my one hand comes to encircle the main body of the bottle while my other comes to grasp the cap between thumb, index and middle finger, twisting it off in union with a raised arm that is angled-in from the elbow like the hand from the wrist. Just as unthinking is the bringing of the bottle up to my mouth, and its being recapped and returned to the side of my desk when my thirst is slaked.

In none of these movements are we proceeding as Schneider and D.F. must do some of the time, and as other patients who have lost their body schemas completely must do all of the time, incessantly objectifying their bodies and surveying their movements. One such case is that of Christina, a former patient of Oliver Sacks who suffers from polyneuritis or damage to the peripheral nerves. She cannot stand up or reach to manipulate something without visually guiding her limbs, and though her movements have become more fluid with practice, she still depends utterly on her eyes.[18] Jonathan Cole and Jacques Paillard have documented an injury with a similarly extreme outcome. Ian Waterman has lost all of his mylinated or insulated nerve fibre functioning below his neck, and consequently lacks the senses of touch and of immanent positional aware-ness in stasis and in movement. His limbs were initially uncontrollable, though he managed to master everyday tasks over two years of intensive treatment. Like Christina, he needs to visually locate his limbs and monitor

[18] Sacks 1985, 44, 47, quoted in Morris 2012, 53–4.

their movements from start to finish. When walking, Ian cannot daydream but must focus on his legs and overall gait to maintain progress and not fall over; when writing, he must concentrate on his upper body posture and grasp; and when picking up an egg, he must monitor effort and applied force to avoid breaking it. He has constituted a new schema without the ease and anonymity of the ordinary one.[19]

So long as our motor intentionality remains intact for different situations and attitudes, our movements will almost always manifest what Cole and Paillard have entitled 'topokinetic' and 'morphokinetic' accuracy.[20] Our bodies are exhibiting their ordinary and unthinking proficiency in their routes towards certain things, in their adjustments to their usable forms or features and in the ongoing itineraries in which these things are employed towards the ends we have envisaged. Motor intentionality is that part of the art hidden in the depths of the soul that ensures a sensorimotor unity of perception and action and perception in action. Its articulations of things are analogous to Kant's schemas for empirical concepts, since the taking up of scissors and cloth for tailoring or pen and paper for writing presupposes the unthematic apprehension of these figures towards the appropriate end before one gets to grips with them. '[E]ach particular focusing is wrapped into a general project' (*PP*, 265), and in their combined value, the tools define a situation 'that calls for a certain mode of resolution, a certain labour' (*PP*, 108–9). Motor intentionality is also analogous to Kant's schematisation of the pure concepts of the understanding in that it mediates the general and the particular. Its plan for the taking up of the seen towards the desired outcome reconciles the tasks and skills that are recursive by their nature with the unique contours and features of this phenomenal field.[21] As the projective organisation of one's posture that gears it into a sector of the world, it comprises a context-sensitive action solution and route to realisation. It is the body schema schematising or prefiguring how body and limbs will be deployed in just this context. Putting it another way, it is the schematisation of how one will skilfully negotiate this particular environment. Even habitual actions demand their own schematisations, for one's body and affordances never

---

[19] Cole and Paillard 1995, 245–66. Quoted in Gallagher 2005a, 43–5, 109–26.
[20] Cole and Paillard 1995, 256; Gallagher 2005a, 113–14. See also Paillard 1991, 461–81.
[21] One should not overplay what is analogous. A big difference is that for Kant the concept has priority over its schematisation, in that the concept provides the cognised unity of the content intuited and anticipated in the schema. For Merleau-Ponty, the body schema serves to organise the phenomenal field, predelineating action possibilities within it before concepts come to work through their dedicated schematisations. My thanks to my second reviewer on this point.

stand in precisely the relations they did before, however small the changes in their relative location might be. The projective appropriation of the current milieu towards the outcome is at once an advance accommodation or conformation to the peculiar details of that milieu, constituting what Merleau-Ponty calls an embracing and a fit (*PP*, 141, 143).

All this helps to flesh out the operative, passively synthesising intentionality adverted to by Husserl that carries me along, determining me practically in my entire procedure. Motor intentionality undergirds signitive, imaginative and volitional act intentionality as the bodily plan for fulfilling the not yet given. It is not empty and undetermined, for drawing on vision and other sources it horizonally predelineates and polarises body and environment. Its schematised body is the tacit third term in the figure-background structure as articulated in advance towards an outcome (*PP*, 101–3, 115). Whether I perceive something for itself or towards an ulterior end, my body is geared into the world 'when my motor intentions, as they unfold, receive the responses they anticipate from the world' (*PP*, 261). When moving towards my chosen outcome immediately, smoothly and accurately, what I am doing, why I am doing it and the way of doing it (if and so far as it is conscious) pertain to act intentionality. The subconscious way of proceeding and how I am proceeding that way pertain to motor intentionality, which does not attend act intentionality from without. The two are moments of one overall intending. Within it the former is invisible, the adverbial moment free of the act-object cognitions involved in learning the skills whose deployments it prefigures (*PP*, 140, 525).

Where absent or deficient motor intentionality reveals itself most clearly, and even as it mediates them, it is recalcitrant to objective thought's abstract categories of objective body in the realm of physical causes and autonomous consciousness in the realm of reasons.[22] It is projectively operative within the world and yet irreducible to causal explanation in being intrinsically perceptual and by extension selective, privileging what will be taken up through its postural plan. Those things are carved out of the milieu in its projected outcome, existing *for* this organising intentionality. Furthermore, its immanently organised body exists ahead of itself. Shaped towards a result in the world, it is at grips with its affordances in advance. As a centre of virtual action, it is not in space and time, but inhabits them (*PP*, 111, 140). What counts in the orientation of the perceptual field is not my body as a physical thing in objective space, but

---

[22] See also Gardner 2013, 126, 131.

instead 'my body as a system of possible actions, a virtual body whose phenomenal "place" is defined by its task and by its situation. My body is wherever it has something to do' (*PP*, 260). Jensen is right to contend that the body in its motile power is not an agency-neutral system of automatic functions. Were this the case it would be intentionally blind, excluding any responsiveness to the meaning of a conscious representation as well as making movement external to the will of the agent. My bodily capacity to move towards an end should be seen as teleologically basic, not demanding that I direct my will at my bodily organs as if from a distance.[23] We need to jettison a story of conscious acts as causes lying behind bare physical movements, stressing their continuity with an intentional awareness involved in and inhabiting our movements (*PP*, 56, 139, 141, 452).

As an operative region of silence, motor intentionality defies all subsequent objectification, something emphasised by Kelly. He notes that the distinction between objective and situational space is between purely represented and behavioural space, with the latter comprising a milieu of dynamically changing relations. The practical comprehension of a thing's location and shape and size in motor intentionality is not of an independently specifiable spatial feature that can be captured by a representation and a concept. Even when I am in a position to reflect on the completed activity, I cannot properly report the bodily understanding that was anonymously operative within it.[24] Thus the gesture of reaching towards something in the pursuit of an end contains a reference to it, not as a representation, 'but as this highly determinate thing toward which we are thrown, next to which we are through anticipation, and which we haunt' (*PP*, 140). This is another way of expressing that the thing is highly determined for the body, which shows a praktognosic awareness of and sensitivity to its features. Every perception has something about it in which 'we merge with this body that is better informed than we are about the world, about motives, and about the means available for accomplishing the synthesis' (*PP*, 248).[25]

6.4 Seeing Solutions and Transposing Skills

Intellectualism has overplayed the diminution of Schneider's productive imagination in relation to his abstract movements, passing over the loss of motor intentionality that prevents such movements being executed immediately. But it is rightly contended that his imaginative shortcomings have

[23] Jensen 2013, 52–9.   [24] Kelly 2002, 381–2, 384, 389.   [25] Translation emended.

closed off a wide swath of other possibilities open to the healthy individual. When the patient fails to recognise Goldstein's house or think of calling there while on an errand, an appropriate motor projection is already impossible. Keeping this in mind, it would be wrong to hold that the productive imagination responsible for our apprehensions of possibilities that are symbolic forms in the perceiving of things can be separated from the perceptual structures on which it rests (*PP*, 115, 126). It would be absurd to solely explain Schneider's imaginative deficiencies causally, in terms of his visual agnosia, yet 'no less absurd to think that the shrapnel collided with symbolic consciousness. Rather, his spirit is affected through vision' (*PP*, 127). Schneider's injuries have damaged his vision in both the literal and figurative senses. Because things cannot be recognised visually outside their habitual contexts, they cannot motivate him to imagine more than one action, such as also calling on Goldstein. Even when communicated to him the things are no longer means for deploying a supposedly uncondi-tioned power of projection. On being told that he passed the doctor's house during his errand, he is still unable to envision a possibility branch-ing off from the original practical situation. Ordinarily our visual deliver-ances are taken up and transformed by our imaginative power. The relationship is not of cause to effect, but of founding to founded. Consciousness develops sensible givens beyond their initial significations, though their colourations persist in the semantic evolution of terms such as 'insight' or 'natural light' (*PP*, 128, 138). This supports Samantha Matherne's claim that not all the patient's difficulties can be understood through a motor-centric reading.[26]

It has already been noted that a possibility envisaged as a positive potentiality is an 'I could' (if it is realisable elsewhere or at another time) or an 'I can' (if it is realisable here and now). When one envisages an immediate possibility on the move and launches into its realisation there is usually little or no interruption in the flow of movement. Imaginative representation and the change of direction are at one as the action is initiated in the world. With most of our skilled and familiar actions, however, we pick out appropriate orientations and affordances without our having to picture anything in acting or in advance. What Dreyfus has called the appropriate 'situational discriminations' are made as we see and in our seeing.[27] For its part, our motility is not 'a servant of consciousness, transporting the body to the point of space that we imagine beforehand' (*PP*, 140). When the ball is passed to our football player, he spots a brief

[26] Matherne 2014, 138.   [27] Dreyfus 2002, 370–2.

opening in which he can swerve to the right and around the opposing midfielder, evade the full-back by accelerating leftwards and turn again to take a clear shot at the goal. He is seeing this route within his phenomenal field and embarking on it as he sees it. What he is discerning, moreover, is no top-down itinerary that his body is copying off as a servile implementation machine. The body is not a thing being called on that is making no original and operatively intentional contribution. In his espying of the appropriate route, his body schema has already initiated the motor plan that will evolve for him to realise it. The schema has begun to provide the highly determined somatic way with the seen way. Just as importantly, the itinerary in view is not indifferent to this hidden action solution. The projective and anisotropic seeing is indissociable from the embryonic motor plan of context-sensitive skill deployments, and they will remain moments of one process through the whole course of the action. The player's consciousness, vision and motility are integrated in the evolving action in his rapidly shifting milieu. His course of movement is not following on a detached seeing as his intention is being fulfilled, and he is at one with his milieu in responding immediately and appropriately to changes within it through these integrated functions (*SB*, 168–9; *PP*, 115, 139).

One often sees an itinerary in one's current perceptual field that need not be pursued when seen, and even then the relevant route will have a motor colouration. Shaped in advance of actual motor projections, it is for all that amenable to possible ones, which is not at all fortuitous. To bring this out, Merleau-Ponty draws on Sartre's famous example of a mountain crag. For the artist, it is something to be admired and sketched or painted and nothing more, whereas for the mountaineer, it is something to be climbed. But only relative to this freely chosen project of climbing, according to Sartre, can it be encountered as an obstacle that will be more or less difficult to surmount. Freedom reveals worldly resistances in the first place; they do not exist in themselves. Though things limit our freedom of action, 'it is our freedom itself which must first constitute the framework, the technique, and the ends in which they will manifest themselves as limits'.[28] In responding, Merleau-Ponty argues that my body schema nonetheless contributes to my tracing out of certain contours when I look at the mountain from a distance. In my visual projection of a climbing situation, I am spontaneously picking out certain obstacles

---

[28] Sartre 1958, 482.

and ways to get around them. The latter are perceived as just those contours into which my actions could be geared:

> We must in effect distinguish between my explicit intentions, such as the plan I form today to climb these mountains, and the general intentions that invest my surroundings with some value in a virtual way . . . [m]y projects as a thinking being are clearly constructed upon these valuations . . . Insofar as I have hands, feet, a body, and a world, I sustain intentions around myself that are not decided upon and that affect my surroundings in ways I do not choose . . . freedom makes use of the gaze along with its spontaneous valuations. Without these . . . we would not be in the world, ourselves implicated in the spectacle and, so to speak, intermingled with things . . . there are no obstacles in themselves, but the "myself" that qualifies them as obstacles is not an acosmic subject; this subject anticipates himself among the things in order to give them the shape of things. There is an autochthonous sense of the world that is constituted in the exchange between the world and our embodied existence and that forms the ground of every deliberate *Sinngebung*. (*PP*, 464–6)

The route that the novice climber traces out will of necessity be different from that of the expert, who will see and may well choose a more difficult route if she is climbing alone or with other experts, enjoying a serious challenge and relishing the satisfaction of meeting it. There will be no need to worry about risks to which the novice would be prey. On making this motivated choice, the whole being will be taken up with the project. Unlike Schneider, who is bound to the actual, the expert and to a much lesser extent the novice have a freedom of intention and action, a power of placing themselves in a situation and seeing the best way to deal with it. When we look at our life in the round – in reckoning with the possible, in choosing and in perpetuating our choices in moving – we find over and again that our perceiving and knowing and willing life is shot through by that intentional arc that projects around us our past, our milieu and our physical, moral and ideological situation.

It should be added that even when we have the appropriate skills our milieus may not be negotiated faultlessly. The operative embracing of and accommodation to the world can always go wrong, with motor intentions *only* gearing into it continually when they receive the responses they anticipate. Even the seasoned mountaineer can slip, and the football player be tackled successfully by the midfielder. But in most situations, the embodied subject can recover, with his or her compensatory movements proceeding of necessity from a rapid recalibration of the evolving motor plan. The latter is not rolled out like a carpet in a direction fixed once and for all. Schilder is right to claim that that the plan develops in continuous contact with the experience of moving, though it also develops and changes as a consequence of what is felt and seen and heard and so on. At the dinner party, I clumsily knock over the wine bottle in reaching for the pitcher, and promptly pull in my arm and bring it back out to right the bottle, minimising spillage and avoiding breakage. Beside the sea, the thrown beach ball is suddenly caught by a gust of wind, and I run sideways and crabwise to catch it without actually having to stop. In large part, such responses show as much immediacy and spontaneity as originally anticipated actions. We roll to accommodate the surprises thrown up in certain situations.

This brings me to the question of whether Merleau-Ponty gets things right as regards the imaginative and motor capacities that we actualise in moving practically. For as it happens, Rasmus Jensen has identified problems in his interpretation of the Schneider case. In those passages that are devoted to abstract movements, motor intentionality is conspicuous by its loss, and in those devoted to concrete movements it is conspicuous by its preservation, taken as identical to that of the ordinary person. In these last places, according to Jensen, Merleau-Ponty assimilates the normal to the pathological, just like the intellectualist. The evidence for this move first appears in his misreading of a quotation from Goldstein on practical situations. Remarking that the normal subject can extricate his body from an ongoing process of habitual movement in the realm of his imagination, Merleau-Ponty adds that this is what the patient can no longer do, and that he reports his concrete movements as a sequence of events resulting from or solicited by his situation. He experiences the movements and his own self as 'merely a link in the unfolding of the whole, and I am scarcely aware of any voluntary initiative . . . everything works by itself' (*PP*, 107). Jensen notes that the words Merleau-Ponty attributes to Schneider are actually Goldstein's, who is not even paraphrasing the patient, but setting out his own view of how the normal subject experiences the flow of concrete or habitual activities. He or she is scarcely aware of any voluntary initiative in living through the sequence or subsequently focussing on it because 'everything works by itself'. In this light, continues Goldstein, the experience of the patient is barely distinguishable in essence from that of the ordinary individual (despite his visual deficiency), and in the same way 'his behaviour in such instances barely deviates from that of the normal person'.[29]

---

[29] Goldstein 1923, 175, quoted in Jensen 2009, 382.

Merleau-Ponty attributes what he thinks is the patient's self-description to the normal case in that he takes it as an accurate characterisation of concrete movement in both, agreeing with Goldstein in spite of his misattribution.[30] His ongoing assimilation move is noticeable when he states that, as I take my place in familiar actions, my body takes over from me. The patient's perceived task in the workshop solicits the relevant movements from him 'through a sort of distant attraction', and in just the same way 'the phenomenal forces at work in my visual field obtain from me, without any calculation, the motor reactions that will establish between those forces the optimum equilibrium' (*PP*, 109). At the level of habitual action, I too am my acting body, the potentiality of certain actions that are solicited in certain worldly situations. By taking concrete movement as effectively identical in the pathological and normal cases, however, Merleau-Ponty veers perilously close to what he criticises in Bergson, the idea of a habit as the fossilised residue of a spiritual activity. The consequences of the assimilation move are twofold; what might be called an alienation problem and what Jensen calls a vacuity problem. The first lies in the suggestion that our habitual actions are not experienced as agential. But even when deeply engaged in habitual movements, as Gabrielle Benette Jackson has argued, we do not experience them as involuntary, and expressions such as 'being in the zone' or 'feeling the flow' do not express the absence of volition, however minimal or different the sense of agency accompanying the habitual or routine performances might be. In fact they suggest quite the opposite, the feeling that one's intentions are manifested in and through one's movements.[31] This does not hold for every practical performance, since what begins voluntarily can take the wrong course when we become absent-minded, as was noted in the last chapter. Yet the sense of agency *does* permeate the vast majority of our movements – even when we do not remain explicitly mindful of what we are aiming at – and this is what Merleau-Ponty here forgets.

---

[30] Jensen 2009, 382–3.

[31] Jackson 2018, 770–1, 777. In these pages Jackson is somewhat sceptical about the ramifications of Jensen's misattribution claim, holding that if the words are Goldstein's rather than Schneider's, they could well have been the latter's. It is plausible that he did describe himself as lacking a sense of agency in his concrete behaviour, perhaps adopting the doctor's terminology. On Jackson's reading, Merleau-Ponty cites what he thinks is the patient's self-ascribed lack in order to contrast it with our normal experience. He does seem to make this contrast at first and later affirms our ordinary sense of agency in which we inhabit our movements (*PP*, 107, 146). But in between he assimilates our concrete behaviour to Schneider's as Jensen contends, notably when writing of movements obtained 'through a sort of distant attraction'. *PP*, 108–9; Jensen 2009, 381–2.

In my view, this is an uncharacteristic lapse, for nowhere else it is suggested that everything works by itself. Certainly Merleau-Ponty goes on to refer to our merging with a body that is better informed than we are about the world, and to 'another subject beneath me' who marks out my place in the world. Such a 'natural mind' is not 'the momentary body that is the instrument of my personal choices and that focuses upon some world, but rather the system of anonymous "functions" that wraps each particular focusing into a general project' (*PP*, 265). But this sub-conscious schematising does not count against my inhabiting my movements. In agreeing to bring my hand to my knee or to my ear, for example, I do so by the shortest and most economical route to fulfil the request straight off. Because this is the very itinerary my body schema plans out for me, it predelineates the realisation of just what I wish and just *as* I wish (*PP*, 145–6). As contended in the previous section, act awareness and operative motor awareness are ordinarily continuous. It would be helpful to add that, even in the most familiar of movements, the overcoming of resistance is not experienced as occurring by itself. To move habitually towards an end while no longer representing it, efforts must still be made to build up and maintain momentum. I do not feel these efforts as dissociated from me and in proceeding successfully feel them with confidence.[32] In 'being in the zone' I have the somatically induced assurance of proceeding the right way. Though the willed along with the willing of it has receded from conscious view, it is being fulfilled with a felt proficiency. If Merleau-Ponty does not say this he would not demur, for he holds that to understand praktognosically in moving habitually 'is to experience the accord between what we aim at and what is given, between the intention and the realisation' (*PP*, 146). This is why the absent-minded deviation from an originally explicit aim is as discomfiting and irritating on its discovery as it is rare.

For Jensen, the vacuity problem in Merleau-Ponty's interpretation of the Schneider case emerges as soon as the normal and the pathological are assimilated. In these passages devoted to concrete movements, the assertion is that motor intentionality is the same in the patient and the normal person. We have a productive imagination that is gravely diminished in the first and the healthy version in the second, but these are not really called on for these habitual performances, which are effectively automatic. The motor intentionality doing its work for each is a highest common factor, a view that a revised intellectualism can accommodate. But if the imaginative power of projection supplies the completing condition for the

---

[32] See the marvellous Jeeves and Wooster illustration in Morris 2012, 93.

immediate execution of both abstract and part-concrete-like and context-strange movements in the healthy person, any appeal to her persisting motor intentionality will be vacuous so long as it is not shown to be determining the action in any way noticeably different from the patient's (since it is just the common condition for immediate execution). Operative beyond her practical movements, the only difference will be that of its persistence as against its absence.[33] If the imagination has to work with a common factor motor intentionality, moreover, it is hard to understand how it can bring the latter outside its habitual action solutions to facilitate novel movements straight off, or putting it otherwise, how imagination can readily recalibrate sub-conscious plans for habitual skill deployments towards other outcomes.[34]

Once it is realised that our envisaged actions are not indifferent to actual or possible motor projections, however, it can be appreciated that they do not run with a common factor motor intentionality for abstract movements and for part-concrete-like mimes. And if our creative imaginings go further down, we shall also find different motor projections for modifying concrete movements, which are not locked into habitual gridlines. Contrary to the intellectualist and assimilationist view, it will turn out that Schneider and the normal person do not have the same practical milieu with the same landscapes. The vacuity problem will be quarantined, which is just what happens when Merleau-Ponty recognises that the intellectualist diagnosis of 'a collapse of consciousness and a setting free of automatic reflexes ... would miss the fundamental disorder' (*PP*, 126), namely, the diminution of the patient's intentional arc ensuing from damage to his founding sight and motility as well as his founded imagination, with his practical space not being unaffected (*PP*, 128, 139). As Jensen maintains, Schneider's condition involves a contraction of what Merleau-Ponty has for the most part characterised as the normal open-ended horizon constituting our awareness of the world as a realm of action.[35] Our practical comportment cannot be the same as the patient's, for his experience does not tend towards speech or raise questions for him, always having that kind 'of evidentness and self-sufficiency of the real that stifles all interrogation, all reference to the possible, all wonder, and all improvisation' (*PP*, 202). The normal person is not confined to a milieu of purely concrete movement and does not inhabit it in the first place, since it is pathological. Even when I move about in the familiar and relatively

---

[33] Jensen 2009, 381, 383.   [34] From here to the section end I cite parts of Mooney 2011, 366–75.
[35] Ibid., 386.

constrained world of my house, 'each gesture or each perception is imme-diately situated in relation to a thousand virtual coordinates' (*PP*, 131). This is expanded upon in passages where Merleau-Ponty considers our ordinary facility for imitating the movements of others:

> The space and time that I inhabit are always surrounded by indeterminate horizons that contain other points of view. The synthesis of time, like that of space, is always to be started over again … [in imitation] the change of coordinates is eminently contained in this existential operation. This is because the normal subject has his body not only as a system of current positions, but also, and consequently, as an open system of an infinity of equivalent positions in different orientations. What we called the 'body schema' is precisely this system of equivalences, this immediately given invariant by which different motor tasks are instantly transposable … in order for us to be able to imagine space, we must first be introduced into it through our body, which must have given us the first model of transposi-tions, equivalences, and identifications that turns space into an objective system and allows our experience to be an experience of objects and to open onto an 'in itself'. [36] (*PP*, 141–3)

It is our capacity to immediately improvise in certain situations that precludes a common factor motor intentionality and the vacuity problem. We saw that the patient can only take requests for part-concrete-like mimes as those for completely concrete-like and context-familiar ones, imagina-tively placing himself in the affective situation as a whole and using his entire body as he would habitually. When actually engaged in his habitual tasks, he must of course make minor adjustments like we do to use his tools efficiently. Within a task, these adjustments involve small recalibrations of motor anticipations. Hence the speed and dexterity of his habitual move-ments (*PP*, 105, 106–7). Yet he cannot immediately abbreviate acquired skills and deploy them in novel combinations. He is unable to cut them down and transpose them to meet new or unexpected situations, the kind that demand novel postures. Extrapolating from Merleau-Ponty's observa-tions that we can change coordinates and instantly transpose our motor tasks, a transposition capacity can be taken as intrinsic to the normal person's motor horizon. The body schema does not schematise with acquisitions that are fossilised when sedimented in the habitual body, but with an open repertoire of skills for adaptation and combination. When I productively imagine a novel action in my daily odyssey of negotiating the world, and in so doing apprehend it as an 'I can' or

---

[36] Translation slightly emended.

immediate possibility for me, my body must project or be able to project a route for the straight-off realisation of that action. Because the somatic solution for the imagined action would frustrate the latter's immediate fulfilment if it were to prefigure sheer reiterations of existing motor skills, it must of necessity prefigure the transposition of the skills, their adaptation and combination to attain the relevant outcome. All those novel action possibilities that are immediately realisable are dependent on anonymous schematisations of novel skill deployments, which cannot comprise common factor motor intentionalities.

So far as I know, Merleau-Ponty never provides examples of transposing skills onto different practical ends or of copying such transpositions, even if his account avoids a dichotomy between practical action and creativity.[37] But some illustrations can be given consistent with this story. On picking up the ringing telephone in one or other abbreviated manner – say by stretching out my arm further while maintaining my slouching posture – I promptly crook it between ear and shoulder, taking notes during the conversation as I have seen a colleague do. On another day in midwinter, I find myself rushing to a birthday party with a large, boxed cake in my hands. Coming round the corner I see that the kitchen door is shut and want to minimise delay, while guessing it was shut to keep the heat in. The course of action I envisage in response and the appropriately discriminative seeing and motor projection are at one, which is why I gear into the action so quickly. Out and downwards goes my forearm on the lever to open the door and, once through, sideways goes my foot to close it. Holding the box

---

[37] I concur with the view that some actions are more rooted in one's actual environment and current task, that others involve reckoning with the possible to a greater or lesser extent, and that for the healthy person the concrete and the abstract are located on a continuum. They only become [sharply] distinct forms of behaviour or action in pathological cases like Schneider's (Romdenh-Romluc 2011, 100). In this context, Jackson has argued that the appeal to a transposition capacity seems unnecessary. We do not require an extra (sub-)category of concrete movement to explain Schneider's pathology because *all* his performances are pathological. Schneider's problem is that his concrete and abstract movements are disjoined, no matter how good he becomes at integrating them. A better narrative does not have to integrate conceptually contained or distinct events, while allowing bodies and situations to be equally 'centrifugal' and 'centripetal' within a single performance. Motor intentionality realises a dynamic fundamental function (that of the intentional arc) composed of body and situation and joined through projection and solicitation (Jackson 2018, 8, 10–13). But if all normal movements are amenable to transposition, then there is no sub-category of concrete movements to be set against those that are not transposable. The only distinction is between transposable movements and those actually transposed. All of Schneider's movements *are* pathological, and my claim is that this is because they are fossilised. They cannot be transposed, that is, readily recalibrated and combined to constitute creative ones, either from the outset or in a course of movement that begins habitually. I accommodate the better narrative, and my birthday cake example is of a course of movement that is equally centrifugal and centripetal. See Mooney 2011, 371–2, 374–6, 377.

all the while, I need not recall pressing down on a suitcase or a bin lid with my forearm, or of diverting a football with my foot. Even if I do momentarily recall some habitual application, I do not thereby proceed in an overwrought manner, adopting the overall postures that went with the luggage or garbage compressing or the football tackling. These acquired movements have undergone abbreviation and combination, co-existing successively with the carrying of the cake. All the actions serve the major task, with the last attending to heat retention as well as candle lighting and quenching and cake sampling for the invitees. The results of the relevant actions are anticipated within the overall intentional arc, and in my continuously evolving posture 'the tasks divide themselves up among the segments in question' (*PP*, 150). My body schema's transposition capacity allows me to imaginatively meet many practical situations that have thrown up unexpected problems and take them in my stride. Operative in modified and abbreviated actions, the capacity contributes to a life that is most often untroubled in its prime. I can and do negotiate obstacles within action sequences – and for that matter multi-task – without actually breaking or appreciably slowing the flow and tempo of movement.[38]

6.5   Reflective Objectification in Action

It goes without saying that our pre-reflective reckonings with the possible and motor intentional transpositions only bring us so far in our daily odysseys. There will be situations where no skill combinations can compensate for the lack of an appropriate technique, or where strength or bodily flexibility or feeling are not up to the task. We will then have to stop and reflect, explicitly attempting to cognise a solution to our difficulty. Improvisation will follow on from questioning or interrogation (*PP*, 202). Here again our productive imaginations will go beyond that of the unfortunate patient, not least because we can envisage our making use of implements outside their typical and habitual applications, re-schematising them so that they acquire new affordance values. If he cannot transpose skills, he will hardly be able to transpose the tools integral to them onto other ends. His fulfilment of his wallet-making task would seem to be contingent on things running smoothly and predictably (though whether this is incontrovertibly the case must remain speculation). In any event, we can imagine an ordinary worker who has gained proficiency in

---

[38] For an account that extends to Merleau-Ponty's later work on the body schema and correlative milieu, see Halák 2021, 33–51.

making wallets finding that his sewing thumb and forefinger have become sore and tender and that he cannot continue as before, without wishing to cease altogether. Even if he stops short for some moments without any result, he is reflectively alive to the possibility of an alternative strategy. Then it dawns on him that he can use an industrial safety glove to relieve the pressure of the needle, or hold it with pliers to bring it through the material. Going forward more slowly is nonetheless going forward.

Reflection on one's performances occurs pretty much as often as things go obstinately wrong, that is, when one feels discomfort, when a flow of action is seriously hindered or when perceptual events slide into confusion. The mistake of traditional theories of perception is to bring in intellectual operations 'to which we resort only when direct perception flounders in ambiguity' (*PP*, 358). Usually our current experiences link up with our earlier experience and those of others without having to involve any explicit verification. Perception in its original form so occupies me that I am unable to turn to my conscious act and perceive myself perceiving. If every experience involves a latent knowledge and has something anonymous about it, 'this is because it takes up an acquisition that it does not question' (*PP*, 247). Merleau-Ponty will go so far as to suggest that all reflections on and objectifications of the body are marked by objective thought:

> The body, then, is not an object. For the same reason, the consciousness that I have of it is not a thought, that is, I cannot decompose and recompose this consciousness in order to form a clear idea. Its unity is always implicit and confused ... Whether it is a question of the other person's body or of my own, I have no other means of knowing the human body than by living it, that is, by taking up for myself the drama that moves through it and by merging with it. Thus, I am my body, at least to the extent that I have an acquisition, and reciprocally my body is something like a natural subject, or a provisional sketch of my total being. The experience of one's own body, then, is opposed to the reflective procedure that disentangles the object from the subject and the subject from the object, and that only gives us thought about the body or the body as an idea, and not the experience of the body or the body in reality. (*PP*, 204–5)

We are left in little doubt that reflection involves a disengagement from our active and somatically engaged life, and that the real understanding of the body consists in being immersed in it. It could be countered that Merleau-Ponty is only referring to the objectivist version of reflection, but he contends that, in practical action, '[w]e never move our objective body, we move our phenomenal body ... since it is our body as a power of various regions of the world that already rises up toward the objects to grasp and perceive them' (*PP*, 108). Whenever we do objectify our bodies, we turn them away from the world. Suppose I am walking with my friend in the park. Having pulled ahead while he rummages in his bag, I look over the parapet of a bridge, glimpsing a fine heron standing in the stream. My friend is a birdwatcher, and I silently beckon him to come near. In such a situation, maintains Merleau-Ponty, there is not first a perception followed by a movement. Though my waving arm is within my visual field, it is the unthematic vehicle of my intention and continuous with it. In signalling to my friend, who has lagged behind, my action is a systematic whole that will be modified as a whole. When he fails to respond to my summons, my increasing impatience and beckoning more sharply will also be at one. Later on in my apartment, I can refine or embellish the movement, aiming it at an imaginary other. I may even perpetuate this movement in a more objective attitude, zooming in on my arm as a signifying instrument of muscles and tendons, or make it in an abstract attitude as an end in itself, as an oscillating shape for my amusement. The movement is maintained as the end changes. But in all these reflective acts the body has shed its anonymity and I have broken with my ordinary involvements in the world, carving subjective and self-centred zones of reflection out of it. So too with all those situations in which I lend my body to experimentation (*PP*, 111, 113–14, 292).

Yet dancers comfortable in one phase of a performance often reflect on their bodily readiness for a strenuous phase to come, just like sportspeople in competition situations.[39] The football player may well consider his knee injury before the ball is passed to him. Shaun Gallagher gives the example of an expert racing skier who is reflectively anticipating changes in the snow further downhill. Reflective deliberation – and the capacity to know just where and when to employ it – should be considered part of what it is to be an expert in the flow of skilled action. In reckoning with the possible, one goes beyond the current field to think about a future one.[40] The skier is conscious of a thaw that has made the borders of the run very slushy. She reckons quite consciously that, well before the next bend, she will lean a little more to the right and angle in her skies. The alternative is an abrupt correction that could easily ensue in disaster. And outside public performances and competitions, as Joseph Berendzen has contended, the capacities to accept coaching, review earlier performances and continually refine a skill are as much part of the person's life as moving unreflectively. The

---

[39] On dancers' reflective objectifications, see Montero 2013 and Bergonzoni 2017.
[40] Gallagher 2009, 1106.

sort of reflective revision found in coaching and in many aspects of ordinary life involves a latent yet readily available ability being put to work.[41] It is this reference to the reflective objectification of bodily comportment in everyday life that I would like to expand upon.[42]

On my way to see a friend in hospital, I realise that visiting time will soon be over, and that I need to proceed more quickly so we can spend more time together. As I am running along, I develop a contingency plan about what to do if his close family are gathered around the bedside, the very family that may have made a long journey across the city. At the doorway, I will peep into the ward while staying largely out of sight, and I will be poised to slowly turn around and retrace my steps down the corridor. My friend is on the long road to recovery and I can talk to him tomorrow. Others aside, I often approve or decry my behaviour or handiwork and think about how to proceed with more finesse. Such reflections are not waiting on breakdown situations; rather they are pre-emptive or corrective strategies formulated within the flow. These situational thoughts might well be called little reflections. They are not characters in an extraordinary tale of becoming lost in reflection after turning away from the world, but parts of an ordinary story about negotiating it. In responding to interruptions, most of them facilitate successful adjustments to skill deployments to reorient them towards their ends. They can do so because our motor projections have an inbuilt plasticity. Our transposable skills subtend much of what is thought, and we are not usually at risk of disaster in resorting to reflection, unlike the dancer or athlete in the middle of a fast and difficult move.

Little reflections are once-off responses to once-off situations. Ordinarily they fade quickly from awareness and let us return to moving anonymously and indeed to theorising. In these last instances, they follow from interruptions to the skilled coping that has been allowing for such theoretical activity. They are then practical and productive interventions bridging longer and abstractive episodes of reflection, the kind that are involved when planning far into the future. As transitory ways of thinking our way around barriers and distractions, these strategies are needed to quickly restore the bodily composure and correlative stability of milieu required for long-term planning and theorising, which makes them much more than psychological peculiarities. They are as vital to these episodes as they are to renewed coping in the flow. And if the situations of daily life do

[41] Berendzen 2010, 644–5.
[42] From here to the chapter end, I rework ideas from Mooney 2019, 71–5.

not continually throw up difficulties needing reflectively mediated revisions, it is rare to see out the day without them. Now a bad handlebar hold cycling or a rough fingernail typing demands a reflexive articulation and response, and then an overburdened shoulder or an itchy arm. But when Merleau-Ponty casts sedimented acquisitions and their anonymous work as enough for us, and reflection as following on floundering, he is evoking a world in which no such self-objectifications lie between the two.

His more extreme passages can nonetheless be reconstructed in order to accommodate little reflections. It is true that the experience of the body is opposed to that reflective procedure that disentangles the object from the subject and vice-versa. It is also true that in objectifying our bodies for amusement or experimentation we turn away from the world of involvements. Yet this only holds for cases where such amusements or experiments are exclusively self-directed. For the ordinary commuter and worker as for the skier, there is another mode of reflection in which we objectify both poles of a situation through some of its course, but without splitting them apart and without thematising the body in its own tactile reflexivity. What is objectified is an engaged area of the body as we wish to rest or re-deploy it, as we wish it to be freed from or optimally geared into a thing or contour in the overall situation. The reflectively mediated change of a movement or hold allows us to restore or maintain momentum or even increase it. Such explicit acts can be taken as breaks in absorption alone that do not hinder our actual coping. And we can still affirm that we move our phenomenal body and not our objective one, just not doing so exclusively. In objectifying some engaged area, we continue to be cradled by the body schema's organisation of everywhere else, and the schema will usually furnish the how for the reflectively represented way.

When Merleau-Ponty is not so concerned about objectivism he gives us a better take on our perceptual lives. For *us*, sedimentation runs with spontaneity. What at our disposal is not a final gain, for it 'expresses, at each moment, the energy of our present consciousness'. What is acquired is only truly acquired and utilised 'if it is taken up in a new movement of thought' (*PP*, 132). We are fortunate that our experience tends towards expression, suggesting questions to us. Unlike Schneider's ours does not have the self-evidence and self-sufficiency stifling 'all interrogation, all reference to the possible, all wonder, and all improvisation' (*PP*, 202). Admitting little reflections does not threaten that fundamental function or intentional arc in which we find the unity of the senses, their unity with intelligence, and the unity of sensitivity and motility. Ordinarily we express this unity in being towards the world, and in their own ways the pathological cases express its diminution or loss. Which is to presuppose phenomena not yet properly thematised. Through these pages, others have been considered expressly as doctors or patients or philosophers. Still further, others have been implicitly present on the horizon of our experience when we are reading in our homes or trains or libraries. It is these ongoing senses of others and of our public world that remain to be unpacked.

CHAPTER 7

Others Expressive, Engaged and Exposed

7.1 Introduction

Just as the realm of inanimate and biological nature intertwines with my personal life, remarks Merleau-Ponty, so do social and personal behaviours intertwine with nature. They are sedimented in the very sense of my environment, which I only apprehend against the cultural world. I never encounter a bare milieu of soil and air and water, since I have around me a world of cultural objects, of utensils, roads, houses and farms. All these consciously wrought products cannot help but bear references to their creators. They appear as if placed *on* the natural world rather than as inexhaustible things immanent within it. The implements and milieus of other selves can be remarkably determinate, for example in exploring a house following an invasion. People had to leave in a hurry, and I feel their recent presence within a veil of anonymity. The traces of others are far less determinate when unintended, such as footprints left in the sand (*PP*, 338, 363). But even when I am alone on a beach or in a forest that seems unmarked by others, it has the sense of being a locale of the world available to all, an inherently public world (*PP*, 354, 371).

With the advent of mechanistic theories of the living body, two inter-linked questions came to be posed in sharp relief, namely, whether others can be present to me as conscious beings and known veridically as such. Descartes refuses to take our awareness as an epiphenomenon of the parts and processes comprising our living bodies. But because his human body is a purely physical entity, the ego must be a transcendent cause lying behind bodily movements, not an awareness that is actually inhabiting them. I have already referred to Merleau-Ponty's contention that Cartesian and intellectualist accounts of the living body cast it as an exterior without an interior, and subjectivity as 'an interior without an exterior, that is, an impartial spectator' (*PP*, 56). But even when the body is no longer under-stood by way of the mechanisms of first-generation objective thought, it is persistently taken as the visible container of an ego or mind that cannot show itself through it. Consciousness is inaccessible, and can only be apprehended indirectly by way of inferences based on analogies. I begin this chapter by considering Husserl's static endeavour to explicate one's experience of the other in terms of analogical appresentation. I then outline Merleau-Ponty's alternative theory of the intercorporeality and activity that founds the experience of the other, arguing that his founding story needs to be filled out further. Following on this, I set out his views on the expressivity of bodies, on style and on enculturation. In the last section I turn to his view of one's body for others, contrasting it with Sartre's conception of the body for another. Merleau-Ponty argues that one's body is at once for oneself, and cannot be estranged from its engagements.

7.2   The Other as an Analogue

Because we see our physical bodies moving in diverse ways, according to Descartes, we distinguish voluntary and intelligent movements from involuntary and automatic ones. Through the first we meet most of the contingencies of life as mere automata could never do, and we consequently judge that each body is directed by a rational awareness, as we also do when we hear intelligent speech.[1] This awareness is not utterly impartial, however, since the passions or emotions aroused in the mind or soul through external causes move it to direct the body. Gleaned from facial expressions and tears and laughter and so forth, these passions do not disappear when brought under the control of the will, though they only exist in the spiritual side of my existence. Sensory appearances are nothing but their signs or indications, as they are for all mental contents.[2] Without being committed to an immaterial soul, John Stewart Mill is the first to clearly propound a now familiar argument from analogy. I know from experience that others have bodies like mine, and once their bodies come to closely resemble my own body when I have certain feelings, I judge by analogy that they are having similar feelings. I work from my affective and consciously registered 'inside' to my corporeal 'outside' on which I observe signs of my feelings, and from others' observed outsides to their conscious insides.[3] Bertrand Russell takes up this account, contending that I infer their cognitive states to the extent that their outward bodily behaviour resembles my own when I have such states.[4]

[1] Descartes 1984a, 139–41.   [2] Descartes 1984c, 338–9, 342–3, 367–9.   [3] Mill 1878, 243–4.
[4] Russell 1948, 501–5.

Merleau-Ponty is blunt in assessing the arguments by analogical infer-ence. In our original experiences of the other, we find nothing like a reasoning from analogy at work (*PP*, 364, 367–8). Here he refers to a difficulty pinpointed by Scheler. If I go from my inside to my outside and take the reverse path with the other, inferring from its outside to its inside, I am presupposing what I want to explain, knowing that I myself am on the scene and by implication knowing about the other, as Russell is likewise aware.[5] If we appeal to the Husserl of *Ideas II*, we might seem to circumvent the difficulties of an inferential account. In this ordinary attitude there is no concern with proof or probability. Within it our belief in other centres of awareness is lived unquestioningly, as an experiential rather than epistemic certainty. Even when others are not focally present as friends or strangers, they are marginally on the horizons of my experience. When seeing the lived body of another, my sensuous apprehension is not aimed at it, but goes right through it without being aimed at a spirit joined to that body. What I intend perceptually is the person there who is dancing or laughing and chattering. In the standing and sitting and walking and dancing, that lived body is 'filled with soul through and through' (*Ids2*, 252). In every human performance, the lived body is full of soul in that it is thoroughly animated and expressive, which is reminiscent of Wittgenstein's contention that our ordinary attitudes towards others are attitudes towards souls – we are not of the *opinion* that they have souls.[6] But if consciousness is essentially embodied and shown through the lived body, there is one genuine sense in which it is hidden. I see and hear your conscious awareness, but not from *your* point of view (*Ids2*, 208, 254).

The Fifth Cartesian Meditation is Husserl's most sustained effort to explicate the appresentation of another ego. Granting that we already have a sense of the other (and of communities of others), the fundamental problem is to uncover its original constitution (*CM*, 90–1, 121). To this end, Husserl formulates a second and quite different reduction following on his initial procedure of bracketing the entire natural attitude. In this peculiar reduction, he places my adult and embodied self with all its somatic capacities in a 'sphere of ownness' (*Eigenheitssphäre*), a fictional situation without any experience of others whatsoever. It is not as if a plague has spared me alone, but as if I have never experienced them, having no sense of being alone. This procedure is explicitly static and abstractive, having no concern with the genesis of the sense in human infancy. Nor is it concerned with the apprehension of a human ego, only of

[5] Ibid., 503; Scheler 1954, 240. [6] Wittgenstein 1958, 178e.

an alien one in general (*CM*, 106, 108, 121). However use is made of genetic concepts such as similarity and passive synthesis.[7]

In the solitary sphere, no things in my milieu such as books and paintings and brushes have the sense of being made by them, and that selfsame environment is a 'mere nature', not amounting to a world proper. Within it my own lived body stands out uniquely. Some imagined outcomes are still immediate possibilities for me; my awareness of available agency is still founded on this skilled body in which and over which I hold sway. It is present with me in the reflexivity of touching and being-touched and kinaesthetic feelings of moving. I feel all of my activities from within when I look down at my legs walking or when I see my hands pushing or pulling, and remember what it looks like to do these things as a result of self-objectifications of my acting body (*CM*, 93–7). In this abstractive domain, anything beyond the edge of my body or range of action retains the sense of being outside or alien to me (*CM*, 98–9). Let us now suppose that the body of another enters my visual field for the first time. Constituted for me is the 'pairing' of our bodies, without any initiative or act intentionality on my part. Pairing is a passive synthesis of association; in seeing that moving configuration resembling my own body, their 'unity of similarity' will motivate the sense of it being a second lived body. This is the first and assimilative moment of 'analogical appresentation', the taking of the moving shape as an analogue of my own lived body. On foot of somatic self-experience, I cannot help but attribute sensing, sensitivity and self-movement to it – in the appresentation I co-intend activities and experiences not directly present. This is consistently confirmed so long as the movements of the alien body appear as those of eyes seeing, feet walking and hands grasping and pulling (*CM*, 110–4, 119–20).

Such an appresentation itself motivates me to take that *Leib* as the body of another ego governing it, the second moment of analogical appresentation, though the two come together in temporal terms. The analogising is not a thinking act, according to Husserl, because the appresentation of lived body and ego from the one sensuous presentation is not inferential. This is rather too quick, as will be argued below, though he is far more careful about the first moment – it *seems* that the other body appropriates from mine the sense of being an alien lived body, but the appresentation may not be so transparent. What is it about the phenomenon that motivates the sense of its being the lived body of another, rather than a second one of mine? (*CM*, 111, 113). The answer lies in the unique ways that my

[7] Staehler 2008, 107–8.

living body is present with me in my ownness. It is always experienced as the zero-point of all orientations, as an absolute here, but never as a here *and* a there. And it is always experienced as the *only* body under my control, immediately and spontaneously movable by me but never accompanied by a second body I can control remotely. Furthermore, all those movements converting my changeable here (rather than absolute here) into a there involve quite determinate systems of experience. Visual appearances change as I am changing position, and the exercise of my kinaesthetic capacities or skills in sight and locomotion and manipulation is accompanied by the correlative kinaesthetic feelings. Quite apart from being unable to feel myself from beyond the edge of my body, I am not having the visual and kinaesthetic experiences that I would be having if I were moving like that lived body is moving over there. The paired bodies are presenting dissimilarities together with their similarities, and the former are as striking as the latter. The dissimilarities motivate me to analogically appresent that lived body as belonging to another ego and governed by it (*CM*, 97, 116–19).

Perceiving from here alone, I can imagine myself moving to take the place of that lived body there, but am not perceiving a duplicate perceiving *as* I could. In seeing the other seeing and acting and what is seen and acted upon, I am aware that I could only experience the latter *like* the other is experiencing it if I were moving from over there in the same way (*CM*, 117, 119–21, 123). And to apprehend that the other *is* perceiving what I *could* perceive in a like manner is to constitute what we have in common, a world of mutually accessible objects. The other will also come to perceive my body here. From over there it will analogically appresent my visual shape as that of another lived body governed by another ego, in this case mine. Just as the other's body is within my perceptual field, so my body is within its perceptual field. In these ways, the advent of the other changes the sense of my environment quite radically. It is no longer a mere nature for me as the sole absolute here, but a realm for another absolute here that surrounds it from its own standpoint, the perspective of an absolute here that is always a 'there'. And when others again come into presence, each is a further absolute here that is a there, and I am another lived body for each. My body for myself is at once a body for others in being actually or potentially perceived by them. To apprehend the public world of things and lived bodies far and near is to unseat the fictionally subjective and solipsistic spatiality, which is destroyed on being discovered. But it is not just my body that comes to presence as one among many in *our* common world, but my own ego. Only in bringing another egoic awareness to explicit awareness can the ego contrastively gain the sense being 'my' self. In this mutual transfer of sense, subjectivity, intersubjectivity and world are constituted together, as they are genetically (*CM*, 113, 115, 120–4, 128–30).

Husserl stresses that it is still correct to speak of perceiving someone else. I am not seeing a sign or a mere analogue, but your own lived body manifesting your own lived experiences, even if not from your own point of view. In seeing another in the constituted sense 'what is grasped originaliter is the body of a psyche essentially inaccessible to me originaliter, and the two are comprised in the unity of one psychophysical reality' (*CM*, 124). The appresentation of the hidden sides of a thing is capable of fulfilment in principle if not always in fact. The appresentation of the alter ego's standpoint is different in kind, for no experience can ever reveal it. We are confined to appresentation as an indirect mode of intentionality. The experience of the other is the phenomenon of a non-phenomenon, of an awareness in and beyond the world, indicated by way of the body there but forever beyond my reach. If I could occupy your egoic pole in its stream of awareness or live it first-hand, then it would be a moment of my own essence and we would be the same. Separation is essential to the very sense of the alter ego (*CM*, 109–11, 122).[8]

7.3   Anonymity, Engagement and Separation

Merleau-Ponty does not refer directly to Husserl's endeavour to get to the other from the sphere of ownness, though it is one of his targets. In original perception there is no thought correlation of one's consciously lived experiences with one's observed body, and no analogical inference following on from the observation of the other's body. But neither is there any *unthought* visual pairing that could found an appresentational analogue of one's body as lived (*PP*, 190, 368). Everything in the static account depends on an associative pairing of our bodies in a unity of similarity of shape or configuration. Yet the said unity is not in place originally, either in genetic terms or in the fictional sphere of ownness. Husserl has himself noted that the way I appear to myself outwardly is not like the way that the other body appears to me, and I may have no access to pools or mirrors to familiarise myself with my image in full profile so it can be associated with that full profile over there. Even if I have had access to reflective surfaces, I may not

---

[8] For a very helpful account of the split within the embodied self, of the other as a double and of the other's sublimity, see Waldenfels 2011, 47–57.

recognise the visual image as my own visual reflection. Such an apprehension needs to be learnt (*Ids2*, 155, 167).

As a supposedly primary necessity behind any kind of progression, the unity of similarity thesis falls down when we look at the responses of infants to others. For Merleau-Ponty, babies show that a more original relationship is in play from an early age. In one of its moments, this is affective, for infants can and do apprehend the joyful signification of a smile before ever seeing their visual reflections, and so too the sense of menace or melancholy as it is mimicked. They respond appropriately when they have not yet exhibited similar states in their own facial expressions, not having any contents furnished by prior experience (*SB*, 156). Joy or melancholy or anger or grief is visible in the lived or phenomenal body over there, directly expressed rather than indirectly signified. Following Scheler, we do not have a physical body as an initial datum, for this is a theoretical abstraction from the primary phenomena.[9] The states are experienced as affective variations of an expressive being in the world whose presence is undivided between body and consciousness (*PP*, 372). This is consistent with *Ideas II*, though it has no proper place in the Fifth Cartesian Meditation, which zones in on a body seeing, walking and pushing. In the initial experience of the other, the apprehension of emotional states is passed over (*CM*, 119–20).

Ordinarily the infant apprehends that lived body as animated through and through, with its movements already perceived as having a bearing on the infant's own body; these have immediate and affective significations for it. I see this if I pretend to bite the finger of an infant of fifteen months. The baby has scarcely seen his face, let alone his teeth, but immediately responds by opening his mouth. He apprehends a certain intentionality in my body (that of biting, the outcome of the movement as mimicked thus far) and responds with a counteracting intentionality (that of stopping the bite there with his jaw here). Our baby has an embodied sense of what biting is in terms of what it does and of forestalling it, and more than this has intermodally correlated my seen jaw with his felt jaw as a common instrument (*PP*, 368). What is perceived is a behaviour with an immanent signification that is again undivided between body and consciousness (the perception of a directed or outcome-oriented action is not the appresentation of a *being-directed* by a conscious and volitional awareness). In Gallagher's words, there is an experience of affection and action that involves the direct body-reading of a perceptual consciousness as against

[9] Scheler 1954, 10, 260.

the indirect mind-reading of a cogitating one.[10] Responses show an affective, intersensory and sensorimotor relationship *between* our lived bodies:

> The sense of the gestures is not given but rather understood, which is to say
> taken up by an act of the spectator. The entire difficulty is to conceive of this
> act properly and not to confuse it with an epistemic operation.
> Communication or the understanding of gestures is achieved through the
> reciprocity between my intentions and the other person's gestures, and
> between my gestures and the intentions which can be read in the other's
> behaviour. Everything happens as if the other person's intention inhabited
> my body, or as if my intentions inhabited his body. The gesture I witness
> sketches out the first signs of an intentional object. (*PP*, 190–1)

In early life there is a sense that shines forth in the concordance of one's
experiences with each other and intersection with those of others, such that
there is 'a sort of gearing' of the one into the many that facilitates one's
eventual and explicit experiences of rational subjects (*PP*, lxxxiv). Shogo
Tanaka makes a convincing case to the effect that Merleau-Ponty has all
but reached the conception of intercorporeality expounded in his final
writings, of a perception-action loop in which the other's action prompts
the same action in me or the awareness of its possibility in me, and in which
my action prompts the same in the other.[11] This is at once a passive or sub-
egoic pairing of our body schemas and an active responsiveness to movements that are perceived as there. As the latter will remark in one of his late
works, the notion of pairing (suitably understood as an internal reciprocity
before any visual unity of similarity) is anything but a metaphor (*PrP*, 118).

It should be stressed that this reciprocal and inter-intentional inhabiting
is anonymous, in that the internal correlation of an awareness here with an
awareness there is not yet the primitive sense of the own as against the alien,
which must in its turn found the reportable signification of the 'I' as against
the 'you'. In this light, Merleau-Ponty does not wish to lay too much
weight on our intercorporeality. If we only related to the other in this way
we would introduce the impersonal into the centre of subjectivity to an
inordinate extent. Were the existents perceiving each other to remain
anonymous, a plurality could not appear within this collective consciousness (*PP*, 372). We need a more detailed story bridging this elementary
stage and the eventual appresentation of the other *as* the other, and in
which other and world are revealed together. It commences with the
perception of lived bodies as implicated in action situations, and here
Merleau-Ponty takes advantage of an account already developed by

[10] Gallagher 2005a, 227.   [11] Tanaka 2015, 461–3.

Gurwitsch.[12] From the start, the baby encounters behaviours that are geared into the world. As suggested earlier, the infant perceives this or that awareness as directed or outcome-oriented. In their behaviour or comportment, other lived bodies are not perceived as alongside things in the world, but as sketching out certain manners of dealing with them, such that the senses of these dynamic configurations transcend their bodily boundaries to include the relevant things (*PP*, 192, 199, 333, 367). In pointing towards a goal, the practical spectacle or situation gives a living sense to the child's own impulses and possibilities, for it appears like a question, lighting up specific areas of the world as invitations to be replied to.[13] Once the thing has been perceived in its use, it is no longer like a meteorite, for it has been diverted from its first and immediate sense. This is how the gesture sketches out the first signs of an intentional object, which is present and understood praktognosically as soon as the powers of the infant's body adjust to and gear into it. The child takes up for herself the mode of existence laid out before her (*PP*, 190–1, 370).

One first learns about the way to employ an implement from what it looks like for it to be used there, later acquiring hands-on and head-on competence (the accomplishment of which is obscured in the fictional sphere of ownness). When the infant takes possession of something on learning to use it 'his body schema assures the immediate correspondence of what he sees done and what he does', and the thing assumes its shape 'as a determinate *manipulandum*' (*PP*, 370). As the thing becomes determinate for one's own body, moreover, 'the other person takes shape as a centre of human action' (*PP*, 370). Lived or phenomenal bodies become concretised as centres of actions radiating over and across their milieus, and only by way of their embodied engagements can others eventually be found at the virtual origins of their visible behaviours (*SB*, 157; *PP*, 457). When I have learnt to use things towards an outcome and my gaze falls on another performing the same action, the relevant implements are not just what

---

[12] Gallagher 2005b, 101–4; Gurwitsch 1979, 35–6, 66, 97.

[13] Helena De Preester contends that imitation for Merleau-Ponty is a matter of common goals. To imitate the other is not usually to do the same, but to arrive at the same result or outcome. What is prioritised intentionally should be supported at the explanatory level, and is with mirror neuron theory. On this model, certain neurons enable individuals to recognise actions made by others because the neural patterns produced in their premotor areas in observing the actions are similar to the neural patterns generated in the production of these actions, mirroring the latter in the main. The discharge of mirror neurons correlates with an overall action rather than its moments, and the neurons only become active when a particular type of action is performed to achieve a particular type of goal (De Preester 2008, 137–9). On the limitations of mirror neuron theory, see Zahavi 2014, 154–63.

I could do with them, but what *this* behaviour is about to do with them. I experience my body as a power of certain behaviours opening up a certain milieu of possibilities, only being given to myself as a hold on that milieu, and yet a certain handling of things is occurring over there. The perceived world can gain its sense as available to all when one arrives at the appreciation of multiple centres of action bearing on things in ways now familiar to me. This founds the developed sense of the world as the correlate of every consciousness I *might* encounter (*PP*, 354, 368–70). Scheler would recognise such a progression, having claimed that we do not impute experiences to others on foot of our supposedly discrete experiences:

> What occurs, rather, is an immediate flow of experiences undifferentiated as between mine and thine, which actually contains both our own and others' experiences intermingled and without distinction from one another. Within this flow there is a gradual formation of ever more stable vortices, which slowly attract further elements of the stream into their orbits and thereby become successively and very gradually identified with distinct individuals.[14]

Scheler adds that the self to which the experiences are given is already individual, but which individual it may be having an experience need not be apparent in the way it is presented. This is to raise a problem that Merleau-Ponty does something to address in referring to another activity occurring over there, the aforementioned problem of how a plurality comes to appear, and more particularly of how the own and alien spheres get to be achieved as senses, that is, apprehended as separate and distinct from each other. Yet Merleau-Ponty does not address it at length. If he does not wish to lay too much weight on our intercorporeality in the pre-conceptual stages, his overriding emphasis is still on our intercorporeal synchronicity, in which our bodies form one system, 'a single whole, two sides of a single phenomenon' (*PP*, 370).

The problem remains because the infant can perceive multiple standpoints and centres of action – in each case a there – without necessarily apprehending them as the bodies of separate, distinctive others outside the single system. With the help of some of Husserl's enduring insights as reconstructed genetically by Gail Soffer, however, we can provide a more detailed story about how pre-conceptual differentiation is achieved, reconciling a psychology of human development with an a priori account of how the experience of that lived body there comes to differ *noticeably* from this

---

[14] Scheler 1954, 246.

one here. Soffer argues that when an infant learns imitatively to grasp and shake a rattle, practice allows her to correlate the tactile and kinaesthetic feelings of her own hand movements with the visual appearances of these extremities. These are *then* paired visually with those of others, founding the derivative appresentation of these feelings in those other hands. But when the infant sees those hands grasping and picking up the rattle, she does not have the bodily feelings anticipated in that very activity. The frustration of horizonal expectations facilitates the differentiation of the acting bodies. Those hands there are apprehended as sensate, but not like these ones here. And as she grows, the infant gradually gains mastery over her body, moving ever more of it immediately and spontaneously and gaining the expectations of so doing. The running up of the infant body is accompanied by a running down of what other bodies do for it. In the earliest stages of post-natal life, the infant accomplishes far more through others' bodies than she does through her own. When the movements made for the infant diminish as her own powers widen and deepen, she is in a position to realise that the bodies resembling hers in certain ways of moving are not a part of a single intercorporeal system. Her holding sway over her body and sense of direct efficacy here but not there constitutes her original sphere of ownness, which only emerges or attains its sense in contrast to the alien spheres.[15]

The persisting bodily reflexivity in touching is also needed for this agential sense of ownness, but if I read it correctly, nothing in this account goes against Merleau-Ponty's narrative, and it supports his contention that in early life I become given to myself as a certain hold on a certain milieu, not handling things as the other is doing over there. In our *developed* perception of the other, moreover, differentiation is experienced with someone's affections as well as actions. I simultaneously perceive and appresent the experiences of my friend Paul. Though they are directly visible on his phenomenal body, I am aware that that I cannot be accessing them from his own viewpoint; he suffers because his wife has died, or because someone has stolen his watch, whereas I suffer because *he* is grieving or because *he* is angry (*PP*, 372). Merleau-Ponty remarks that language will play an essential role in the perception of the other, most notably in dialogue (*PP*, 370), and he also allows for analogical inferences. If the correlations that are observed between our intentions and our gesticulations and the gesticulations occurring over there do not first teach us about the existence of others, they 'can certainly provide a guide

---

[15] Soffer 1999, 157–8, 160.

in the methodical knowledge of others and when direct perception fails' (*PP*, 368).

Without a language, distinctions could not be drawn between intentions and volitions and actions. And though others' lived experiences are embodied and directly perceived, Søren Overgaard has pointed out that there is still a role to be played by inferences in recognising *that* they are lived by others, that they possess first-hand significances for them which I can only access mediately.[16] Inferences are surely implied in my asymmetrical awareness of ego and alter ego as poles of experience for themselves, that is, in my awareness of 'my view upon myself and the other's view upon himself' (*PP*, lxxvi). In my perceiving of purposive movement, furthermore, I appresent an intention as being on the scene, and someone else can appear in control of his phenomenal body (*PP*, 367, 369). An infant can well perceive another pole of affection and action and appresent another's bodily feelings, which like affection and action are undivided between body and consciousness. But to appresent another as an existent whose awareness is for itself and who is governing its body is to appresent the *psychical* aspect of a psychophysical being comprehended as such. In these last performances – and hence in what Husserl takes as the second moment of analogical appresentation – theoretical inferences and convictions must be doing duty. My acts cannot be unthinking or free of conceptual cognition. Merleau-Ponty does not provide such an argument, even if it could be built up from some of his other remarks.[17] I think that the reason is his ongoing wish to foreground the work of the preconceptual domain. After intercorporeality, his focus is on the motivations behind transfers of sense and inferences (*SB*, 156; *PP*, 391). The being-directed of a lived body by an ego could not be appresented without the prior awareness of an outcome-oriented course of action emanating from a centre of action.[18]

Though the child comes to apprehend centres of action as distinctively own and alien and subsequently learns to use personal pronouns, the 'I' and 'You' are still levelled out as experiences shared by many. If we were to characterise self and other in this manner the alter ego would follow on the variations of the ego, erasing the individuality of perspectives. The 'we'

---

[16] Overgaard 2017, 76–7.   [17] See *PP*, 187, 450–1.

[18] Merleau-Ponty later states that positing another myself and having a conception of that other self as constituting is impossible without language. Speech is an eminent way of behaving that is pre-constituted for me and that gives certain objects the values of subjects. Its significations allow the leap to 'the *I* of *this* body of mine, *this* incarnate life's thought' and the *I* of a body objectified as that of another myself. *Sns*, 93–5.

would be the same as the 'one' (*PP*, 364, 372). The child enjoys a naive and unarticulated belief in the world as immediately and universally accessible, presumptively taking things as having the same allure and value for everyone. It is not suspected that we are limited to certain points of view, since we are all 'blank minds directed toward a single self-evident world where everything takes place', a realm in which 'others are so many gazes inspecting things, they have an almost material existence, to the point that one child wonders how these gazes are not broken when they meet' (*PP*, 371). When others impinge on the child's spontaneity and do not manifest the same enthusiasm for something, the child cannot comprehend why. Leaning heavily on Jean Piaget's theory of development, Merleau-Ponty holds that we reach the age of reason at around twelve years.[19] I discover myself as a sensible and intellectual awareness and as a point of view called upon to transcend my particularity, to attain objectivity at the level of judgement. In contesting my views, the other becomes more than a behaviour in my transcendental field. He or she gives me the idea of an individual centre of perspectives, and the dialogue teaches me as much about myself as about that other (*PP*, 353, 370–1).

7.4 Expressivity and Enculturation

As has been suggested, the notion of behaviour has a rich and multi-faceted extension for Merleau-Ponty, well removed from the scientistic behaviourisms having little or no concern with sense and meaning. All behaviour is expressive of something, from the simplest of gestures and gesticulations down to the reflex movements that are responses to situations rather than reactions to stimuli. If our initial datum is not a physical body but one that is thoroughly animated and expressive or filled with soul, it would be better again to say that its being animated is already its being expressive, as seen in its coming and going and laughing and dancing and so forth. And in working with things, as we noted, lived bodies are sketching out and expressing certain manners of dealing with them, some of which the infant will soon take up. We would go wrong in casting the body as one expressive space among others, for that would be the constituted or objective body as isolated from or cut out of its myriad engagements. Instead, the phenomenal body is the origin and the very movement of expression in projecting significations beyond itself, first giving them their place by ensuring 'that they begin to exist as things,

---

[19] See Piaget 1922, 222 ff.

beneath our hands and before our eyes' (*PP*, 147). Things gain senses from others before being logical subjects of attributes, and thus the expressive value of experiences 'grounds the pre-predicative unity of the perceived world prior to intellectual significations' (*PP*, 244). Expressive experiences precede *meant* acts of signification (*PP*, 304).[20]

When it takes shape as a centre of action radiating over a milieu, drawing things and others into its vortex towards practical and affective outcomes, the body is 'no longer a simple fragment of the world, but rather the place of a certain elaboration and somehow a certain "view" of the world' (*PP*, 369). A drama is apprehended as taking place in and through it and beyond it over there, and as an expressive unity lighting up itself and its milieu, the lived body can best be compared to a work of art. A poem would eventually be lost from memory were its text not preserved on pieces of paper, fragile of themselves. Like every work of art, it is never independent of some material support and does not subsist eternally like a logical truth. In its words it has an expressive fecundity that is modulated and amplified in its recital through pitch and tone and timbre and emphasis. A painting or a piece of music also illustrates the lived body's expressivity. These works cannot communicate anything apart from their peculiar arrangement of colours and sounds. Only from the perception of the painting can its analysis take on its sense, and the musical significance of a sonata is similarly inseparable from hearing its sound. No examination of its score can anticipate it, and once it is heard, all analyses must refer back to the actual experience. And even if one learns to distinguish subtly different ways of performing the sonata, it will never be actualised apart from these modulations in a pure and heavenly realm (*PP*, 153–4, 188). Poems and paintings and pieces of music are individuals, in that what is expressed is inseparable from the manner of expressing it. These 'send forth their significations without ever leaving their temporal and spatial place'. In this sense, the expressive body is comparable to a work of art, 'a knot of living significations and not the law of a certain number of covariant terms' (*PP*, 153).

Once the unquestioned beliefs in sensations as discrete units of experience and in an occult psyche have been overcome, a bodily behaviour and a face cease to be simple 'visual givens'. They are wholes 'impregnated with an immanent signification' through the spontaneous organisation of their parts (*PP*, 58). Everyday perception shows an affinity and meaningful unity between a person's tone of voice and smile and gestures as integral

[20] See also Cassirer 1957, 67–8.

moments of an overall attitude. The relaxed face and smile and cheerful gestures 'actually contain the rhythm of the action or of this joy as a particular mode of being in the world' (*PP*, 192). For all that, the face is what the infant is first drawn to, the centre of expression par excellence. In original experience it is 'the transparent envelope of the attitudes and desires of others', and in developed perception it remains 'the place of manifestation, the barely material support for a multitude of intentions' (*SB*, 167). The face is perhaps the supreme exemplar of the gestalt and phenomenological insight that pattern and pregnancy are decisive for recognition. Prior to and with epistemic cognition, we can already identify this or that face and apprehend a gaze or attitude without being able to describe the specific lines of the face or colour of eyes and hair (*SB*, 166; *PP*, 294). And if a part or detail of the face is pregnant with the whole, the latter is more often dependent on that part for its overall determination. This was well understood by Cézanne, who arrived at the awareness that the sense of a facial expression is not behind it but *upon* it in its light and colour, and that a simple dab of colour can transform an entire physiognomy or facial expression in a portrait (*PP*, 336–7). In death as in life and their depictions, furthermore, we are ultimately condemned to expression and therefore to sense. A face in repose or the face of a corpse will still express something, even if nothing more than peacefulness or surprise (*PP*, lxxxiii–iv, 478–9). From the human point of view, it is impossible to apprehend a face or a corpse as a mere thing, for they 'are sacred entities, not the "givens of sight"' (*SB*, 167).

To perceive another is at once to perceive a unique and once-off existent with his or her peculiar style of being. Members of groups typically have shared professions, pursuits and standards of living, but these they have taken up singularly. In the richest sense, someone's style expresses their personhood and whole way of being in the world (*PP*, 463, 469). Even on those rare occasions when it is not immediately to the fore, we expect a person's style to be discernible. This is what motivates our strenuous – and not infrequently anxious – efforts to pick out distinctive behaviours on meeting identical twins. When recognised later on, someone's style presents itself with an 'irrecusable evidentness', for it is re-experienced as a whole, having been conserved through different milieus as a peculiar mode of comportment or 'certain way of handling situations that I identify or understand in an individual' (*PP*, 342). And we are almost invariably correct when we anticipate its continuance, believing that the person in question will handle future situations in more or less the same manner. As with their world, a person's comportment 'is carried along by intentional

lines that trace out in advance at least the style of what is about to arrive'
(*PP*, 439). Romdenh-Romluc has glossed this well – someone's life has
a style and unfolds in accordance with it, but the path pursued is not
detailed in advance. A jealous nature will continue to colour his or her
engagements with the world, without having to determine the course that
life will take.[21]

Even in the absence of opportunities to discover very much about
someone's character, their comportment will succeed in conveying something of their singularity, if only by means of gait, gestures, finger movements and voice. It will communicate their peculiar dexterity or clumsiness
or calmness or nervousness (*PP*, 294, 455). The very reflexes of a person are
singular, in that 'the style of each individual is still visible in them just as
the beating of the heart is felt even at the periphery of the body' (*PP*, 87).
Along with existence, someone receives a style as a way of existing accessible
to others, though no matter how extensive the knowledge of that person
may become, no definition can embrace it (*PP*, 342, 482). Recognised
readily and yet elusive, to the extent of being ineffable, the other's style is
recalcitrant to philosophy 'which can only penetrate the individual
through the illegitimate process of the *example*, that is, by stripping it of
its facticity' (*PP*, 64). What is singular is of course mediated by what is
general, and must be if one is to negotiate the lifeworld. When I take
someone to be trustworthy, I am drawing on my personal and communal
understanding of that virtue. But it is something of their style that must
strike a chord if we are to become genuine friends or partners, something of
'the singular manner of being that is the person herself' (*PP*, 397).

With every human existent, generality as socio-cultural mediation goes
all the way down. I have noted that, for Merleau-Ponty, one can only
encounter one's natural environment against the cultural world. Nature is
'but a vague and far-off being, driven back by the towns, roads, houses, and
above all by the presence of other men' (*PP*, 25). As planned and executed
the things exhibit human work, which Hegel saw with such acuity (*SB*,
162).[22] They express embodied intelligence as the creations of beings whose
original sociality is not a factual state, but a condition of developing
somatically and consciously as humans do. Everything is necessary for us,
in that to have our world we must have these particular bodies with
opposable fingers and thumbs, bodies that will also let us stand upright.
Everything is contingent 'in the sense that this human way of existing is not
guaranteed to each human child through some essence acquired at birth'

---

[21] Romdenh-Romluc 2011, 242–3; *Ids2*, 283.   [22] See Hegel 1977, 117–9, 295 ff.

(*PP*, 174). On this conception, the social is already the cultural, and for the young infant, '[t]he very first cultural object, and the one by which they all exist, is the other's body as the bearer of a behaviour' (*PP*, 364). Our intercorporeality is realised as a sociality prior to language and reason:

> It is impossible to superimpose upon man both a primary layer of behaviours that could be called 'natural' and a constructed cultural or spiritual world. For man, everything is constructed and everything is natural, in the sense that there is no single word or behaviour that does not owe something to mere biological being – and at the same time, there is no word or behaviour that does not break free from animal life, that does not deflect vital behaviours from their direction through a sort of escape and a genius for ambiguity that might well serve to define man ... [b]ehaviours create significations that are transcendent in relation to the anatomical structure and yet immanent in the behaviour as such, since behaviour can be taught and understood (PP, 195).

From the beginning, we take up the expressions of others in responding to them, and usually without reflection. We never cease to be situated in a socio-cultural lifeworld that solicits us silently as well as thematically (*PP*, 379). In entering a room, 'the customs of our milieu or the arrangements of our listeners immediately obtains from us the words, attitudes, and tone that fits with them' (*PP*, 109). Socialised ways of proceeding are literally incorporated into our body schemas, our gestures expressing our cultural 'habitus' or inherited manner of meeting a situation and living it (*PP*, 139, 194–5). An acquired habit, as Pierre Bourdieu puts it, 'speaks directly to the motor functions, in the form of a pattern of postures ... charged with a host of social meanings and values'.[23] On this question, Dreyfus remarks that to talk of 'first' and 'second' nature is mistaken. With socialisation, there is no ground floor of individual instincts or objects on which cultural significations are then imposed. Instead, neonates are 'absorbed into a holistic web of interconnected meanings that they pick up directly by imitation'.[24] Babies need little encouragement to explore their milieus, but studies show that Japanese babies tend to be more quiet and contented, attuned to a culture valuing social integration, tradition and consensus, whereas American babies are attuned to a culture of more aggressive individuals valuing progress and cultivating interactions with compromises. Existence is mediated for both, since they are already developing *as* Japanese or American babies.[25]

---

[23] Bourdieu 1977, 87.   [24] Dreyfus 2013, 25.   [25] Ibid., 24–5.

Originally encultured, cognising itself through the implicit and explicit norms of its socio-cultural lifeworld and transforming the latter to a greater or lesser extent, the human being is a historical structure and a historical idea, not a natural species (*PP*, lxxxiii–lxxxiv, 174, 379). Putting it more soberly, each of us is a particular structure and signification of nature and history (*PP*, 482). We are born into and take up our communal existence unknowingly and in our singular ways, and only grow in knowledge and change things through what history offers at this or that juncture. Hence there is no unconditioned and centrifugal subject of history, and we cannot determine where the forces of history end and where ours begin (*PP*, 177, 474–6). And as adult and infant comportment teaches us, our affective lives are historically and culturally mediated in tandem with our behavioural norms. Only in some cultures, for example, is love expressed through the kiss. Like clothing and jewellery, love transforms the biological needs from which it originated, without its current expressions comprising its destiny. Many bodily expressions are nonetheless too close to us to be easily identified as the historical a prioris of a certain epoch (*PP*, 90, 195). Our implements display the particular forms of our lifeworld more easily. Clothes are irreducible to artificial skin (*SB*, 163, 174), since they express desires for adornment and for conveying roles. The 'genius for ambiguity' that might define humanity extends to the apprehension of divergent symbolic forms in the one blow. We can use a branch as a stick and see that same thing in its different functions, *as* a branch that has become a stick. And distanciation allows us to create implements to create further ones again. We achieve ends at several removes with planning, and our implements transcend our anatomical means (*SB*, 175; *PP*, 89, 148).

Like the intentional consciousness that of its essence goes beyond itself, the lived body is more than it is under any single conception, 'always rooted in nature at the very moment it is transformed by culture; it is never self-enclosed but never transcended' (*PP*, 205). Taken in isolation, however, our somatic core would be meagre (*PP*, 307). The bodily existence 'which streams forth through me without my complicity, is but the sketch of a genuine presence in the world', even if it grounds the latter in establishing 'our primary pact with the world' (*PP*, 168). A more adequate phenomenology will explicate the embodied human spirit as it has been concretised historically in certain forms of interpersonal relations and artefacts. If the regulative conception of a totality is an 'Idea in the Kantian sense', the 'Idea in the Hegelian sense' is the ideal of uncovering these forms for each civilisation (*PP*, lxxxii). This is why the constitution of others does not elucidate that of society, which is not shared by two or three, 'but is rather a coexistence with an indefinite number of consciousnesses'. Whether we are concerned with the vestiges of a lost civilisation or with living speech, the task is to show how 'an intention, a thought or a project can detach from the personal subject and become visible outside of him in his body and in the environment that he constructs' (*PP*, 364).

7.5 Exposure, the Gaze and Otherness

While I find myself always already situated in a socio-cultural and natural world, according to Merleau-Ponty, I am for all that an existent who maintains a faculty of withdrawal from factual situations. Sometimes I may 'live like a stranger in society, treat others, ceremonies and monuments like mere arrangements of colours and lights, and strip them of all human signification' (*PP*, 377). I can also retreat to some fastness, plug up my ears and close my eyes, lie down and hear the blood pulsing through those ears. At certain times in my life the world itself recedes or appears strange, for I can become absorbed in my bodily existence or have recourse to my thinking nature, throwing into doubt every perception as taken in isolation. Here lies the real truth of solipsism, not that I am the only awareness, but that my acts can become conspicuous as the only ones lived first-hand and that my experiences do not exhaust my being, which withdraws and evaluates and is more than any of them. But even when living in solitude, I am never enclosed in this situation like an object in a box. The socio-cultural and natural world will always intrude in some way, and my intentionality will sketch out something parasitic on this realm, even if only in the imaginary. If I had not already been presented with others, I could not speak of solitude. Nor can I throw an isolated perception into doubt except in the name of one correcting it. Solitude and communication are not mutually exclusive terms, but two moments of one phenomenon. Shut off in reflection the philosopher cannot fail to drag in others, and solipsism could only be true of an existent observing itself without being or doing anything determinate, which is impossible. Nothing would be taken as other than self and nobody would be addressed (*PP*, 168, 374, 376–8). A sphere of radical ownness cannot even be delimited as a fiction.

The retreat to some fastness is never unmotivated, for be in the world with others is to be exposed to their gaze (*PP*, lxxvi). Husserl realises this and Sartre does everything to prioritise it in positing three 'ontological dimensions' of the body.[26] First, there is the acting body 'for itself and for

---

[26] Dillon 1998, 140–2.

me', pre-reflectively present with me as a touching thing, as a point of view on the world and as a point of departure taking up implements. 'I exist my body' as what I am and as what surpasses itself towards some way of being.[27] Second, there is the 'body for others', whether it is my body as it appears to the other or vice-versa – the two are equivalent. The body for others is always apprehended in a situation as a 'tool of tools' or instrument for transcendence towards determinable ends.[28] Finally, there is the body existing for me as thematically *known* by the other, where I myself know that other as a subject for whom I am an 'object in itself', a dimension that is only revealed in language.[29] Martin Dillon has noted that the body for itself and for me is taken as fundamentally different from the body for others, before we get to the third dimension. A cleft is instituted between my body in action and my body for others.[30] According to Sartre, the hand that I see touching things reveals their resistance to me, but is not known by me in the act of touching them. Not revealing itself or its efforts, I only see my engaged hand in the way I see this inkwell in front of me. On this account, the feeling of touching and the feeling that one is being-touched are two species of phenomena that can never be united, and '[i]n fact they are radically distinct, and they exist on two incommunicable levels'. The body is either a thematic thing among things or that by which they are revealed to me, and it cannot be both at the same time.[31]

Merleau-Ponty replies that the dimensions of the 'for itself and for me' must already be the structures of the 'for others'. If one only recognises oneself inwardly and not with an outside, then the bodies of others cannot come to life with their insides. And if agency and intelligence are expressed outwardly, so are our feelings of our bodies from inside (*PP*, 58, 391, 474). Though he does not base the last claim on a sustained argument, he does appeal in passing to Husserl's account of touching and being-touched. When my gaze crosses another's 'I re-enact the foreign existence in a sort of reflection (*une sorte de réflexion*)' (*PP*, 367). Writing some years later, he makes it clear that this 'sort of reflection' is an extension of the body's reflexivity or feeling of feeling. The touching and being-touched cannot be thematised at the same time, yet these two moments of the phenomenon are not thereby incommunicable. When I shake someone's hand, her hand is substituted for my left hand as previously touched by my right. Feeling like my left hand from the outside, her hand is perceived and apperceived as an outside with its own inside, just as my hand is in hers. We appear to

---

[27] Sartre 1958, 304, 326, 329, 340.   [28] Ibid., 339–40, 344, 347.   [29] Ibid., 351, 354.
[30] Dillon 1998, 139–42.   [31] Sartre 1958, 304.

each other like the organs of a single intercorporeality, for the active and passive moments are effecting a communication between our two hands as they do between my own hands. The apperception is foregrounded when I switch my attention from touching that hand to the being-touched *in* that hand; I am unable to directly experience its being-felt from within, since it is not *my* previously touched hand that I am touching. When our gazes cross, I have yet another perception of a sensitive body exposed in the world. Because my internally felt flesh has been correlated with certain areas of my body in my visual field, I concurrently experience myself in touch and vision as an inside having an outside. This is how I appresent the sensitive interiority of another's body when seeing it without touching it (*Sns*, 168; *Ids2*, 174). Because my body for itself is at once for others it is not a monoform density; the junction of both is found in and upon it (*PP*, lxxvi, 391, 517). When taken up cognitively, this relation is not purged of its ambiguous two-sidedness, which remains in play in the developed perception of the psychophysical other. What Merleau-Ponty finds in our tactile reflexivity is woven into our intercorporeal expressivity:

> When I turn toward my perception itself, and when I pass from direct perception to the thought of this perception, I re-enact it, I uncover a thought older than myself at work in my perceptual organs of which these organs are merely the trace. I understand others in the same way . . . [t]here is, between my consciousness and my body such as I live it, and between this phenomenal body and the other person's phenomenal body such as I see it from the outside, an internal relation that makes the other person appear as the completion of the system. Others can be evident because I am not transparent to myself, and because my subjectivity draws its body along behind itself. [32] (*PP*, 367–8)

I will discover and eventually report that I am not immersed in a synchronous system with others, without either abandoning or diminishing our original intercorporeality. In Merleau-Ponty's view, our separation from others is a separation within a unity, an incision that is not a severing or slicing all the way through. In somatic sensitivity as in affection and action, it is through our anonymous unity that our bodies are more than mere objects for each other (*PP*, 368–9). But might this primordial intertwining be thoroughly effaced? Might one agree that the body for itself and for me is also for others, while conceding that its transcendent character falls out of view with Sartre's body in its third dimension, my body as *known* by the other? For his other as subject, my

[32] Translation slightly emended.

lived body and my embodied consciousness alike amount to nothing more than an object in itself. In Sartre's notorious theory of 'the gaze' or 'the look' as a relation that I have to undergo daily, to be seen by another is to experience the calcification and therefore the alienation of my own possibilities. I experience my exposure and my transcendence transcended, no longer maintaining control of whatever situation I was in before coming under that gaze.[33] By contrast with Hegel's dialectic of master and servant that ends in the mutual recognition of consciousnesses, this event cannot be surmounted once and for all.[34] The gaze of an autonomous consciousness surveying me as an item within its perceptual field fixes me into my current activity as a mere thing, and I become a slave or degraded consciousness for a transcendence that is not mine. I find myself frozen as if under a basilisk's eyes. And the potentiality of the objectifying gaze is always on the margins of my awareness, whether I am a voyeur looking through a keyhole who trembles at every noise or a traveller in the twilight who is ready to discern a face in the trunk of every tree.[35]

For Sartre, the gaze must and will be countered. As someone caught within it, I will perpetuate my objectification by the other if I consensually reduce myself to the latter's representation of me, though this attitude cannot endure. As someone who reasserts or who will come to reassert my free selfhood with its possibilities, I will realise that the gaze is only contemplative and respond by staring back, reducing that other to an object for *my* subjectivity. The struggle to assert one's freedom through one's body is interminable, for the other as object can again be transfigured as free subject and re-objectify me.[36] On one familiar line of criticism, Sartre presents a caricature of the richness and complexity of human relations, failing to capture the nature of many (if not most) of them.[37] Merleau-Ponty concurs and holds that the story falls short on several counts. I cannot be completely enclosed in the other's perspective because it is not a private spectacle, always being in some way towards our public and intersubjective world even as it focusses in on me. By the very same token, I cannot enclose the other in my perspective. I cannot transmogrify another being towards the world into an isolated object because my perspective has no definite limits, and 'because it spontaneously slips into the other's perspective, and because they are gathered together in a single

---

[33] Sartre 1958, 257, 263.   [34] Hegel 1977, 117–19; Sartre 1958, 297.
[35] Sartre 1958, 270, 273, 277, 280.   [36] Ibid., 285–7, 292–3, 297, 378.
[37] Carman 2020, 134–5; Romdenh-Romluc 2011, 148–9.

world in which we all participate as anonymous subjects of perception'
(*PP*, 369).

Only if we were purely thinking and knowing natures would we ever
gaze inhumanly, interpreting each other's actions as those of insects
surveyed from on high (*PP*, 378). But we never are, and hence our sociality
and situated possibilities cannot be completely abolished in our ways of
looking. I can only perceive the other as bare existence or as pure freedom
as much or as little as I can myself, and never at either extreme. The other as
mere thing 'is only an insincere modality of the other, just as absolute
subjectivity is only an abstract notion of myself' (*PP*, 474). A domineering
gaze and postural attitude is expressive, but so too is the impassive gaze of
a stranger. There *is* an objectification that I perceive as harmful – without
any shame or shyness on my part – when it is experienced as the lack of
a possible communication, when the other refuses to 'join in' with me in
any way, as Sartre would put it.[38] Yet this refusal to express anything in
particular is still a mode of expression. The impassive existence appears as if
devoid of sympathy, so its suspension of communication does not thereby
annihilate it. And as soon as that other becomes committed to some line of
behaviour through speaking or some impatient gesture, a way of thinking
and acting that seemed inaccessible has opened up (*PP*, 378).

Sartre is highly attuned – in his inimitably bleak fashion – to the
dramatic character of some of our engagements with others. But if his
human world is too much a realm of degrading objectification and unceasing struggle, Merleau-Ponty errs in the opposite direction. His world is too
convivial overall, built on a romanticised realm of peaceful coexistence in
childhood (*PP*, 372). We have seen that the 'for itself and for me' must
already be the 'for others', and it is added that both my lived or phenomenal body and my objective body are for others *and* myself (*PP*, 517). Yet he
does not elaborate on this, passing over the sheer extent to which we may
reflectively objectify our bodies in response to the judicative gazes of others
and socio-cultural idealisations. We may then train ourselves to move in
different ways and even have our bodies reshaped to our genuine or illusory
advantage. Such activities can entail extensive commerce between the body
image and body schema. To modify the former is often to rework the latter
and acquire new habitualities. In a related vein, Merleau-Ponty does not
have Michel Foucault's understanding of the body as the socio-political site
of disciplinary practices. That we fit in with the customs of our milieu and

---

[38] Sartre 1958, 287.

with other norms in our images and postures is never problematic for him.[39]

On the credit side, Merleau-Ponty is remarkably sensitive to what is strange and enigmatic in our intersubjective engagements. There are difficulties inherent in our perceptions of others, he states, that do not result from objective thought. Nor will all of these difficulties be dissolved through the recognition of the significance of gestural and linguistic behaviour. I only experience at a distance what others live first-hand, and our situations can never be superimposed on each other (*PP*, 373). Often I suppose and even flatter myself that I see 'right through' someone. When I discover a falsehood, for example, I may read off from this a person's whole character and way of being in the world. And having done this, I might further assume that they will collapse in the face of adversity. But Sartre is right that the *way* people take up their situations is unpredictable.[40] For some, the onset of blindness does not immediately derail their existing lives and worlds, since they persevere as long as they can. Others give up on their prior existences before these have become impossible (*PP*, 81–2). In my perceiving of the other, I overcome in *intention* the 'infinite distance' that will forever separate my subjectivity from another's. And this is the very heart of the matter; the signitive, memorial and imaginative intending of an alter ego's lived experiences cannot ever arrive at first-hand fulfilment or access from his or her perspective (*PP*, 457). When I say I know someone very well or like him very much, I am aiming beyond perception 'at an inexhaustible background beyond his qualities that indeed might one day shatter the image that I have formed of him' (*PP*, 379).[41] The perceptual act is violent in so far as we presume that we can objectify another or a thing as a shot through transparency. We most often predelineate the future as more of the same without surprises, though ineliminable transcendence is the price of there being others and things for us in the first place.

Merleau-Ponty maintains that the problems involved in perceiving others and the intersubjective world are only concerns for adults. In having a naive belief in the world as the same for all, that is, as presenting itself to everyone else as it presents itself to him or her, the child cannot comprehend such concerns. But if the very young have no conception of different points of view, they do have the primordial certainty of being with others in an inherently public world. Because this originary faith still sustains us as

---

[39] Foucault 1991. On body images and their ideological colourings, see Weiss 1999.
[40] Sartre 1958, 328.   [41] Translation emended.

adults, children are correct against ourselves and against Piaget, who valorises the truths we access on reaching the age of reason. In practice, the world remains indubitable to us, and hence 'the barbarous thoughts of the initial stage must remain like an indispensable acquisition beneath the thoughts of the adult stage' (*PP*, 371). Furthermore, Piaget reads far too much rationality into adult awareness, as if our thoughts were sufficient onto themselves and capable of resolving all contradictions. It is not just that our original relations with others carry into the age of reason, but that they never get to be saturated by rationality and that we can never live as absolute spirits free from their sway. And we can better understand our earlier and later relations when we explicate the domains of speech and affectivity.

CHAPTER 8

Language, Speech and Affectivity

8.1 Introduction

For Merleau-Ponty, the faithful description of language in its use will foreground it as the amplification of our projective existence. In its very origin, it is indissociable from our affectively and actively being towards the world (*PP*, 186, 191–3), and it remains indissociable from the relations with others that were required to found it and that were reshaped on being articulated. The appearance of reason in and through language 'does not leave intact a sphere of self-enclosed instincts' (*SB*, 181). We find ourselves within a world of others and things in which our speaking acts have transformed the embodied existence preceding linguistic activity (*PP*, 56, 189, 194–5). The task is to uncover the existential and pre-linguistic conditions of language without passing over its remarkable efficacy. In dialogue most notably, a common ground is established between myself and the other, constituting our 'consummate reciprocity' (*PP*, 370).[1] The medium that facilitates intimacy is no less distinctive in enabling distanciation. Supposing bodily skills – and itself an acquired skill that each of us feels in its employment – language lets us distance ourselves from our milieus to inspect and articulate them in shareable ways. Speech achieves and expresses our *thought* separation from the world. The purely lived, moreover, 'is not even found within man's speaking life', for there is no sanctum of lived experience utterly devoid of linguistic mediation (*PP*, 353).

In addressing the phenomenon of speech, according to Merleau-Ponty, 'we will have the opportunity to leave behind, once and for all, the classical subject-object dichotomy' (*PP*, 179). There is no question of rejecting the subject, only of re-situating it so that it is no longer the first and final foundation of human knowledge. One does not begin with thoughts

---

[1] Translation emended.

before oneself in the interiority of consciousness and then compose words to declare them to others.[2] Language is not a mode of bodily expressivity externalising thought, for its acquisition enables and inhabits the conscious and cognitive acts of the epistemic subject. I commence this chapter by outlining Merleau-Ponty's treatment, firstly of the behaviourism that leaves the speaking subject and ideality of meaning out of account, and secondly of the intellectualist alternative. This last view sees language as expressing thoughts and experiences ordered according to principles, but holds on to the idea of pre-expressive meanings. On the phenomenological alternative, words are the bodies of meanings. The latter persist and evolve through our living expressions and are inseparable from their founding and material supports. I go on to outline Merleau-Ponty's story about our induction into language by way of existential significations before we understand ideal meanings and use them to create situations. I then expli-cate his distinction between creative or speaking and habitual or spoken speech. Finally, I turn to his view of our affective lives in theoretical research and more mundane pursuits. Following Heidegger, the world is always revealed through some affective state, and although Merleau-Ponty's world is too much of a happy one, he does much to bring out the drama of human lives decentred starkly by thwarted love or delusion.

8.2 Words as the Bodies of Meaning

Methodological behaviourism is an extreme form of empiricism in which the study of language from an external and third-person perspective is to reveal it as a stock of verbal or aural images. When words are heard they are linked to certain stimuli, and the two are inscribed together in brain tracks or in associations with no discernibly physical base, though which is the case is of little importance. In early life, the child learns to link a unit of sound to a certain image and behaviour. The word 'water' will evoke an image of drinking and the words 'bath' and 'pool' the images of washing and swim-ming. Later on, certain interoceptive or exteroceptive stimuli reawaken the memory of the behaviour and the associated word, so that speech can take place. Without doubt words are combined in particular ways, but these have been built up through experience and inherited, so we need not appeal to occult mental states or faculties behind what is experienced.[3] We can speak on

---

[2] Descartes 1984a, 140.
[3] It is unclear what theory Merleau-Ponty has in mind, though his presentation appears to refer to part of an account advanced by Pavlov. If our sensations and ideas of the external world are the first and

foot of causes 'in the way an electric lamp can become incandescent' (*PP*, 179–80).

In Merleau-Ponty's view, such a crude theory is easily refuted by explicating the phenomenon of hearing someone speak. The theory makes no appeal to a speaking subject, since it posits nothing but a flow of words that occurs without any intention to communicate motivating and carrying into that flow. We cannot then distinguish conscious speech from thoughtless recitals following on stimuli and rote learning. Yet our ordinary experience tells us over and again that to speak to another is to act. We can and do distinguish between what is said and the way it is said, the one showing the intentional attitude of the speaker towards the other (so as to have an effect in the hearer). This extreme theory also falls short in regarding linguistic sense as context-dependent, as we discover when we examine cases of aphasia as against anarthria. The latter condition is a motor disorder ensuing from lesions in the central nervous system that cause the partial or total loss of articulate speech with consonants. The former condition involves the partial or total loss of speech itself, resulting from injuries to those brain areas devoted to producing and interpreting language (Broca's area and Wernicke's area). Merleau-Ponty notes that some partial aphasics are able to use words quite appropriately in contexts that have a vital or experiential significance. If they are tired, for example, they will agree that it is good for someone to take a rest when in this condition, though they cannot comprehend this recommendation when they are full of vigour. Words usually function as context-sensitive instruments of action and sometimes as more disinterested denominations, yet the patients cannot understand them the second way. They have been deprived of access to the ideality or abstractive sameness of word meaning, in which a signification is recognisable through different contexts without what is referred to being accessible perceptually.[4] By ignoring the ideality

---

concrete signals of its reality, then words in speech are the second, the signals of signals. See Windholz 1990, 163–73.

[4] We can distinguish between free and culturally bound ideality and between 'objective' or univocal expressions (for instance of logical and mathematical truths) and the context-sensitive meanings in what Husserl entitles 'essentially occasional' expressions. These include all personal pronouns and demonstratives, and are occasional or indexical in that their meanings are bound up with the peculiar circumstances of their utterance. In their use, they have an *indicating* meaning, a minimal ideality or sameness, and an *indicated* meaning, the indicative function as exercised for a singular presentation or state of affairs in perception, memory or imagination. Husserl adds that most expressions used in everyday life are vague, having no one meaning content and awakening cognate concepts and personal associations. Any attempt to model ordinary language on fixed or objective expressions and eliminate its vagueness and ambiguity is doomed (*LI 1*, 218–24). Merleau-Ponty agrees. See *PP*, 408–12.

of linguistic signification, empiricism distorts developed experience from above, its model of sensations and stimuli having already distorted original experience from below (*PP*, 53, 180).

On the alternative and intellectualist approach, ordinary language is permeated by ideality, and our own speech and responses to requests show that we are depending on it. More than this, our bodily comportment in following certain instructions shows that we organise what we are at grips with in accordance with cognitive and categorial insights into ideal essences or types, ideationally abstracted from earlier experiences and doing their work pre-reflectively. When the ensuing behaviour displays a lack of accordance, this suggests that the heard words are deficient in meaning. Gelb and Goldstein draw this conclusion after examining patient 'Th.' and some of his fellows, diagnosing them as cognitive amnesiacs because of their difficulties with colour names. The patient describes green as 'grassy' and red as 'like a cherry', and on request assembles ribbons having an identical colour.[5] But when asked to sort red and green ribbons into different piles, he invariably goes off-track. He successfully assembles samples with a similar hue, but just as readily lumps in pale or bright red with pale or bright green, as do some of the others. For the doctors, the brain injuries of such individuals have caused them to regress into the concrete attitude that is to the fore in early life. In this attitude merely empirical similarities or resemblances are predominant (pale red looks like pale green *more* than it looks like dark red), whereas in the categorial and intellectual attitude we perceive and organise empirical things according to essences such as redness or greenness. Patient Th. and others cannot see and organise things in ways that transcend and often go against immediate similarities because they have no principles from which to proceed.[6]

Merleau-Ponty agrees that in the categorial attitude we break away from a thing's unique properties, with the name conveying an essence or category. It is not just knowledge that is in question, moreover, since our very experiences of colours and of other features of things are altered in and through the founded intellectual acts. Unlike the patients we do not associate things through merely empirical similarities, for once in place a categorial activity is a certain manner of relating to the world, with thought and objective language being two manifestations of the intentional arc or fundamental function of projection (*PP*, 181, 196–7). As Gurwitsch observes, there is an existential turn in the doctors' account in which categorial and concrete attitudes and behaviours are integrated.[7] But the

---

[5] Gelb and Goldstein 1924, 133–4, 148.　　[6] Ibid., 148–53, 162.　　[7] Gurwitsch 1949, 189–90.

downside of Gelb and Goldstein's analyses and of similar ones when left unqualified is that language seems conditioned by thoughts that are behind it and occurrent without it. Using empiricist terminology, we might say that patient Th. still possesses the verbal images of the words 'red' and 'green', and only encounters difficulties because these are not informed by the categorial attitude that does its work in advance of linguistic external-isation (*PP*, 181). A similar story is recounted in Husserl's early period when he distinguishes between indications and expressions as two functions of signs. Every sign must function as an indication, pointing to something that is not directly present and that might no longer be extant. When a conscious being sees smoke it is indicating fire in the associative sense, but it need not *mean* fire. Indications in the simplest sense are things that point beyond themselves and that motivate beliefs without conceptually or categorially meaning anything (*LI 1*, 183–4).

For a mark or sound to indicate expressively, it must be informed or animated by intentional awareness. What makes an expression say some-thing *of* something or refer to an object communicatively, in Husserl's view, is a meaning-conferring act. Through it, the sign, with its referent or objective correlate, has a meaning and not a mere sense. But when thinking silently about oneself there is no need to communicate anything *to* oneself (because one is living through one's acts), and hence no necessity to use words (*LI 1*, 190–1, 197–200). We think conceptually and categorially before we animate marks or sounds to constitute them as words, so that when our pre-expressive significations are given linguistic expression, the spoken or written words do not add anything. The sounds or marks have no product-ivity beyond what is put into them by the animating intention (*Ids1*, 296; *Ids2*, 252–3). Though empiricism seems to be radically opposed to these intellectualist stories, there is actually a close kinship between them. In the one view, the word is evoked through stimuli or associations. In the other, it is informed by conceptual and categorial work, but has no significance of its own that could be evocative. The meaning lies in the thought alone and the word is its sensible container (*PP*, 182). Language is stripped of its efficacy because the word is just the outer sign of the inner recognition:

> In the first account, we exist prior to the world as meaningful; in the second account, we are beyond it – in the first, there is no one who speaks; in the second, there is certainly a subject, but it is the thinking subject, not the speaking subject. With regard to speech itself, intellectualism hardly differs from empiricism, and it is no more able to do without an explanation through automatic reflexes. Once the categorial operation has been accom-plished, the appearance of the word that accomplishes it [expressively]

remains to be explained, and again an explanation is found through a physiological or psychological mechanism, since the word is an inert envelope. (*PP*, 182)

We can only move beyond intellectualism and empiricism if we recognise that the word itself *has* a meaning.[8] It imports a significance that we come to appreciate rather than constitute spontaneously and centrifugally, and that we still depend on (*PP*, 182, 426). If the act of speaking only referred to its object through a prior epistemic intention followed by associative work awakening certain verbal images, 'then we could not understand why thought tends towards its expression as if toward its completion'. Because there is no pre-expressive stratum of meant signification, what we entitle the thinking subject 'is in a sort of ignorance of his thoughts so long has he has not formulated them for himself, or even spoken or written them' (*PP*, 182–3). Even thinking silently about oneself – as in Husserl's solitary and self-directed monologue – has to be linguistically mediated, being another mode of speech. Language is the language of thought itself, its clarification and its stabilisation. It is true that we give our thoughts to ourselves, that we make them our own, but a thought could never exist for itself and for us outside the constraints of communication, since it 'would fall into the unconscious the moment it appears, which amounts to saying that it would not even exist for itself' (*PP*, 183). Our recognition of types of things as such also takes place through language, with the most familiar object appearing indeterminate when one attempts to articulate it themat-ically without remembering its name. If I zone in on something and say 'there is the brush', the designation of the object does not happen after the act of recognition, but is essential to and coextensive with it. I am conscious of having reached the object, but without subsuming it under a concept that is then linked with the word through frequent association, for the concept only has its referential function through the name (*PP*, 182–3).

On this theory, our speech does not translate fully formed thought but rather accomplishes it, and even the abstractive ideation in categorial

---

[8] This seems to strain against the arbitrary nature of the linguistic sign, the long-recognised lack of any intrinsic and motivated relationship between the signifier and signified outside of onomatopoeia, and beyond this the specific way that words colour the concepts that they give life to in expression and hence their way of intelligibly articulating the world. Merleau-Ponty clearly affirms the arbitrariness of the word-thing link (*PP*, 192–4), and his statement that the word *has* a meaning is best understood as the claim that the link is *as if* natural for the child entering a linguistic community, and that the word's aural shape embodies a certain socio-cultural heritage, style and emotional essence, or a certain way of singing the world (*PP*, 188, 193, 425). Even though word meanings are ideal and translatable, there is no pure ideality that is untouched by its transmigration into another linguistic body.

thinking has to be realised linguistically. Thought and expression are constituted simultaneously, so that the words we speak are not the empty envelopes of thoughts or their mere clothing, but their bodies as well as their emblems, their genuine presences in the sensible world (*PP*, 183, 187, 412). But why then is there a widespread belief in an 'inner' thinker who possesses her thoughts before and behind language and world? Merleau-Ponty's answer is that we are tricked into believing in such a private and self-contained realm by sedimented language. We do not represent words as we use them, rather what they refer to, and they can function as anonymously as our bodily habitualities. We have 'already constituted and already expressed thoughts that we can silently recall to ourselves and by which we give ourselves the illusion of an inner life', though 'this supposed silence is buzzing with words' (*PP*, 186, 188–9). And if there is no domain of conceptual meaning-conferring and intending prior to linguistic expression, neither are there any meanings that could come to float above and beyond their verbal expressions. When we consider the ideality and longevity of the meanings with which we intend things and states of affairs, thought 'seems able to detach itself from its material instruments and to take on an eternal value' (*PP*, 411). And yet every 'idea' is necessarily interwoven with an act of expression. It is just as much a cultural object as a church or a novel or the Ninth Symphony. Words and other symbols are quite literally the bodies of their meanings, and if they are destroyed the said meanings will themselves disappear from the world. New acts of creative expression would then be required to restore them. This does not entail that the time of ideas must merge with the time of buildings or books or musical scores, but it does entail that the former cannot persist for very long in the absence of the latter. The most ideal and abstract of meanings must be inscribed on a material surface if it can no longer be (or cannot just be) communicated verbally. Otherwise it could not survive the community in which it was expressed after all the members of the latter have died (*CES*, 359–61; *PP*, 410).

8.3   Existential Significations and Beyond

In projectively being towards the world, we seek to communicate with others, to learn from them and inform them, to engage with them towards further outcomes and at best to be kind and fair to them. And if there were not some predisposition for speech in the child who hears it, according to Merleau-Ponty, it would be one sonorous phenomenon among others, and could not play its guiding role in the constitution of the perceived world.

Yet at first the 'linguistic ceremony' and its 'nasal melody' has no hold on the infant, since it cannot make anything happen for him. He is like a spectator who is badly placed to see and hear a play in a theatre and who cannot follow it (*SB*, 169; *PP*, 422–3). For the child, words begin to take on their senses as 'existential significations' that inhabit and that are inseparable from them. Words are stylised as the singular expressions of a person, are 'gestural' in having an affective or emotional value in their expression and are intentional in referring to things and states of affairs before communicating with meanings or concepts.

The affective or emotional content of spoken words is exhibited by accent, tone, facial expression and posture, and by infants' responses. The linguistic gesture sketches out its own sense because the expression of an emotion is the emotion itself or the inducing of that emotion in others. The sorrow is expressed in the tears and hands and the anger in the red face and trembling, and just as much in the sad and angry voices. And when we range over the spoken and written, we find an emotional richness in poetry going beyond that expressed in everyday language. The vowels and phonemes in their recital are 'so many ways of singing the world' that are expressive without objective resemblance or onomatopoeia. Because the affective or emotional values in words are socially-culturally coloured, however, the full sense of a language can never be translated into another. There is no *bald* conceptual expressivity. To assimilate a language it would be necessary to take up the whole world it expresses, a task that defies completion (*PP*, 187–8, 192–3).

The intentional significations of linguistic expressions are initially read off from expressively speaking faces, and more again will be appreciated when the child gains the skills of tracking other persons and things and apprehending states of affairs at a distance. Adults often suppose they teach language to the very young by pointing to objects as they utter their names. Pointing arm and index finger are aligned with the adult gaze in catching the child's attention, motivating the latter to follow arm and eyes forwards towards their target. Wittgenstein famously observes that this way of teaching (or 'ostensive teaching') is usually modelled on a primitive notion of a language more primitive than ours. It is an exclusively representational model, and though this is an essential function of language, it is only appropriate for a narrowly circumscribed region of communication. The meaning of the word 'five' does not itself picture anything and is found in how it is used in a language that is woven into actions (in the widest sense). Linguistic significance is irreducible to one-to-one relations with isolated things in fixed and unchanging relations.[9] Merleau-Ponty's view of learning a language shows affinities. While we must find correspondences between words and things, poetry shows vividly that language goes beyond them, and the sentence gives each word its sense within its configuration (*PP*, 192, 408). I do not inspect the one indicating word and one indicated thing to arrive at the verbal signification. Instead, 'I learn it just as I learn the use of a tool – by seeing it employed in the context of a certain situation' (*PP*, 225).

Such a view suggests that there is an element of truth in behaviourism, since the first and existential significations of words *are* living or vital ones and refer to what is proximally accessible in practical contexts. These emotional and indicative powers of the uttered words can be discerned in the behaviours expressed in and around them. In accent and tone and other bodily gestures, the adult is expressing an emotional and evaluative attitude to a situation (*PP*, 152, 188). He or she is conveying whether it should be avoided as dangerous or unpleasant or pursued as useful or pleasant. The sense of the sentence is already given pre-conceptually as a broad aim or an intention, as a point of departure towards and arrival at something intended from a particular point of view (*PP*, 454). As heard, the spoken word 'is first an event that grasps my body, and its hold upon my body circumscribes the zone of signification to which it refers' (*PP*, 244). Taken up by embodied awareness from without, the word's elementary sense is a precondition of our coming to understand its conceptual signification. Since it is usually heard in sentences, we go from whole to part in learning its meaning, akin to the process of refining part of a dance after traversing the entire movement. Through its use in different sentences and contexts, the word gradually assumes a significance that cannot be fixed absolutely. The passage from pre-conceptual sense (already a schema for imagination if functioning nominatively) to ideal and intelligible (and more often context-sensitive) meaning is from the immediacy of existential significations – which remain efficacious when worked over cognitively – to the mediacy of verbal concepts for making explicit and articulating otherwise (*PP*, 408, 424–6, 539).

We can be taken to have learnt a language in the substantive sense when it can create a situation for us and when we can use it effortlessly to create situations of our own. Language has a peculiar power to report situations that are not present to the hearers or readers or no longer extant, and to frame situations that are only objects for the imagination. It is the medium

---

[9] Wittgenstein 1958, 2–5e.

for thinking in empirical absence, for conveying a landscape not immediately given to everyone or even capable of perceptual fulfilment. In language our powers of articulating situations are at their height (*PP*, 194), and some articulations are attributable to a whole host of people. Alone of all expressive operations 'speech is capable of constituting an intersubjective acquisition' (*PP*, 195–6), as witnessed by the oral traditions preserved in the earliest written histories. For language to create a situation it must be taken up by the productive imagination (*PP*, 198) as the power of 'bringing the expressed into existence, and of opening routes, new dimensions, and new landscapes to thought'. This power is as obscure for adults as it is for children, in that the vista produced in the reader's awareness 'magically appears during the linguistic incantation, just as the story emanates from the grandmother's book' (*PP*, 423).

Once I create situations of my own through language, I have acquired the word as one acquires a tool, for it is part my equipment, having a place in my world as linguistically articulated and articulatable (*PP*, 186, 425). I count on and reckon with my words as I do with other skills, for 'they constitute a certain field of action held around me'. Through them I make things real, and Merleau-Ponty contends that I can say of the word what can be said of my body as schematised posturally. There is no need to thematise it in its use, for 'I possess its articulatory and sonorous essence as one of the modulations or one of the possible uses of my body' (*PP*, 186). By way of 'the contraction of the throat, the sibilant emission of air between the tongue and the teeth' (*PP*, 200), I throw bodies of sound ahead of myself as implements affording outcomes. The phonetic gesture is a genuine structuring of experience for the speaking subject and for those listening, investing segments of the perceptual field with particular significations pointing beyond it (*PP*, 199). It is a distinctive opening of the transcendental field of possibilities, going far beyond the edge of my body and what it expresses silently. When some request is fulfilled immediately, the intellectual and motor significations will have been intimately at one.

So long as I stay in direct contact with others or even indirectly through their writings and recordings they continue to contribute effectively to the thoughts and situations that I take myself as creating. In the dialogue with the other that establishes a common ground and that constitutes our consummate reciprocity, communication is not first and foremost with representations or thoughts, but 'with a speaking subject, with a certain style of being, and with the "world" that he aims at' (*PP*, 189). More properly, I communicate with the other person, though this does not prevent me from lapsing into objective thought after we go our separate ways. On remembering the other's objections and my responses, I suppose that he or she drew out thoughts I had no idea I possessed, which is to misinterpret the dialogical phenomenon. Often these are thoughts that I did not possess, and that were only possible within and from the speaking relation. They were co-constituted of their essence, and as such were never exclusively mine. Speech gives the power of thinking according to others, of reflecting them in oneself. Their thoughts as taken up allow me to enrich and even formulate my own (*PP*, 184, 370). If I lend thoughts to the other in my words, 'he makes me think in return', and I forget that his words inhabit my replies, turning the latter into episodes of my private history (*PP*, 370–1).

8.4   Speaking and Spoken Speech

Just as we can come to identify bodily movements as more or less creative or habitual, so too we can distinguish 'speaking speech' (*parole parlante*) from 'spoken speech' (*parole parlée*). Merleau-Ponty also calls the former authentic, originary and transcendental speech (*PP*, 202–3, 408–9, 411), and he characterises creation in diverse ways. These include the 'first man' ever to speak, the first words of the child, the discovery of an emotion by the lover and the words of 'the writer and the philosopher who awaken a primordial experience beneath traditions' (*PP*, 530). Yet little light is cast on the ancestral leap beyond existential and gestural significations to conceptually communicative speech, or on the emergence of syntactical forms and vocabularies (*PP*, 192–3). And because so much weight is placed on the continuity between pre-verbal expressivity and verbal articulation, it is difficult to isolate the time that the child begins to learn or display meaningful speech.[10]

Speaking speech brings new thoughts into existence. The lover who has discovered an emotion for the first time silhouettes its power on articulating it, and may determine it further again in writing. Along with dialogues and poems it is great speeches and novels that are Merleau-Ponty's privileged media for speaking speech, since they impose their own meanings on us (*PP*, 202–3, 335, 408–11). Through metaphors and analogies and imagery their authors frame and colour in the picture of a certain place or time and draw out the nuances of this or that emotion or affective state, of this or that fundamental life project and of this or that character. When I read Stendhal I already have a notion of what it is to be a rogue, but words in

---

[10] Kee 2018, 422–4.

this writer's hands take on a whole new twist. Cross-references are multiplied and a flawed way of being is understood as never before.[11] Other ways of combining words can depose their existing meanings and result in new thoughts, jolting us out of customary ways of seeing and evaluating. We need not venture far into the works of Woolf or Joyce to find the most catachretic of changes, though Merleau-Ponty's particular focus is on existential or gestural significations. When new ways of expressing words in speaking have repercussions for their future understanding, they show to striking effect that we transcend ourselves in our *uses* of our bodies (*PP*, 188, 199–200, 408). It is true that I need this particular body, which is 'something like a natural subject, or a provisional sketch of my total being' (*PP*, 205), but no less true that my anatomy and my psychophysical equipment leave open possibilities that cannot be read off from them (*PP*, 195). An 'open and indefinite power of signifying' is an ultimate fact 'by which man transcends himself through his body and his speech toward a new behaviour, toward others, or toward his own thought' (*PP*, 200).

In sharp contrast, spoken speech is characterised as constituted, sedimented, empirical and secondary, the public manifestation of already completed thoughts (*PP*, 409, 411). Its long-since acquired word meanings are so habitual and familiar in their employment as to be banal, leading to second-order intendings 'which are in turn translated into other words that require no genuine effort of expression from us, and that will demand no effort of comprehension from our listeners' (*PP*, 189). In spoken speech, he adds, the linguistic and intersubjective world no longer has any wonder for us, not being distinguished from the silence that is only broken by the creative speech that brings more of the world's contours into view. It is difficult to disagree with Baldwin when he contends that spoken speech is by implication 'inauthentic'. Even if Merleau-Ponty does not employ this term, his account cannot help but remind us of Heidegger's critique of 'idle talk' (*BT*, 211–14), the superficial chatter that is both second-order and second-rate.[12] Forgetting that the spoken is as much the instrument of justifiable practical action, long-term planning and solidarity as it is of prattle or gossip, Merleau-Ponty has slid into an unduly harsh and indeed one-sided view of everyday speech. Yet he moves in a much better direction when he suggests that purely spoken speech is pathological. All those who exhibit it seem incapable of transcending it. We saw that Schneider can only comprehend metaphorical and analogical language through painstaking analyses. His vocabulary and syntax appear intact, yet he cannot grasp counterfactual statements or express possible situations.

---

[11] Merleau-Ponty 1973, 12–13, quoted in Hass 2008, 180–1.   [12] Baldwin 2007, 94.

The questions he asks are as formulaic as his answers to those asked by others. After his release from hospital, inquiries addressed to his children when they arrive home from school follow patterns that are as stereotypically repetitive as his bodily comportment more generally (*PP*, 129–30, 201–2).

As already noted, the productive imagination is that which allows for 'all interrogation, all reference to the possible, all wonder and all improvisation' (*PP*, 202). Its diminution does make Schneider's speech automatic, but it does congeal it. Ordinarily the intention to speak is an open experience; in speech the spoken may suggestively lead into the speaking, and this is the essence of normal language (*PP*, 198, 202). The latter is an 'ever-recreated opening in the fullness of being . . . that like a wave gathers itself together and steadies itself in order to once again throw itself beyond itself' (*PP*, 203). In this better and more persuasive account, the distinction is not between two kinds but between two *functions* of speech, each feeding into and conditioning the other. Spoken speech is the sedimentation of what was once speaking speech and enables still more of the latter. Roberta Dreon has indicated a helpful manner of understanding this relationship between the two functions. Although the creative transgression of habitual usages and significations is unpredictable, it cannot be arbitrary, precisely because it depends on these previously established connections. Instead of a conception of *creatio ex nihilo* (set against constituted and supposedly empirical speech), we can work with a circular model of the speaking and the spoken without an asymmetrical subordination of the second to the first. And wherever we discern modified and transgressive word usages we must already have an awareness of the stable yet open meanings that were modified and transgressed. Otherwise the changes would be unrecognisable and unintelligible.[13]

On the better account, the acquired is the springboard for the new, and 'only truly acquired if it is taken up in a fresh movement of thought' (*PP*, 132). To express creatively is 'to ensure that the new intention takes up the heritage of the past . . . to incorporate the past into the present and to weld this present to a future' (*PP*, 413). But if the speaking subject constituted by way of inherited significations constitutes when changing them, this is not all the way down. A paradox of expression is that language transcends us in our most creative acts, for its expressiveness never finds its completion with them. The expressed is not a signification that ceases where the signifying thought ceases, since it outlives the thought itself (*PP*, 412). Even if the philosopher dreams of

---

[13] Dreon 2016, 61–2, 65.

a comprehensive and transparent speech to end everything (*PP*, 196), there is an ineliminable fertility in the medium of expression:

> Language transcends us, not merely because the use of language always presupposes a large number of thoughts that are not present and that each word summarises, but also for another deeper reason: namely, these thoughts in their actuality had never themselves been 'pure' thoughts either, there was already in them an excess of the signified over the signifying, the same effort of thought already thought [*pensée pensée*] to equal thinking thought [*pensée pensante*], and the same provisional joining of the two that makes up the entire mystery of expression. (*PP*, 410)

Merleau-Ponty is not rowing back on his claims that language is needed to form and stabilise thought, allowing for its recognition and its perpetuation in individual and collective memory, but is qualifying them heavily. If the meaning of the phrase that one utters appears transparently intelligible throughout and as nothing more than the realisation of what one intends to communicate, this is 'because we presuppose as given all of the participations that it owes to the history of the language and that contribute to determining its meaning' (*PP*, 194).[14] With our gestures and the terms that we use we often express much more to our hearers than we wish to, and the expressions may work far beyond us. Due to the excess of the signified over the signifying the speaking subject cannot be sure of grasping all the ramifications of his or her utterances, and it holds in principle 'that the expressive operation in every speech act can be indefinitely reiterated, that one can speak about speech, whereas one cannot paint about painting' (*PP*, 196). Our words 'accomplish communication without any guarantee in the midst of incredible linguistic hazards' (*PP*, 194), and just what was expressed will never become totally clear and unambiguous through reflecting on it afterwards (*PP*, 411–12). It is not just that speaking speech and spoken speech call on each other, but that they are mutable in relation to their hearers and contexts of use. Hayden Kee has observed that profound words lost on one person will be revelatory for a second, and that a person might only come to appreciate the deeper import of a lover's words many years later. So too with the untimely works of the artist or the philosopher, lying dormant and in wait of a public that will understand them decades from now. Any endeavour to sort speech acts into isolated units (of gestures and words and so on) and place them in the categories of the creative and the derivative 'risks falsifying the intersubjective relationality, the temporality, and indeed, the holistic mereology of speech'.[15]

---

[14] Translation emended.   [15] Kee 2018, 426.

8.5 Affective Life and Life Decentred

Objective thought and the use of scientific language sometimes lead us to suppose that an existence devoted to explanation and discovery is a disinterested as well as austere one. A person has come to live 'the life of the mind' and has transcended an ordinary and mundane existence. A life that is lived in the pursuit of enduring accomplishments is of course easily distinguishable from one of short-term pleasure seeking. The first has a history of training and sacrifice behind it; the second is monopolised by desires with little or no evidence of sublimation. Its most valued accomplishments are transitory episodes of enjoyment that are more difficult to sustain as the years advance. For the most part, however, we are well aware that the so-called life of the mind is one with an all-consuming interest; scientists and artists and philosophers *want* to do what they do. Aristotle points out that all human beings desire to know, though this desire can only put down roots and thrive when certain circumstances are in place for its fulfilment. Affectivity is at the origin of every project, and philosophy is motivated by an affective state of wonder that triggers this very human pursuit, the endeavour to rouse oneself from a naive existence and make the meaning of life and world explicit (*PP*, lxxvii, 309).

As already suggested, Kant's Third Critique is greatly admired by Merleau-Ponty because it brings out the affective as well as imaginative aspects of aesthetic experience and knowledge in general. For Kant, philosophy also commences with the desire to know (and to know and act autonomously), and when someone makes a philosophical or scientific or practical discovery the experience has its own manner of being pleasing. One appreciates oneself 'as a nature spontaneously conforming to the law of the understanding'. With every discovery – not just in my experience of the beautiful – I judge that this experience holds for others too and can be accessed by them because it is expressible (*PP*, lxxxi). That which is impressive and pleasurable and communicable is almost always what we *wish* to communicate. We saw that the child has a naïve belief in the world as the same for everyone, as presenting itself in the same way (*PP*, 371). When the child communicates an experience, it is assumed that everyone will find it just as exciting and attractive. Yet the child lives on in the adult researcher who wants to convey a discovery to those with the abilities to understand it and verify it for themselves.

These are founded achievements of lives that have been affectively as well as posturally geared into the world. We always live in some affective state, or in what Heidegger calls a mood. This is a mode of affective attunement to the world, not something that we can isolate introspectively. When we encounter it we are also and of necessity encountering the way it has revealed the world anterior to epistemic objectification. Even when we come to master a mood, we can only do so by replacing it with a counter-mood; we cannot free ourselves from *some* mode of affective attunement (*BT*, 175–9). At their most elementary in childhood and even in adulthood, moods are ways of living 'according to the emotional categories of our milieu' (*PP*, 399). For Schneider, however, faces are neither pleasant nor unpleasant if he is not conversing with them, and a rainy or sunny day is neither sad nor joyful. People and things at a remove from concrete tasks do not interest him because in affective terms his world is more or less neutral, and even his concrete tasks are pursued without any overt enthusiasm (*PP*, 156, 159–60).[16] We have seen that others and things pull us out of ourselves long before we embark on our own projects, and even in adulthood they may still enchant us (*PP*, 221, 307). Repulsion is no less forceful; the storm-tossed sea is genuinely ferocious and the city of ill-tempered pedestrians and huge buildings genuinely intimidating. The lifeworld is never a metaphor, but the affective homeland of our thoughts. Within it, our existence is a drama we take up through our bodies (*PP*, 25–6, 205).

We are affectively geared out of the world of possibilities when assailed by and caught up in what Heidegger calls a bad mood. We can no longer pursue our projects with our usual proficiency, and when such a mood is at its worst these grind to a halt because they do not matter anymore (*BT*, 175). In such a situation, the most fundamental of life projects will be interrupted. Nor will a different and short-term possibility exercise a pull on us, since our skills, imagination and our habitual diversions are insufficient on their own. A perception, thought or suggestion can only motivate us if our mood is attuned to it, allowing it to appeal to us (*PP*, 132, 156–7). All this being said, many of the moods that assail us are sourced in traumatic events, and these moods can all too often solidify into habitual attitudes and inclinations that reveal the world in some ways and yet occlude it very badly in others. Although Merleau-Ponty takes up the notions of organic and abnormal repression to help us understand pathologies, to silhouette undamaged performances and to account for distanciation, he agrees with Freud that abnormally repressed traumas always return, ensuing in anxieties and fixations and repetition compulsions (*PP*, 85, 88). Events that are still personal and datable may be no less efficacious. The drama of life at its most intense is shown in our rejoicing at births and

---

[16] See also Steinfeld 1927, 176–7.

recoveries and relationships gained, and in our grieving at illnesses and deaths and relationships lost.

Merleau-Ponty's focus is predominantly on the happy events, and his perceiver almost invariably comes across as resilient in the face of sad ones. In resuming my course of life, I have learnt where to avoid reminders of my friend's death, and when not preoccupied or tired or ill-humoured I attend to the world that retains something of its original beauty, and to the things that retain something of their fascination, each one inviting me to perceive more of it (*PP*, 82–3, 242, 261). Even when I am overcome with grief or completely absorbed in my sorrow, my gaze will wander out before me and take an interest in some bright object. My body has again sided with the world that has intruded on a personal episode (*PP*, 86, 221–2). Yet this will not hold for every human life, and is hardly the story of a grieving adult. It resembles nothing so much as a child who has been pulled out of some momentary misery to take up a joyful if tear-stained investigation. For the adult, the colour and vivacity of the world may have been lost without any chance of return, with talk of closure or moving on being worse than useless. A sudden death or the news of a terminal illness may leave in its wake a Sisyphean struggle to keep on living.[17]

When he focusses on the phenomenon of love, however, I think that Merleau-Ponty shows far more acuity. Attraction to a would-be life partner is one of our most ecstatically affective ways of being. Frustration in this domain can ensue in a radically decentred existence, manifested starkly and painfully in its integrally psychosomatic unity. The emergence of love from desire he calls 'miraculous', and no more explicable than the emergence of the figurative from the literal. The love I discover is neither hidden in the unconscious nor an object standing in front of consciousness. It is rather an overall turning towards someone that works in advance of any decision, a total 'conversion' of thought and behaviour of which I am aware but which has worked through me rather than being accomplished by me, constituting an existential situation lived in ambiguity (*PP*, 200, 400). What we give the name of love is in Merleau-Ponty's eyes always fragile and frequently delusional. Pascal argues that I may love someone for her beauty, but disease can destroy this and the love with it. Should I love her for her intelligence and acuity, these too can be destroyed. I may then contend that I love the substance of her soul, but this is an abstraction, so it turns out that I have never loved anyone, only qualities.[18] Certainly this touches on the perceptual fundaments of love, but it says nothing of the

---

[17] Here I draw on Mooney 2017, 73.   [18] Pascal 1966, 245.

beloved's personhood as expressed in their style, what has been called 'the singular manner of being that is the person herself' (*PP*, 397). When I promise myself to someone, writes Merleau-Ponty soon afterwards, I am aiming beyond qualities and body and time at the person, even if I could not love without them. Pascal is for all that remarkably insightful. For one thing, I cannot promise my future feelings, which may well pass away when the other changes or when I myself change (*PP*, 398; *PrP*, 26–7, 35–6). For another, what I believe to be essential to the other may be comparatively superficial features or roles on which I have become fixated due to my own history and which cannot get me to their personhood in the round. It *is* that I only love qualities or some incidental facets of their being. I return to myself in recognising that a false love has died, and that my life was mistaken when oriented around it (*PP*, 398–9).

In each original situation, I was motivated through and through by the depth of the feeling. My experience of the person mediated all of my relations with the world, 'and my life really was engaged in a form that, like a melody, demanded a certain continuation' (*PP*, 397). If the relationship is broken off by the other or destroyed by others again, my entire world can shrink or collapse, as illustrated by a young woman treated by the existential psychanalyst Ludwig Binswanger. On being forbidden to see her lover, she became an insomniac, found it difficult to swallow and finally became an aphonic, losing her voice. She had lost it twice in childhood after frights, but quickly recovered. No physiological source of the current aphonia can be found, and a doctrinaire Freudianism would seek an explanation in the oral stage of development. In early infancy the mouth is the primary organ of pleasure, as seen in suckling and in sucking the thumb. The passive phase carries into the more active enjoyment of the mouth in later life, as witnessed in chewing and kissing. When the patient was frightened or closed off from the activity of kissing she relapsed into the oral phase. For Binswanger, such an explanation assigns too much primacy to actual physical contact, forgetting that the mouth is intimately linked to communal existence through speech – it is the organ of coexistence par excellence. The patient's future was threatened in childhood by death, the violent cessation of coexistence. Later on happy coexistence was invested in her lover, and the prohibition symbolically reawakens the earlier threat of death and irremediable solitude and brings back the earlier aphonia. And if she finds it difficult to swallow, this is because swallowing symbolises the movement of existence in which we assimilate events that we have undergone and move beyond them. Her swallowing problem symbolises her refusal to accept and assimilate the prohibition, with this refusal having at the same time accentuated her peculiar sensitivity of throat and mouth.[19]

Both approaches are correct in denying that the woman is putting on a show for effect. She is not like the politician shaking hands with a train conductor to look like a man of the people, or the friend refusing to speak to me because he feels insulted. Only someone able to speak can choose silence. If Binswanger transcends orthodox Freudianism, however, he lays too much weight on the childhood threats of death and solitude. He is not as sensitive as he typically is to the patient's entire being in the world. Some events that befall us do not just close off a particular possibility; as we have seen, they can radically change and even close down our whole world. For Merleau-Ponty, the current aphonia cannot be reduced to the outer indication or symbolisation of a past and inner state. It is not a sign that only conveys significance externally, like stripes on a sleeve an officer's rank. It is right to see the swallowing difficulty as directly expressing the rejection of the prohibition, but the aphonia expresses it no less directly, and along with it a loveless and grief-laden future. The prohibition is not just the threat of death and total solitude, but the actual interdiction of a joyful, vibrant and cherished coexistence. A life of great emotional and sexual intimacy has been closed off as actuality and possibility, and aphonia is the extreme exhibition of this unhappy situation (*PP*, 163–4).

To the extent that it takes bodily expressions as mere indications of conscious or affective states that are not themselves inhabited by these states, existential psychoanalysis slides towards a spiritualism that passes over our integrally psychosomatic being in the world. But this does not mean that the lived body should be taken as the transparent envelope of spirit (*PP*, 163–4). The young woman's situation is ambiguous and does not exclude the possibility of a choice at the outset. She *may* have chosen silence, for once the tie with her lover was broken familial coexistence would have appeared to her as pale and formulaic, and even as a cruel parody or mockery of the exhilarating intimacy denied to her. If she deliberately refused such coexistence she would have cast herself into a situation that resembles aphonia closely. This would have been a variant of Sartrean bad faith, the psychological hypocrisy of hiding powers we know we still possess.[20] Yet the choice to mime some attitude or affect can actually throw us into it. On going to bed, we consciously put ourselves in the position of the sleeper, turning on our sides, pulling up our knees and breathing slowly. Once sleep comes to us, the will fades away

[19] Binswanger 1935, 113 ff.   [20] Sartre 1958, 48–54.

and the mime becomes the reality. A refusal to speak may have initiated the onset of aphonia, though the choice would have become irrelevant as soon as the latter commenced, since the young woman could not then will herself out of it. Psychological hypocrisy can develop into a metaphysical hypocrisy in which the deceiver is entrapped by the deception. What was a facade can become genuinely expressive of someone's existence (*PP*, 164–5, 166–7). One way or another, the woman only regained her speech when she was treated *and* permitted to meet her lover again. With the recovery of the longed-for coexistence, earlier regions of comportment were reactivated. The overall movement of projective existence could resume like a river that has thawed (*PP*, 164–6, 168).

A centred existence is not so easily restored when separation is permanent, or when someone habitually frames scenarios that are only remotely realisable or not at all. The intentionalities of such a person's productive imagination are affectively and effectively sundered from others and milieus that might moderate them and with which they could be realised. In discussing the 'Bovary Syndrome', Merleau-Ponty draws on Jules de Gaultier's incisive portrayal of that pathologically dissatisfied and disappointed consciousness for whom 'real life' is always happening somewhere else, and for whom the here and now is so dreary and sterile as to be rendered incapable of transformation. A disposition to idealise others in idealised relationships with oneself becomes the gravedigger of an existence projecting and pursuing live possibilities.[21] Extreme as it is, such a condition tells us something about our ordinarily affective and imaginative lives. An unexpected invitation to a gathering can be so appealing as to drain the present phenomenal field and locale of their force and vivacity. For me as for my interlocutor, the most attractive and enlivening landscape is soon to be somewhere else, and the only possibilities that are now salient in my perceptual field are those affording my journey to that event and place (*PP*, 299). Situations like this put into relief our lived time and personhood and sometimes our finitude and fragility, all topics for my concluding chapter.

---

[21] Gaultier 1902, 216 ff.

CHAPTER 9

Temporality, Subjectivity and Idealisation

9.1 Introduction

Though Merleau-Ponty pays far more attention to our lived spatiality of situation than to our lived time or temporality, he remarks that this last topic is not of lesser importance. It is necessary to analyse lived temporality without being governed by a pre-established understanding of time, and a phenomenological analysis when pursued to its conclusions will lead us to revise our conception of subjectivity. It will be shown that the conscious subject is temporally constituted through and through, and of inner necessity (*PP*, 432–3). At the outset of this chapter, I traverse Merleau-Ponty's criticisms of theories of time marked by objective thought, and turn to consider his preferred alternative, the formal account of immanently experienced time proffered by Husserl. The theory is highly abstractive, and with Heidegger's help we must also address the existential meaning of temporality, which in its optimal mode gives the subject a self-transformative orientation. But if the formal story leaves out the long-term future, the existential story assigns too little importance to the present. Both narratives neglect the temporality of one's body, which is towards the future within the present by virtue of its immemorial past.

The embodied and conscious subject presupposes its temporal constitution and is taken as having an early and confused self-awareness or 'tacit Cogito' running with a fundamental perceptual faith. Following on this one's self-certainty and world-certainty are coextensive in the expressed or 'spoken Cogito', and the awareness of living one's experiences inalienably shows that subjectivity is indeclinable. I go on to argue that Merleau-Ponty's embodied subject is fundamentally the person, or what he calls the concrete subject. Personhood embraces the reflective, pre-reflective and anonymous or sub-reflective facets of existence. Against dualism the concrete subject is integrated in both its character and development, with the operatively intentional body and act intentional consciousness or mind standing in an internal union of the founding and the emergently founded. In my closing section, I consider the objections that Merleau-Ponty regards the human existent as an unceasing project of appropriation – with others and things being at first the means to its ends – and that his idealised body is marked by ageist and ableist presuppositions. If these criticisms can only be met in part, their force is tempered by his emphasis on our finitude and fragility, on solidarity with others and on the limits of philosophical and phenomenological reflection for life and world.

9.2 On Immanent Temporal Awareness

In our spoken or habitual speech, we say that time flows or passes by, employing the metaphor of a fluid and flowing substance like a river of water. When this Heraclitean metaphor is given a more determined content, it is claimed that the flow is made up of a succession of 'nows', each of them being a punctual present. But such time is not a stream of itself, for we have surreptitiously introduced a *view* upon time, an observer seeing it as if from a riverbank or floating in the flow. Unlike a river's downward course, however, the experiential past does not drive the present into being, or the present the future. The latter is not prepared behind us but planned out in front of us, so the metaphor is confused. If time itself is a sheer succession of 'nows', moreover, only the current now will have any existence for me as a being that has its own awareness in that selfsame now, which is the plenitude of presence. The wooden table with my initials carved into it will not refer to the past, which is dead and gone. The theory of an atomistic present in itself entails a perceiver imprisoned in that present and destroys the very notion of time, of different nows and of succession. If I respond that a now is physiologically or psychologically preserved and can be reproduced or reawakened, this presupposes what it seeks to explain, a view of the past that would let me recognise the reawakened as a memory (*PP*, 433–7).

The foregoing view of time is a construct of objective thought, indebted to constituted time as understood through the metaphors of the flowing and the discrete. Although these spatialising metaphors are unavoidable, Bergson has shown an acute appreciation of their limitations, arguing that what we call 'time' is really experienced as continuous duration, involving internally interlinked moments as against externally juxtaposed pieces.[1] If he rightly stresses its essential continuity, however, his claim that we move

[1] Bergson 2001, 128–9, 132–3.

from past to present to future through imperceptible transitions confuses these dimensions. If consciousness is like a diluting liquid in which moments melt together, then we cannot get to know them in their multiplicity and their passing away (*PP*, 444, 543–4). We need an account more sensitive to metaphor in which the temporal 'stream' is experienced through the non-representational articulation of the dimensions, and this has been furnished by Husserl (*PP*, 239). As we have noted, the experience of a transcendent thing like a house presupposes a 'transition synthesis' letting the changing aspects of that object be experienced in an unbroken or sliding succession of appearances, a prerequisite of any synthesis of identification. The experience of a spatial object is necessarily of a unity in time that enjoys temporal extension in itself (*PCIT*, 24, 118). In the phenomenology of 'internal' or constituting time, we work back behind our naive intentional experiences of objects (granting that not all objects are perceivable spatially). First, there are the transcendent objects themselves in what we call the 'objective time' of clocks and chronographs, measured in seconds, minutes, hours and days and so forth. Second, there are these things as immanently experienced, particular durations and successions apprehended without being objectified as such. Third, there is the time-constituting flow of awareness, which itself appears in its flowing (*PCIT*, 77, 80, 393).

Husserl's transcendental account begins with the immanent experience and its contents. For Kant, we reproduce earlier moments of our objects in a synthesis of imagination, but this is to neglect the perception of these pasts. Temporal awareness is not a punctual or isolated present, but a 'living present' or field that embraces and articulates its object's temporal extension. When the current phase of the experience lapses into the past, a 'retention' or 'primary memory' apprehends this immediately becoming lapsed, constituting it as 'just-past'. It is the perception of an absence that was a presence, a holding and awareness of a present thus modified. Furthermore, each retention is of a present having its own retention, so a chain of these primary memories is carried in and behind the current phase of experience like the tail of a comet, running off into the depths of the past (*PCIT*, 30–2, 43). The retentional chain does double duty, holding the moments of the experienced transversely and the experience of it longitudinally, thus constituting the unity of the temporally extended experience itself.[2] Thanks to this articulating continuum of retentions we

---

[2] Substituting 'longitudinal' for 'horizontal'. Brough's rendering of *Längsintentionalität* as the latter captures Husserl's sense well, at the risk of confusing the horizontal and horizonal.

perceive something in its duration and succession 'all at once' without confusing its pasts with its present. If preceding moments were reproduced in their original and unmodified presence they would then be superimposed on the current experience. The seeing of something moving would be laden with visual after-images, and in playing the tenth note of a piano piece it would be heard with the preceding nine notes as if all the keys were struck together (*PCIT*, 13, 81–2, 85–7).

The present that comes to be retended is constituted by what Husserl calls the 'primal impression'. This is a direct and unmodified perceiving contemporaneous with the perceived, such as the sound heard when a key is struck. The primal impression of the 'now' is the 'source-point' of a continuum of retentions, most evidently when it is that now in which the transcendent thing first appears (*PCIT*, 30–2, 35–6). And because intentional awareness arcs beyond itself, the living present has a primary expectation or 'protention' constituting the 'just-about-to-be'. Protention is the expectation of the proximate future to arrive, coloured by context, memory and imagination as the expectation of what is about to arrive and the way it will arrive. There are always several protentions at work, since in hearing a melody I anticipate several notes ahead, and in reaching for the door I anticipate seeing the passage and then the garden. Each predelineating horizon is open to frustration, for the notes heard may not be those expected, or the passage or garden seen as expected because the door is jammed. We have a trail of retentions and a horizon of protentions, and once the melody finishes and the garden is seen we are aware of completion. Some future is still expected but no longer *this* one (*PCIT*, 54–5, 89, 118, 142).

If a punctual and isolated now is a fiction, the actually experienced now is not, though it only reaches its unthematic articulation or constitution in being contrastively mediated by the constituted and unthematic not-nows (*PCIT*, 30–2, 42, 90, 172). No protention is separated from primal impression and no primal impression is separated from retention. All function together as an integrally triadic structure constituting immanently experienced object and intending experience. In doing its longitudinal work, the structure is a time-constituting flow given to itself while never coming into direct view. In constituting the living present, it is at once the abiding and unchanging *flow* and *form* of structuring, the ceaseless and invariant mutation of protention into primal impression and of the latter into retention (with the just lapsed now constantly being added to the retentional trail and its predecessors pushed back). The form is 'absolute' as ultimate and immutable; the destruction of its structure would be that of experiential unities apprehending durations and successions and consequently of all experience. Yet in its primordial unity of structuring it is only metaphorically a flow, for its ceaseless mutation is not that of a thing. Only *things* flow and pass away in whole or in part (*PCIT*, 78–9, 87, 118). In what sense is this flow given to itself? The contention is that the longitudinal unity of a constituted, temporally extended experience is implicitly registered as it unfolds, which is not only to register its unbroken flow of modifications, its just-about-to-be *becoming* now *becoming* just-past as it intends its object, but also the unity of the longitudinally constituting flow in its modifying. The latter's structuring is not given as such, for the flow-awareness is not an act, not being intentionally directed to the flow as a second object. This would require another flow of objectifying awareness to be objectified in turn in an unending regress. It is not awareness *of* the flow, but the flow's internal and oblique self-manifestation (*PCIT*, 87–8, 123, 384–6, 393). The constituted experiential time of an act in its modifications and the constitutively self-given and modifying coincide like two sides of a single thing, inseparably united in one flow. For this deepest flow-awareness 'we lack all names'. We will always fall short in applying predicates of constituted time to what enables it (*PCIT*, 78–9, 87–8).

The absolutely constituting flow is a passive synthesis and takes away nothing from the being of the temporal objects constituted. The objects are intentionally rather than actually immanent, as the transcendent temporal things in their constitutively being experienced (*PCIT*, 24, 79, 95–6). And flow-awareness is a condition of constituting a subject that consciously owns its acts and that constitutes in turn. The intentional experiences must be longitudinally constituted and apprehended in their unbroken unity to be explicitly grasped as successively mine. Subjectivity can only take root within the flow, and any active phase in which I reflect must bear on a phase upon which I reflect, which before being reflected on has to include an implicit self-awareness. The phase in which I reflect cannot retroactively endow the prior phase it objectifies with such awareness; it must be there to be reflectively *made* explicit. A pre-reflective self-awareness is first constituted in the flow, longitudinally retended with its trail of pasts and able to become my thematic object. An implicit 'I think' accompanies its presentations as an extended pole of self-conscious experience and protentionally anticipates further presentations (*PCIT*, 122–3; *Ids2*, 119–20). In its constitutive role it is transcendentally but not ultimately absolute, having 'its primal source in what is ultimately and truly absolute' (*Ids1*, 193).

9.3 Existential and Embodied Temporality

In this phenomenology of temporality that moves decisively beyond a schema of act, interpretation and interpreted object, according to Merleau-Ponty, the operative and passive synthesis of time designates a problem that is clarified when I learn that the different temporal dimensions are accessed by me without my having to undertake the necessary synthesis. I am no more the author of my essentially temporal being than of my heartbeats. The structure of temporal constitution has already thrown me outside myself into the past and the future, though only through my constituted subjectivity can there be time *for* me (*PP*, 250, 441–2, 451, 527). The living present or 'field of presence' embraces an immediate past with its trail for reflective regard, and its constituted unities or temporal objects can later be reproduced by what we ordinarily call memory, recollection or 'secondary memory'. For its part, the protentional horizon of the living present gives me an immediate future of determined although open possibilities (*PCIT*, 47–9; *PP*, 446–8). And it is perfectly consonant with the 'I can' awareness to claim, as Gallagher does, that the double intentionality of protention (of anticipated and anticipating) in subjectivity involves an agential sense of what is about to happen, of what *I* am about to do or experience.[3]

An account looking like this one is briefly touched on by Merleau-Ponty, but only very broadly (*PP*, 440, 452, 454). This is to transgress the bare, formal account of time-constitution, to recognise that subjectivity is not enclosed within the founding time flow or within disengaged reflection 'because it takes up or lives time and merges with the cohesion of a life' (*PP*, 446). An explication of how we existentially take up or appropriate time must encompass the projects we formulate, decide upon and work towards. In turning to these Merleau-Ponty draws on Heidegger's idea of the ecstatic and primordial temporality that comprises the ultimately lived *meaning* of time and of being. In our temporalising or taking up of time, according to Heidegger, the interlinked 'ecstases' or standing-outs of the future, past and present have always already lifted us out *of* ourselves (albeit *for* ourselves) and do not arrive in succession. The future is not 'later' than the past or having-been, and the having-been is not 'earlier' than the present. In this movement that is definitive of our existence '[t]emporality temporalizes itself as a future which makes present in the process of having been' (*BT*, 401). My lived temporality is not implicitly understood (and is

---

[3] Gallagher 2005a, 193–5.

not to be explicitly understood) from the standpoint of a theoretically privileged present. Projecting this or that future is not so much what I do as my dynamic and definitive way of existing as an orientation towards action. This lies behind the epistemic subject's supposedly detached theoretical inspection of isolated, present-at-hand objects in a homogeneous clock time.

In Heidegger's existential analysis, Dasein is not towards a future to come as something later, for as projective it is *in* it. Because the future is real it exerts an attraction on me, pulling me out of myself towards what I am to be. Rather than *going* towards what is yet to be, I am ahead of myself, for I am *coming* towards what already exists efficaciously, for the sake of this virtual existence (*BT*, 372–3). In this light, the past as having been is not something earlier than the present. It is not lapsed, since it inhabits the present as the open yet finite range of possibilities that I have been thrown into by virtue of my birth, social situation and education and so forth. To project a particular possibility is to take up a past that remains real for the former's actualisation in the world. And it is from the future and the past apprehended in futural terms that the present is revealed or made present as the situation for taking up the ready-to-hand to realise the possibility, virtually existent and efficacious as it is. On this story the projection of an authentic future is an anticipatory coming towards my 'ownmost' being as self-transformative, not a passive, stagnant awaiting of more of the same. The past as authentically projected is not understood as the dead and gone or completely constraining, but as a reservoir of acquisitions for exploitation. It is a fertile soil to be reactivated, developed and repeated productively, to be reformed in being renewed. And in the light of these ecstases, the authentic present comes to awareness as the moment for insightful vision and decisive choice, for the gathering of oneself towards one's ownmost being in taking up a window of opportunity, as distinct from the bare perpetuation of habitual being and the distracted, dispersed pursuit of short-term attractions. In factical terms, inauthentic temporalising precedes the authentic variant, and the authentic existence that Dasein projects and works towards is not to be reached once and for all and settled into complacently. Authentic existence is a work in progress; self-transformation is the springboard for further such transformation, effected against the horizon of death as the near or far cessation of all of my possibilities (*BT*, 305–10, 373–80, 387–9).

The triadic and ecstatic structure of meaningful future, past and present in its authentic form reveals itself to Dasein as the structure of its care, of its caring about and taking care of itself, here of its ownmost existence. In projecting an authentic possibility, Dasein is committed in its entire being to what matters to it, affectively as much as cognitively and volitionally. It reckons with and appropriates time, taking it up towards its possibilities, and its anticipation would not be genuine if it did not take unexpected accidents in its stride, and if its resoluteness did not let it project another authentic possibility when this one is frustrated unavoidably (*BT*, 363–5, 374–82, 443). It goes without saying that none of this would be feasible for a disengaged cogitating subject. We saw that Merleau-Ponty takes up this conception of human existence as involving a fundamental function of projection or intentional arc in which it is ahead of itself. Ordinarily we reckon with the possible, and beneath all the meanings of the word sense 'we find the same fundamental notion of a being who is oriented or polarised towards what he is not' (*PP*, 454). My existence itself is an act or a doing, since 'an act, by definition, is the violent passage from what I have to what I aim at, or from what I am to what I have the intention of being' (*PP*, 401). And it is 'by resolutely taking up what I am by chance, by willing what I will, and by doing what I do, that I can go further' (*PP*, 483).

Indebted as he is to Heidegger's conception, Merleau-Ponty contends that the endeavour to undo the privileging of the present goes too far. The authentic future that is already given in advance through resolute projection would be impossible if the other two dimensions were to be demoted to consequences of this ecstatic future. For if this were the case I would cease to see time from the point of view of the present, and I could not then escape from inauthentic existence. I am always centred in the living present or field of presence, if not centred absolutely, and all the decisions that emerge from this 'now' have been placed in relation to my past to have their conscious motives, even if they open up the new in my life (*PP*, 443, 451). Heidegger himself claims that my awareness of having fallen short of what I could be is the 'voice of conscience' that motivates me to survey my whole existence and project authentically, an awareness lived in anxiety and guilt about my being as possibility, for which I alone am responsible (*BT*, 314–30, 373). The authentic future in which one is indeed ahead of oneself must be projected with and from this awareness in the present. In this self-transcending way of existing, the productive imagination is indispensable, as the representational power resting on and coloured by a groundwork of available acquisitions (*PP*, 126, 137). And any further acquisitions needed to reach the ultimate goal will be founded on actions that are immediate possibilities for me. When I embark on a founding action, my body schema will have projected its realisation, and this spatialising schema of posture and milieu is also temporalising. By means of this operative intentionality continuous with volition, my body too is ahead of itself, being in the 'there' and 'then' virtually:

> At each moment in a movement, the preceding instant is not forgotten, but rather is somehow fit into the present, and, in short, the present perception consists in taking up the series of previous positions that envelop each other by relying on the current position. But the immanent position is itself enveloped in the present, and through it so too are all of those positions that will occur throughout the movement. Each moment of the movement embraces its entire expanse and, in particular, its first moment or kinetic initiation inaugurates the link between a here and a there, between a now and a future that the other moments will be limited to developing. (*PP*, 141)

Here as ever it should be added that the succeeding moments only develop on the original motor plan when everything goes just as expected. Postural adjustments are only minor ones when 'my motor intentions, as they unfold, receive the responses they anticipate from the world' (*PP*, 261). In the face of unexpected obstacles, motor projections may be recalibrated extensively, to the extent of transposing skills, though in each and every plan of movement as a context-sensitive schematisation of skills '[t]he synthesis of time, like that of space, is always to be started over again' (*PP*, 141). Thanks to these motor projections, often aided and abetted by little reflections, as has been argued, I can explicitly plan (and virtually occupy) the far future without undue distraction. The founding tasks of the present and the proximate future do not flood my consciousness. It can be reiterated also that the skills learnt consciously are founded on simpler skills that were never acquired consciously, situating me in a bodily past opaque to reflective recuperation. This is not just my own past, since my early movements imitated those of others (*PP*, 362, 457).

Merleau-Ponty does not cease to emphasise that we must continually draw on this bodily 'past of all pasts' or immemorial 'past that has never been a present'. Lying at the origin of projective and volitional being, our individual life feeds on and cannot transcend this reservoir of capacities for enabling, conditioning and actualising our decisions (*PP*, 87, 252). Taken up in one's authentic as well as inauthentic projections, this past is in principle incapable of being held in a trail of retentions for recollection (even if it is renewed and reformed whenever one gains or improves on a skill). Retention of a content of which we are unconscious is impossible (*PCIT*, 123). We draw on a reworkable 'body memory', non-objifiable at its root yet implicated in the agential present, with every present of action and of anticipation having this past immanent within it (*PP*, 87, 366–7, 444). For Edward Casey, the habitual body is the only plausible bearer of this past in its entirety (though not even then, since the body can and does lose skills). And if one's so-called body memory precedes the episodic kind, one's habitualities soon included sedimented thoughts and convictions as well as skills and affects, each a moment of one's socio-cultural nature and history. The thoughts and convictions were *once* present and then forgotten, and it is not the case that all were sedimented so thoroughly as to lie beneath the reach of recollection. Yet none can be recollected transparently. If one always transforms a conscious past in the process of taking it up there is no way of recovering it as it was, even if one has only altered its significance slightly (*PP*, 131–3, 482).[4]

To do justice to the situated character of temporality, according to Merleau-Ponty, we must also acknowledge that the time of our past and living present and long-term projects is intertwined with the 'natural' or 'generalised' time of the world and of our biological functions (*PP*, 86, 478–9). As the time of day and night or light and darkness (and for that matter of the seasons), this time is natural in so far as it is experienced as cyclical and as indifferent to us, and generalised in so far as it is common to the entire human community and all terrestrial species, albeit moderated differently by these organic and lived temporalities. It is always around us and at the margins of our experience. On the horizon of my work in the living present are the morning gone by, the afternoon passing away and the evening soon to arrive. When I am not thinking about the latter and what it will entail it is still 'there', like the back of the house whose front I am currently painting. Because this cycle of days and nights and seasons is experienced as unceasing, it motivates the illusory conception of an unending and unchanging time (*PP*, 362, 438, 447). By extension, it facilitates the ideas of an objective clock time and of fixed calendric dates. Through my circadian rhythms and other bodily processes I am fitted into this natural time, though it cannot be a sheer succession of natural objects or events unmarked by subjectivity (*PP*, 86, 479). The day for completing an urgent task will always be shorter, and the day before meeting a loved one longer. Within limits, however, I can appropriate and extend a day or night and month or year with shutters or artificial lighting.[5]

9.4 Tacit and Spoken Cogito and Perceptual Faith

In our untroubled perceptual involvements, according to Merleau-Ponty, we do not think the object and neither do we think of ourselves thinking it. Instead, 'we merge with this body that is better informed than we are about

---

[4] Casey 1984, 291–3. [5] On a phenomenology of natural time, see Ciavatta 2017, 163–7, 171–6.

the world, about motives, and about the means available for accomplishing the synthesis' (*PP*, 248).[6] He adds that I live the unity of the subject and the intersensory unity of the thing without focussing on them intellectually. Yet he criticises Bergson's distinction between what we think about in reflection and what we immediately live through in inner and undivided experience, the latter taken as a 'fundamental self' that is confused, ever-changing and inexpressible.[7] If there were such immediate inner experience it would not just be incommunicable but meaningless. The awareness of my gesture would be an ineffable quality that could never tell me anything about the movement (*PP*, 543). We must find instead a 'tacit *Cogito*' or existential presence of self to self that conditions language, but which is not an inarticulate hold on the world 'like that of the child's upon his first breath, or of the man who is about to drown and who frantically struggles back toward life'. It cannot be thought but only revealed, and only knows itself in limit situations 'in which it is threatened, such as in the fear of death or in the anxiety caused by another person's gaze upon me' (*PP*, 426).

For Merleau-Ponty, this fundamental consciousness is neither the thematisation nor the ignorance of the self. It not hidden from itself, in the sense that 'there is nothing in it that is not in some way announced to it' without having to know it explicitly (*PP*, 310). The only awareness withheld from it 'is objective thought, or the thetic consciousness of world and of itself' (*PP*, 427). To merge with one's body in perceiving is not to collapse into it as into a thing, but to have a pre-reflective and psychosomatic self-awareness in which there is an embodied someone who perceives, but in which empirical self and body 'are not immediately objects, and never fully become objects' (*PP*, 215). The point is that is this pre-reflective and unthematic self-awareness does not distinguish the psychic and the somatic, which can only be done from an objectifying and theorising standpoint. This 'silent consciousness' only apprehends itself as an 'I think in general' in the face of a confused world 'to be thought'. All knowledge is founded on this original awareness, though 'it is also true that this first perspective waits to be reconquered, fixed and made explicit through perceptual exploration and through speech' (*PP*, 426).

On this narrative, Descartes is already aiming at the tacit Cogito through his spoken Cogito, crossing the distance between the reflective self who is analysing perception and the pre-reflective self who is actually perceiving. The real significance of the Cartesian Cogito is that it observes 'this *fact* of reflection that simultaneously overcomes and maintains the

---

[6] Translation emended.   [7] Bergson 2001, 128–9.

opacity of perception' (*PP*, 45). But because he is not attentive enough to his situation, Descartes does not mention the constitutive role of language, a condition of his communicable Cogito. Forgetting that expressions efface themselves in their use, he passes over the thickness of the cultural acquisitions between his own existence – which he has in sight at the outset – and the most austere and impersonal of truths about this existence. He has the spoken certainty that he is without the speaking elaboration of what he is, an embodied structure of nature and history with an opaque past and an open future. The coincidence with myself that is expressively accomplished in the Cogito is an intended and presumptive coincidence, never a real one. Even the self who reflectively thinks of its thought is not the self who had that thought (*PP*, 360, 422–4). Yet this is not quite fair to Descartes, who never claims I can plumb the depths of my being or make all my ideas of myself clear and distinct. It is also to be wondered how the tacit Cogito so insistently distinguished from Bergson's fundamental self can enjoy an expressible hold on itself and on the world without already being marked by language.

As noted in the last chapter, Merleau-Ponty claims that a thought cannot exist outside the constraints of communication, for it 'would fall into the unconscious the moment it appears, which amounts to saying that it would not even exist for itself' (*PP*, 183). In the same vein, 'the subject gives itself emblems of itself in succession and in the multiplicity'. Were this not the case 'it would be like an inarticulate cry and would not even reach self-consciousness' (*PP*, 450–1). But with his tacit Cogito he is positing a pre-linguistic awareness of self and world, a form of thought that is not altogether devoid of articulation and yet somehow prior to expression. He seeks to resolve the discrepancy in his late work when he states that no pre-reflective contact of self with self is possible outside language, and that the world of silence has pre-linguistic significations that are never positive for the perceiver (*VI*, 170–1). The second claim is not entirely persuasive, however, for the earliest contact of self with self could hardly fail to take advantage of a more primitive awareness of exposure *here* to worldly exigencies and the doings of others *there* that limit situations come to accentuate. In its most developed form, this earlier and more primitive awareness may be read as one's awareness of efficacy here as distinct from there, or to put it another way as the sense of ownness that will be subsumed in the linguistically mediated self-awareness constitutive of subjectivity proper. In this light, we can agree that the Cogito 'is only a *Cogito* when it has expressed itself' (*PP*, 426). There is no mute Cogito, but the first and admittedly expressive 'I think' would still be impossible on foot of an utterly confused hold on the world.[8]

Merleau-Ponty is on much more accessible ground when he asserts that the consciousness of the world is not founded on self-consciousness because they are contemporaneous. Descartes does not appreciate that the certainty of his spoken and written Cogito – entailing a thought separation from the world – and the certainty of the world as a spectacle set against this Cogito are strictly bilateral (*PP*, lxxiii, 311). Though we must maintain the distinction between seeing and thinking that we see, if I think that I see an ashtray there as an item in the world, then in the actual course of events I cannot repress the affirmation that there *is* an ashtray there. In the perceptual act of seeing that gives the word its full sense, 'there can be no question of separating the act itself and the term upon which it bears' (*PP*, 393). Cartesian doubt about perception is ultimately untenable, for if I am really uncertain of seeing something, then my thought of seeing it has not been adequately motivated in the first instance. When I take my idea as that of a mere *impression* of seeing, I have already compared it with cases 'of authentic or actual vision which the thought that one is seeing resembles, and in which the certainty of the thing was then included' (*PP*, 394). This is to anticipate Wittgenstein's argument from the counterfeit case; I cannot doubt that something is genuine unless I know what it is for it to be genuine. All doubts presuppose certainties as the hinges upon which they turn.[9] And while I am right in some situations to doubt that I am seeing as well as what I am seeing, I still doubt inside the certainty of the world. The belief that comprises the natural attitude is an 'originary opinion' (*Urdoxa*) or 'originary faith' (*Urglaube*) in being both original and fundamental (*Ids1*, 252; *PP*, 417). The world's being is not first and last what I think but what I live and communicate with unquestionably, and I am bound to it as to my very homeland (*CES*, 142–3; *PP*, lxxx, lxxvii, 336).

Originary faith is from the outset a 'perceptual faith' (*foi perceptive*) in a milieu of things attractive and repulsive. It is enriched when one apprehends multiple perspectives on a common world, and endures beneath the distanciation following on a linguistically as well as temporally and somatically articulated flow of awareness, in which subjectivity, intersubjectivity and world come to explicit presence (*Ids2*, 300–2; *PP*, lxxxiv, 371, 379, 427–8).

---

[8] On this view, the infant's confused hold upon herself and upon the world (*PP*, 427) does not exclude a comparatively clear distinction *between* the two. A being that cannot yet differentiate body from mind or even the doings of others from natural events may still distinguish between herself here and what threatens and impinges on her from there. See also Baldwin 2019, 29–30.

[9] Wittgenstein 1974, 2e, 7e, 39e. See also *PP*, lxxx.

We saw that every project of embodied awareness is not *at* but *in* the world, presupposing a being involved in it and a working through it, and Merleau-Ponty adds that the world is subjective in the sense that 'its texture and its articulations are sketched out by the subject's movement of transcendence', where transcendence 'is the name we shall give to this movement by which existence takes up for itself and transforms a *de facto* situation'. The world is before us as the means for realising some project of the intentional arc, and behind us 'as the cradle of all significations, as the sense of all senses, and as the ground of all thoughts . . . the primordial unity of all our experiences on the horizon of our life' (*PP*, 173, 454). But this does not quite bring out the ongoing *interweaving* of embodied awareness and world making perceptual faith so unthematically ubiquitous.

Here the phenomenal body and body schema make their pre-reflective and sub-reflective contribution. Returning to the Husserl who has entered the hall of the waxwork museum, we recall that he thinks he sees a woman descending the staircase and smiling at him. What is initially seen in focal terms motivates this conclusion; the seeming face and eyes directed towards him, the out-stepped foot and the hand on the banister rail. The figure seems dynamically synchronised with affordances, as Husserl was with the doors, as he is with the floor and as he will be in ascending the stairs. After the deception is revealed, he can anticipate both passing the mannequin and pausing to better admire the ingenuity of the culprits. Nothing else was strange apart from the wax figure; nothing else in the world was doubted. Ordinarily we see others literally geared into the world, as are we who *feel* ourselves at one with it and whose ongoing and prospective world-certainty is shown in the pursuit of optimal holds. The embodied subject does sketch out the texture and articulations of the world, but only to the extent that the world facilitates or lends itself to these sketches. Every appropriation of things is centrifugal and centripetal; it is and must be an accommodation to them (*PP*, 452–4, 463–4). The schematised and schematising body establishes this pre-predicative unity of life and world before or beneath epistemic perception, supplying the first text that knowledge seeks to make precise (*PP*, lxxxii). The real 'is a tightly woven fabric', my body 'is the common texture of all objects', and in the world it is 'the general instrument of my [praktognosic] "understanding"' (*PP*, lxxiv, 244). Beneath the Cartesian separation of subject and object, the perceived 'remains, despite all critical training, beneath the level of doubt and demonstration' (*PP*, 358–9).[10] We do progress

---

[10] For Merleau-Ponty, this also holds with hallucination (as distinct from misrecognition). His account of hallucination is conjunctivist in that, like veridical perception and misrecognition, it

beyond originary faith in the philosophical recognition of such faith as the foundation of knowledge (*PP*, 360). Yet it is never a provisional form of knowledge to be replaced by something deeper (*PP*, 86, 224, 417).

9.5   The Concrete Subject and Original Union

For Merleau-Ponty, as we have seen, the world that first arranges itself around me in concert with my activities will begin to exist *for* me, even when I am not the author of my experiences. There is someone who perceives and who in some episodes explicitly recognises perceptual fulfilment, or the harmony between what is intended or evoked and what is directly presented (*PP*, lxxii, 23, 224). So far as I am present to myself in experiencing anything my subjectivity is indeclinable; it cannot be disowned because it is inalienable. I am the one who has to live through these acts first-hand, and here again – and here alone – is the living truth of solipsism (*PP*, 340, 374, 422, 450). Outside the living present or field of presence, however, the unbroken unity of awareness – and specifically of egoic awareness – is never actually given from start to finish. Neither my birth nor my death can ever be experiences for me; to imagine them as such is to imagine my pre-existing my birth and surviving my death, and thus to occlude their anonymity. Nor can I exclude interruptions of my reflective or pre-reflective awareness. The unity of the conscious subject through life is presumptive because it is never given as real, though as anticipated and attributed retroactively it lies on the horizon of experience (*PP*, 223–4, 228, 382).

Interdependent with this presumptive unity is my understanding of myself, or my intellectual, imaginative and affective apprehension of who and what I am, of my past and of my possible and likely future or futures. As Merleau-Ponty has suggested, my self-coincidence in the spoken Cogito is itself presumptive. When I explicitly find myself reflecting on an act, I am not accessing all the motivations that have contributed to it (*PP*, 247–8, 360, 426). Given the inevitable colouring of an already perspectival memory by imagination and the acquisitions of later life, my present

does not throw the existence of the wider world into doubt. It is disjunctivist – as Romdenh-Romluc has shown – in that hallucinations do not have some highest common factor that they share with genuine perceptions. When we look at the hallucinations that people actually have, we find that they do not possess the inexhaustibility of real things and people. They cannot appear as intentional objects summoning further experiences that will achieve an optimal hold on them through the exercise of motor skills. In being experienced as private spectacles, they also lack the 'publicness' of real objects, actually or possibly present to others from their perspectives (*PP*, 354–60). They demand a different phenomenology to that of genuine perceptions. Romdenh-Romluc 2007, 79–90.

interpretation of my past life will always be something of an arbitrary reconstruction. Yet as a human I am prey to objective thought as presentism, the conceit that the present is *always* the privileged locus in terms of which our past life is explainable, its events being the terms of an identifiable equation. Thus I tell myself that the happiness and confidence I enjoyed from early childhood into adulthood is explained by the assurance of home life and the parental milieu. This reading is bound up with my current faith in psychoanalysis, and tomorrow I might well explain my past quite differently, foregrounding and configuring other events in another equation. This is why I cannot silence the protest made by the past against any overarching account of its significance or downplaying of its vitality when it was actually lived (*PP*, 361–2). But none of this stops Merleau-Ponty from finding a unity in one's life:

> One day, and indeed once and for all, something was set in motion that, even during sleep, can no longer cease seeing or not seeing, sensing or not sensing, suffering or being happy, thinking or resting, in a word, that can no longer cease 'having it out' with the world . . . [t]here was henceforth a new 'milieu' and the world received a new layer of signification. In the household in which a new child is born, all objects change their sense, they begin to anticipate from this child some still indeterminate treatment . . . a new history, whether it be brief or long, has just been established, and a new register is open . . . even as a thinking subject I am still this first perception, I am the continuation of the same life it inaugurated . . . I am not a series of psychical acts, nor for that matter a central I who gathers them together in a synthetic unity, but rather a single experience inseparable from itself, a single 'cohesion of life', a single temporality that makes itself explicit from its birth and confirms this birth in each present. (*PP*, 429–30)

It is my fate once born to be given to myself as something to be understood, while recognising that I am never at one with my existence (*PP*, 362). But if I am never laid out before myself in being confronted with the present, what makes up the cohesion of my life? The answer lies in my historical thickness (*PP*, 247–8). Were it possible to uncover all the presuppositions contributing to my perceptions and reflections, I could access 'an entire "sedimented history" that does not merely concern the *genesis* of my thought, but that determines its *sense*' (*PP*, 416). All previous events have left their mark to a greater or lesser extent, including traumas and acts of learning that have been organically repressed. As already argued, my skills and socio-cultural milieu opened up a certain world of possibilities and were sedimented with convictions and affects, many anonymous and functioning unthinkingly (*PP*, 85–6, 131–2, 196–7). Some of these acquisitions are exhibited as the expressions of my style. On my view, the single (and stylised) cohesion of life to which Merleau-Ponty refers is in effect that of my personhood, my unity of attitudes, inclinations and manners of meeting and creating situations in which my sedimented inheritances and actions and passions remain efficacious without determining my future life.

On this dispositional model, my personhood embraces what is reflective, pre-reflective and sub-reflective (*PP*, 86–7). Though I may be badly wrong about myself, my ignorance and self-deception are part of who I am. Even the anonymous facets of life are not impersonal, comprising the equiprimordial generality of the biological and socio-cultural as instantiated singularly. I am anonymous in existing as an absolute generality and an absolute individuality, and my being in the world 'is the concrete bearer of this double anonymity' (*PP*, 474). Generality and individuality are not two conceptions of subjectivity, 'but two moments of a single structure that is the concrete subject' (*PP*, 477). But it is important to reiterate that the sedimented is not completely constraining. I have referred to my way of creating situations, and for Merleau-Ponty, '[t]he structure "world", with its double moment of sedimentation and spontaneity, is at the centre of consciousness' (*PP*, 132). I am not a fixed and windowless monad or perspective 'since I am not attached to any particular one and since I can change my point of view' (*PP*, 429). A change in correlative personhood and world may be radical, though instantaneous conversions are rare, and a chosen project of self-transformation is usually long and laborious, depending on a resolve that invariably needs its own nurturing. If my freedom of action and intention can commit me to a new and different direction, it 'does not have the power to turn me immediately into what I decide to be' (*PP*, 473).

In asserting this, Merleau-Ponty is stressing just how difficult it is to break out of one's habitual practices and inclinations, which is why he contests the claim that those suffering from an inferiority complex continually choose themselves as 'base' or 'humiliated' rather than 'great' or 'noble'. For Sartre, they do not desire the unhappiness or despair, but they do complacently choose to remain in a situation in which they are prey to it, perpetuating the gap between the ends that are willed and the ends actually obtained. Appeals to motivations that lock them into the complex are instances of bad faith, since they have ultimately chosen to be their own tormentors.[11] Merleau-Ponty agrees that we have the power of refusing and

---

[11] Sartre 1958, 472–4.

breaking out of such a way of existing, but holds that once an attitude has been inhabited for long enough it assumes a certain weight without having to be a destiny. It is improbable that after twenty years I will escape a complex that has become the very atmosphere of my present, and the probability of the situation continuing provides a phenomenological foundation for statistical thought, whatever the limits of the latter. More intuitively, it warrants the contention that my field of freedom includes proximate possibilities and far more distant ones. Should I ever come to work my way out of the complex, furthermore, the cohesion of life will not be compromised, for the complex will remain just that past against which I exerted myself, and which has been repudiated without being fully annulled (*PP*, 462, 466–7, 473, 481). As a work in progress, an authentic way of being is never immune to regression.

I have taken Merleau-Ponty's concrete subject as the person, and in referring to the cohesion of my life he is insistent that I only belong to myself as an embodied existent oriented towards this or that future in the world, situated psychosomatically in this realm of near and remote possibilities. The concrete subject with its act intentionalities 'only achieves its ipseity by actually being a body and by entering into this world through this body' (*PP*, 430–1). Merleau-Ponty is in fact careful to praise Descartes when the latter writes to Elizabeth that the union of soul and body is lived and cannot be known by the understanding.[12] We are reflecting on something that reflection cannot reach in fact or in principle (*PP*, 44, 205). In this context, Carman maintains that the mind-body problem is an abstract metaphysical one that has no bearing on our experience of ourselves. Existential phenomenology describes our ordinary apprehension of ourselves and of our place in the world, not telling us whether the subject is two substances or one, or how much of the animal and its milieu serves as the vehicle or substratum of cognitive processes.[13] Yet it seems to me that Merleau-Ponty's account bears on the problem, however abstract and recalcitrant to reflection it might be. Everything in his transcendental analyses and explications of concrete essences strains against a substance dualism and a bald property dualism. His phenomenology of lived existence points towards a multi-aspect monism in which mind and body are both interdependent and intercoloured, the impure terms of a substantial union (*PP*, 44, 90–1, 205). And the integral union of these terms is not that of a fixed and closed-off totality. Worldly and relational properties are indispensable for having and sustaining the open-ended and projective self,

[12] Descartes 1984d, 227.   [13] Carman 2020, 220.

and a transcendental phenomenology can run with a phenomenological ontology that eschews extravagant or free-floating speculation by definition.

Merleau-Ponty does I think take the vehicle of cognitive processes to be the organism as a whole with its milieu, holding that we are always geared into the latter and that nothing in our bodily organisation is contingent with regard to our rationality (*PP*, 173–4). And if we read his big book together with *The Structure of Behaviour*, we can find at least the rudiments of an ontological account in which the person is integrally unified in its very process of development. The concrete subject that I am is inseparable from this particular body and world or from '[t]he ontological world and body that we uncover at the core of the subject' (*PP*, 431). The human existent is not a rational animal, that is, not an indifferent body sur-mounted by a mind that unfolds fortuitously over its infrastructure. In its development the body is already oriented towards stages beyond itself, the original union of body and conscious awareness being of the humanly founding and founded. We need only recall the necessities of our having and using opposed fingers and thumbs and of adopting the upright posture. Our somatic processes do not unfold autonomously and are integrated into cycles of more extensive action in which the later stages alter and give new significations to the steps facilitating them (*SB*, 180–1, 184; *PP*, 173–4). It has been contended that the appearance of reason modifies our instincts, that there is no experience without speech and that nothing is lived through purely (*SB*, 181; *PP*, 353).

On such an ontological story the advent of 'mind' entails a real trans-formation of our existence. It does not at first employ the body but realises itself through it, and brings it far beyond its original spatiality by situating it in novel virtualities, in imagined and cognised landscapes that might be realised (*SB*, 208–9; *PP*, 111, 115, 132). Merleau-Ponty is far from advocating a discrete or 'layer-cake' account of the somatic and conscious (which the imagery of sedimentation all too easily suggests), and his descriptions of the founding and founded constitute an emergentist view of cognitive awareness.[14] It does not emerge from the *Körper* of physics, but from a lived existent whose instinctual strivings are succeeded by interested

---

[14] Jack Reynolds has observed that Merleau-Ponty's thought is in alignment with three key features of emergentism, namely novelty, unpredictability and the efficacy of what is emergent. In combination with his reworking of transcendental philosophy and phenomenology, his emergentism points to a more nuanced relationship between phenomenology and naturalism, and specifically to a revised and expanded conception of science and of nature that can accommodate those phenomena recalcitrant to scientific naturalism. See Jack Reynolds 2019, 12, 16–18.

explorations, with organic repression and language allowing for the distanciation in reflecting, willing and planning (*PP*, 31–3, 89, 139, 353). Any attempt to marry a causal object in itself to a mind existing for itself is doomed. There is not 'a single bodily function that is strictly independent of existential structures, and, reciprocally, not a single "spiritual" act that does not rest upon a bodily infrastructure' (*PP*, 455). We can concede that bodily existence is the mere sketch of a genuine presence in the world, while recognising that this creative and unpredictable presence cannot renounce the body it transcends (*PP*, 168, 174, 195, 307). There is no psychical act 'that has not found at least its germ or its general outline in physiological dispositions' (*PP*, 90). If this last claim seems exorbitant, Merleau-Ponty could again point to the hands with which we first took things apart and brought them together. He could add that no conscious achievement is entirely unmarked by our first and embodied experiences of suffering and of doing. The most rarefied scientific theory posits entities whose workings produce certain results, and it can only have these significations because we perceived and anticipated worldly events and the fulfilments of our own projects and those of others, and because we felt the effects of things and of our own efforts in our bodies. Only then could we appresent effects and efforts at a distance.

9.6 Appropriation, Idealisation and Radical Reflection

Science as an outgrowth and amplification of objective thought veers all too easily into scientism, and historically the latter has focussed on the upsides of technological advance, if not so much in our day. And one might wonder whether Merleau-Ponty addresses this focus in the course of his critique. It was noted in Chapter 3 that we encounter things in at least two ways, as useful and as fine-grained objects with distinctive perceptual styles. For the early Heidegger, the use-values are fundamental. In his account of the natural world, the wood is first and foremost a forest of timber, the mountain a quarry of rock and the river a power of water to be harnessed (*BT*, 100). Though Merleau-Ponty never refers to this view, his world for all its openness appears to be taken on occasion as a fund of resources for a self-transcending subject with an idealised readiness-of-hand. He states that, prior to all conscious projection, 'my first perception inaugurated an insatiable being who appropriates everything that it can encounter, to whom nothing can be purely and simply given because it inherited the world' (*PP*, 374). He adds that this existent 'carries in itself the plan of every possible being'. We strive for an optimal hold on what we engage with, and when the outcomes we aim at cannot be achieved with our natural means, we build instruments and in so doing project a cultural world around ourselves that drives back the natural world (*PP*, 25, 148). This raises the worry that each of us is regarded at root as an unceasing project of acquisitive appropriation. Others and things are the means for realising our projects before being anything else, redolent of Hobbesian and Nietzschean narratives if not necessarily as extreme. Furthermore, his embodied and appropriative subject moves its phenomenal body and never its objective one (*PP*, 108, 204–5), and is approximated to most closely by a young adult in the prime of health, strength and proficiency. Such an idealised body appears to be posited from both an ageist and an ableist perspective. It reads as if those who have developed other strategies of moving because of age or injury are only introduced to silhouette the paradigmatically normal and hence normative body.

My surmise is that the rather overwrought remarks about an insatiable being appropriating everything it can encounter hark back to a child whose enthusiasm and curiosity were boundless, and who as an adult still encounters the things of the world as wondrous and inspiring (*PP*, 45–6, 86, 361). On this interpretation, our dealings with others and things are not being thought in fundamentally instrumental terms, and would include acts of bringing lives and things to further expression through speaking speech or another art. Such a reading is consistent with Merleau-Ponty's attentiveness to the transcendence of others and their inimitable styles, and with his contention that the most authentic existence is lived in solidarity with them. He gives an example of farm hands whose labour is no less alienated than that of factory workers. The news that the latter have gone on strike for better wages crystallises the situation of the former, and they make common cause with their urban counterparts for the betterment of both (*PP*, 469–70). A second example is of a resistance fighter under torture, who refuses to betray his comrades because he still feels himself among them and committed to the common struggle, and because they expect such bravery. Freedom is never without its accomplices and its buttresses in intersubjective existence, though only heroes fully live out their relations with others and the world.[15] Each project is 'mine' as my decision and lived by me, though whether my responsiveness is sourced in oppressed people

[15] Merleau-Ponty is emphasising the authentic existence in which solicitude for others has precedence over individual self-realisation. Heidegger himself recognises that one can authentically care for and nurse others and even sacrifice one's life for them. In authentic solicitude, one will not step in ahead of them but free them up for their own possibilities (*BT*, 158–9, 344). Yet when such solicitude

around me or in a loved one before me, I cannot consistently will freedom without willing it for all (*PP*, 373, 479–81, 483).

In relation to the non-human world, however, it seems to me that Merleau-Ponty underplays the tension between the inexhaustible world that transcends us and the one that is useful to us. It is noted that some features of the world and things within the world present themselves outright as obstacles; this crag as insuperable and that road or subway door as frustratingly impassable (*PP*, 144, 464). In our successful projects, moreover, our freedom has sketched out general structures of the world but not everything about its figures, since all the things of the world are determinable indeterminacies that can never be fully determined. That I have a hold on something – and even an optimal hold – does not mean that this is ever complete, and my hold on the wider world around me is no more than a fleeting one (*PP*, 311, 426, 464). Consciousness as a project of the world is at once 'destined to a world that it neither encompasses nor possesses' (*PP*, lxxxii). Yet on closer examination, we find that Merleau-Ponty is focussing on our small-scale endeavours, whereas many large-scale human activities are not accommodations to other living beings and to the contours of the world and show little sensitivity to either. His embodied subject's gearing into things is chiefly into its implements, interposed between itself and the natural world. In employing these – and most notably its machines – the human species has cut deeply into and across that world by damming, diverting, excavating and processing. Yet the vast amplification of the body's power and reach through technology and the driving back (and exploitation and destruction) of flora and fauna and natural things are not of any obvious concern to Merleau-Ponty.

His body that fluidly fulfils its schematisations is without doubt an idealisation from an ageist standpoint, insightful though he is about the body schema and its motor predelineations. Even in the prime of life, as we have seen, everyday situations throw up obstacles demanding little reflections and objectifications of parts of the body. And as Sheena Hyland has argued, few are the days that are utterly free of aches and pains, however minor they may be.[16] As the years advance, little reflections become bigger and more frequent, such that the body always with me is much more present to me, and sometimes always to me. Merleau-Ponty does remark that our freedom 'weakens, without ever becoming zero, to the extent that

---

becomes a way of life self-realisation may not be in view at all. One might struggle to endure because everything is being lived for others after some disaster.

[16] Hyland 2012 passim.

the *tolerance* of the body and institutional givens of our life diminishes' (*PP*, 481). Yet he never thematises that period of life in which one's world of projects narrows down, and in which one's phenomenal field becomes less and less a transcendental field of possibilities. When strength and flexibility diminish, the 'I can' will become an 'I cannot', or an 'I can with difficulty'. Even when an older person's body *is* immediately available, he or she is more likely to ponder the long-term consequences of an action. It is not due to their bodies alone that the older tend to be more careful and hesitant (*Ids2*, 279). In defence of Merleau-Ponty, it should be added that idealisation is hard to avoid. Few of us would not wish to enjoy the health and vivacity associated with youth in combination with the hard-won wisdom associated with old age.

What Merleau-Ponty is highly attentive to is the sheer fragility of embodied existence. As an embodied perceiver I am a surface in constant contact with a world impinging on me. When I am not shut away and in a dreamless sleep, the world 'ceaselessly bombards and besieges subjectivity just as waves surround a shipwreck on the beach' (*PP*, 215). Things break in and disturb us and sometimes damage or destroy us. The great sin of intellectualism is to zoom in on a universal synthesising consciousness, neglecting the contingency in the constitution of sense and meaning by way of a lived, immanently organised body. The latter is 'this meaningful core that behaves as a general function and that nevertheless exists and that is susceptible to illness' (*PP*, 148). Only by withdrawing abstractively into our thinking natures could we have posited a foundational and invulnerable subjectivity. Body and world are interdependent, and our human world always has an air of fragility about it (*PP*, lxxiii, lxxvi, 307). As a consequence of illness or disease, the body can become so present as to drown out everything else, projective perception receding so thoroughly that 'bodily events become the events of the day' (*PP*, 87). Heidegger stresses our anxiety in the face of being-towards-death as the termination of all our possibilities, whereas Merleau-Ponty's emphasis is on our constantly being-exposed to damage and the irrevocable diminution or contraction of these possibilities.[17]

Though he displays a keen sense of the body's fragility, Merleau-Ponty does not seem to refer to the comparative character of health. Richard Shusterman has contended that he works with a simple and indeed extreme polarity between the normal and pathological. Even when free of aches and

---

[17] For two remarkable studies of the world-diminishing and world-destroying effects of pain and illness, see Scarry 1985 and Carel 2018.

pains, fully functional people still have mild incapacities and malfunctions that get in the way of greater success or ease or grace. It is implied that if we do not have the impairments of Schneider or of other neurologically damaged individuals, then our performances will be accurate and our bodies functional to a miraculous extent.[18] Merleau-Ponty *need* not imply this but undoubtedly does in places (*PP*, 108, 204–5). Yet he allows that one may be clumsy and nervous rather than calm and dexterous in one's actions. The unfolding motor intentions that receive the responses they anticipate from the world may not be those of an expert and graceful agent (*PP*, 261, 455). One may even anticipate making many moves (some of them compensatory) to reach one's goals. This being said, he writes from an overtly ableist perspective in which bodily impairments are introduced to silhouette normal bodies. The emphasis is on loss; the consciousness of the injured person 'can be seen attempting to maintain its superstructures even though their foundation has collapsed' (*PP*, 139). His ableism is moderated, however, when he stresses that every new procedure developed by someone who has been injured possesses its own concrete essence and internal coherence (*PP*, 110, 127–8). He would be open, furthermore, to the difference between bodily impairments and disabilities (where the latter are socio-cultural categories imposed from without). We are often inattentive to Sartre's distinction between having some condition and the way it is taken up, in that we perceive reactively and project our own credulous perspectives into the awareness of someone whom we classify as disabled.[19] With no little naivety '[w]e are often amazed that the disabled person or the person suffering from a disease can bear their situation' (*PP*, 458).

Joel Michael Reynolds has made a strong case that Merleau-Ponty is here undermining the 'ableist conflation' that he perpetuates elsewhere, the conflation of disability with pain and suffering and disadvantage.[20] It is perpetuated most noticeably in his treatment of blindness. He only writes of the blind man's cane (stereotypically understood as an extrinsic sign of disability), though some who are blind have long achieved echolocation through mouth-clicks and footsteps. He also assumes that with eyes closed one can incorporate a cane into one's schema *as* the blind person does, learning which objects or within or beyond reach with it (*PP*, 144). This is to forget that blindness is a radical reconfiguration of existence. Nor does he entertain the possibility that it can progress from a privation or something 'gone wrong' to a positive and richer form of life.[21] The blind

---

[18] Shusterman 2005, 166.   [19] Sartre 1958, 328, 337.   [20] J. M. Reynolds 2017, 421–2.
[21] Ibid., 423–5.

person's efforts are described as nothing more than attempts to preserve his or her earlier way of being (*PP*, 81). John Hull has set out a different itinerary towards a new life. Living through late-onset blindness, he came to realise that alternative sources of (praktognosic) knowledge compensate, that one's whole body undergoes a profound transformation in relation to the world, and that the condition is ultimately a world-creating one.[22]

On blindness, Merleau-Ponty is strangely inattentive to his idea of a concrete essence as a complete form of existence. But this is not so very strange. He is invariably drawn to lives or life-stages of conspicuous energy or creativity, like those of the dancer or footballer, the inquisitive child or ardent lover, the climber or great artist. However, other lives can come to clearer presence with the help of insights he has not exploited sufficiently. If we make more of his claim that every concrete essence demands a genetic phenomenology, and more of the way that the anosognosic has positively reconfigured her body schema and world (*PP*, 82–3, 102, 127–8), we can more readily appreciate that John Hull and others are no longer trying to maintain superstructures when their foundations have collapsed. They have built up new foundations and have articulated the superstructures otherwise. Yet Merleau-Ponty could hardly demur, having situated himself within an avowedly revisable approach. Phenomenology is perpetually starting over with unforeseeable results, and 'to the very extent that it remains loyal to its intention, it will never know just where it is going' (*PP*, lxxxv). As intentional analysis of the world, it is the correlative and unending task of bringing to awareness our pre-scientific life, without which our scientific activities cannot make proper sense. We cease to be naively complicit with the world to show the motivations carrying us into it and horizons articulating it, though again the demand that everything be made explicit is absurd, since it would collapse the world into consciousness (*PP*, 59, 61).

Because phenomenology is situated within history like all philosophy, it must draw upon the already constituted world and constituted reason. If it

---

[22] Hull 1997, xii, quoted in J. M. Reynolds 2017, 425. For all of his missteps on blindness, according to Reynolds, Merleau-Ponty's overall project – with his rethinking of oppositions such as nature and history – provides a fertile resource for a new and non-normate phenomenology of world-creating bodies (Ibid., 427). Creation is of course harder when voice, hearing and most forms of motility are destroyed. Richard Zaner provides illuminating and moving treatments of the Jean-Dominique Bauby case as recounted by the latter in *The Diving Bell and the Butterfly* and of the fictional Joe Bonham case as composed by Dalton Trumbo in *Johnny Got His Gun*. He explicates the communication the patients eventually establish with those receptive to their efforts, drawing on Marcel and Alfred Schutz among others. Each of the latter found all subsequent contact on the bond of mother and child. See Zaner 2003 passim.

is to be properly critical, according to Merleau-Ponty, it has to silhouette itself, effecting a 'radical reflection' on its practice and on the inherent shortcomings of its method. It has to undertake a phenomenology of phenomenology that goes from direct description to self-interrogation (*PP*, lxxxv, 382).[23] Radical reflection thematises its own origin and course, recognising that every procedure of philosophical reflection must reflect on what is unreflected, clarifying both its own rational intention and its inherence in lived existence (*PP*, 53, 63). It knows that the positing of an unending task supposes a 'teleology of consciousness' running with a faith that the hidden can be thematised and the already thematic thematised more faithfully (*PP*, 127–8, 309–10). Without this supposition, critique and discovery could have no sense and no impetus. Merleau-Ponty contends that philosophy only becomes truly transcendental or radical 'not by assuming the total making-explicit of knowledge, but rather by recognising this *presumption* of reason as the fundamental philosophical problem' (*PP*, 64). The presumption is that all knowledge which we possess or will possess can be brought to conscious and judicative presence, and that all paradoxes and ambiguities can be dissolved or shown forth as inconsequential.

As ever for Merleau-Ponty, the danger lies in the equation of knowledge with the reportable and supposedly totalisable. Even a return enquiry or questioning back behind act intentionality by means of a genetic phenomenology cannot recover our course of development in its original innocence; it cannot reach or rightfully posit a pure matter of knowledge that is an ideally separable moment of experience, and whose relation to the world could in principle be brought to clarity and distinctness. Philosophical and phenomenological reflection is unable to 'work backward along a pathway already travelled in the opposite direction by constitution' (*PP*, 253). It always arrives late on the scene in which form has been the very appearance of the world rather than its condition of possibility, in which the schematised body or body informed has geared us into the wider *Gestalten*, in which our skills and affects run ahead of our express intentions, and in which our conscious acts presuppose those passive syntheses that were subegoic in their earliest work. Not everything that allows for and bears on our reckonings with the possible and our decisions was once in view. Reflection 'only fully grasps itself if it refers to the unreflective fund it presupposes, upon which it draws, and that constitutes for it, like an original past, a past that has never been a present' (*PP*, 252).[24]

---

[23] See also Husserl 1969, 249, 270–1, 275.   [24] Translation emended.

Bernard Waldenfels has stressed that phenomenology as a radical discipline does not appeal to a rationality that pre-exists the concrete and indeed contingent course of experience. While Merleau-Ponty has drawn on a reason that has arisen in history, he has adapted it to transform the concept of immediacy.[25] In the union of perception and behaviour and psyche and world 'the immediate becomes the sense, the structure, and the spontaneous arrangement of parts' (*PP*, 58). Waldenfels is careful to add that reflection both furnishes and comprises something new. When I become explicitly aware of my reflection as bearing on the unreflected, as Merleau-Ponty remarks, I realise that this act 'appears as a genuine creation, as a change in the structure of consciousness' (*PP*, lxxiii). I can also recognise that phenomenological reflection is creative in the authentic sense as a speaking speech, or as a philosophical event that 'is not the reflection of a prior truth, but rather, like art, the actualisation of a truth' (*PP*, lxxxiv). Only when it comes to presence for consciousness or is freed from the realm of silence does a truth come into being.[26] Creative as it is, moreover, a phenomenology that is faithful to the things themselves can bear much weight in the future, with the mark of its truth more often being its fecundity. Such a truth was actualised when it was understood that 'the natural reference of the matter [of knowledge] to the world leads us to a new conception of intentionality' (*PP*, 253). This has furnished another beginning for a finite and situated perceiver who understands philosophy as motivated by wonder about the world – in its unceasing upsurge a mystery rather than a problem – and true philosophy as the unceasing effort to see ourselves and our world anew.

---

[25] Waldenfels 1980, 29.   [26] Ibid., 29–30. See also Dorfman 2007, 140–1, 147–9.

Bibliography

Aristotle. 1984a. *Metaphysics*, trans. W. D. Ross, in *The Complete Works of Aristotle*, vol. 2, ed. Jonathan Barnes. Princeton, NJ: Princeton University Press, 1552–728.

1984b. *On the Soul*, trans. W. D. Ross and rev. J. A. Smith, in *The Complete Works of Aristotle*, vol. 1, ed. Jonathan Barnes. Princeton, NJ: Princeton University Press, 641–92.

Ataria, Yochai, Shogo Tanaka and Shaun Gallagher (eds.). 2021. *Body Schema and Body Image: New Directions*. Oxford: Oxford University Press.

Bakewell, Sarah. 2016. *At the Existentialist Café: Freedom, Being and Apricot Cocktails*. London: Vintage.

Baldwin, Thomas. 2004. 'Introduction' in Thomas Baldwin (ed.), *Maurice Merleau-Ponty: Basic Writings*. London: Routledge, 1–32.

2007. 'Speaking and Spoken Speech' in Thomas Baldwin (ed.), *Reading Merleau-Ponty: On Phenomenology of Perception*. New York: Routledge, 87–103.

2019. 'Merleau-Ponty's *Cogito*' in Ariane Mildenberg (ed.), *Understanding Merleau-Ponty, Understanding Modernism*. London: Bloomsbury, 19–32.

Bastian, Henry Charlton. 1882. *The Brain as an Organ of Mind*, 3rd ed. London: Kegan Paul, Trench and Co.

Berendzen, Joseph C. 2010. 'Coping without Foundations: On Dreyfus's Use of Merleau-Ponty'. *International Journal of Philosophical Studies*, 18(5), 629–49.

Bergonzoni, Carolina. 2017. 'When I Dance My Walk: A Phenomenological Analysis of Habitual Movement in Dance Practices'. *Phenomenology and Practice*, 11(1), 32–42.

Bergson, Henri. 1991. *Matter and Memory*, trans. Nancy Margaret Paul and W. Scott Palmer. New York: Zone Books.

1992. 'The Life and Work of Ravaisson' in *The Creative Mind: An Introduction to Metaphysics*, trans. Mabelle L. Anderson. New York: Citadel Press, 220–52.

2001. *Time and Free Will: An Essay on the Immediate Data of Consciousness*, trans. F. L. Pogson. New York: Dover.

Bernet, Rudolf. 1990. 'Husserl's Concept of the World' in Arleen B. Dallery, Charles E. Scott and P. Holley Roberts (eds.), *Crises in Continental Philosophy*. Albany, NY: State University of New York Press.

Binswanger, Ludwig. 1935. 'Über Psychotherapie'. *Nervenarzt*, 8, 113–21, 180–9.

Boring, Edwin G. 1921. 'The Stimulus Error'. *The American Journal of Psychology*, 32(4), 449–71.

Bourdieu, Pierre. 1977. *Outline of a Theory of Practice*, trans. Richard Nice. Cambridge: Cambridge University Press.

Brunschvicg, Léon. 1897. *La Modalité du jugement*. Paris: Alcan.

  1922. *L'expérience humaine et la causalité physique*. Paris: Alcan.

Carel, Havi. 2018. *Illness: The Cry of the Flesh*, 3rd ed. London: Routledge.

Carman, Taylor. 2020. *Merleau-Ponty*, 2nd ed. London: Routledge.

Carman, Taylor, and Mark Hansen (eds.). 2005. *The Cambridge Companion to Merleau-Ponty*. Cambridge: Cambridge University Press.

Casey, Edward S. 1984. 'Habitual Body and Memory in Merleau-Ponty'. *Man and World*, 17(3–4), 279–97.

Cassirer, Ernst. 1957. *The Philosophy of Symbolic Forms*, vol. 3, *The Phenomenology of Knowledge*, trans. Ralph Manheim. New Haven, CT: Yale University Press.

Ciavatta, David. 2017. 'Merleau-Ponty and the Phenomenology of Natural Time' in Kirsten Jacobson and John Russon (eds.), *Perception and Its Development in Merleau-Ponty's Philosophy*. Toronto: University of Toronto Press, 159–90.

Cole, Jonathan, and Jacques Paillard. 1995. 'Living without Touch and Peripheral Information about Body Position and Movement: Studies upon Deafferented Subjects' in José Luis Bermúdez, Anthony Marcel and Naomi Eilan (eds.), *The Body and the Self*. Cambridge, MA: The MIT Press, 245–66.

Conrad, Klaus. 1933. 'Das Körperschema: Eine kritische Studie und der Versuch einer Revision'. *Zeitschrift für die gesamte Neurologie und Psychiatrie*, 147(1), 346–69.

Crowther, Paul. 2015. 'The Poetry of 'Flesh' or the Reality of Perception? Merleau-Ponty's Fundamental Error'. *International Journal of Philosophical Studies*, 23(2), 255–78.

De Preester, Helena. 2008. 'From *Ego* to *Alter Ego*: Husserl, Merleau-Ponty and a Layered Approach to Intersubjectivity'. *Phenomenology and the Cognitive Sciences*, 7(1), 133–42.

Descartes, René. 1984a. *Discourse on the Method* in *The Philosophical Writings of Descartes*, vol. 1, trans. and ed. John Cottingham, Robert Stoothoff and Dugald Murdoch. Cambridge: Cambridge University Press, 111–51.

  1984b. *Meditations on First Philosophy* in *The Philosophical Writings of Descartes*, vol. 2, trans. and ed. John Cottingham, Robert Stoothoff and Dugald Murdoch. Cambridge: Cambridge University Press, 12–62.

  1984c. *The Passions of the Soul* in *The Philosophical Writings of Descartes*, vol. 1, trans. and ed. John Cottingham, Robert Stoothoff and Dugald Murdoch. Cambridge: Cambridge University Press, 328–404.

  1984d. 'Letter to Elizabeth, 28th June 1643' in *The Philosophical Writings of Descartes*, vol. 3, trans. and ed. John Cottingham, Robert Stoothoff and Dugald Murdoch. Cambridge: Cambridge University Press, 226–8.

Dewey, John. 1896. 'The Reflex Arc Concept in Psychology'. *Psychological Review*, 3, 357–70.

Dillon, Martin C. 1987. 'Apriority in Kant and Merleau-Ponty'. *Kant-Studien*, 78(3), 403–23.

1998. *Merleau-Ponty's Ontology*, 2nd ed. Evanston, IL: Northwestern University Press.

Dorfman, Eran. 2007. 'Freedom, Perception and Radical Reflection' in Thomas Baldwin (ed.), *Reading Merleau-Ponty: On Phenomenology of Perception*. New York: Routledge, 139–51.

Dreon, Roberta. 2016. 'Merleau-Ponty from Perception to Language. New Elements of Interpretation'. *Lebenswelt. Aesthetics and Philosophy of Experience*, 9, 48–66.

Dreyfus, Hubert. 2002. 'Intelligence without Representation: Merleau-Ponty's Critique of Mental Representation'. *Phenomenology and the Cognitive Sciences*, 1(4), 367–83.

2013. 'The Myth of the Pervasiveness of the Mental' in Joseph K. Schear (ed.), *Mind, Reason, and Being-In-The-World: The McDowell-Dreyfus Debate*. London: Routledge, 15–40.

Drummond, John. 1983. 'Objects' Optimal Appearances and the Immediate Awareness of Space in Vision'. *Man and World*, 16(3), 177–205.

Ellis, Willis D. (trans. and ed.). 1938. *A Source Book of Gestalt Psychology*. New York: Harcourt, Brace and Co and Kegan Paul, Trench, Trubner and Co.

Ferrarin, Alfredo. 2006. 'Lived Space, Geometrical Space in Kant'. *Studi Kantiani*, 19, 11–30.

Fink, Eugen. 1970. 'The Phenomenological Philosophy of Edmund Husserl and Contemporary Criticism' in Roy O. Elveton (trans. and ed.), *The Phenomenology of Husserl: Selected Critical Readings*. Chicago: Quadrangle Books, 73–147.

Foucault, Michel. 1991. *Discipline and Punish*, 2nd ed. Harmondsworth: Penguin.

Freud, Sigmund. 1984. 'Beyond the Pleasure Principle' in *On Metapsychology: The Theory of Psychoanalysis*, trans. James Strachey et al. and ed. Albert Dickson. Harmondsworth: Penguin, 269–338.

1985. 'Civilization and Its Discontents' in *Civilization, Society and Religion*, trans. James Strachey et al. and ed. Albert Dickson. Harmondsworth: Penguin, 251–340.

Gallagher, Shaun. 2005a. *How the Body Shapes the Mind*. Oxford: Oxford University Press.

2005b. 'Phenomenological Contributions to a Theory of Social Cognition'. *Husserl Studies*, 21(2), 95–110.

2009. 'Review of *Reading Merleau-Ponty*'. *Mind*, 118(472), 1105–11.

2017. *Enactivist Interventions: Rethinking the Mind*. Oxford: Oxford University Press.

Gardner, Sebastian. 2013. 'Transcendental Philosophy and the Given' in Joseph K. Schear (ed.), *Mind, Reason, and Being-In-The-World: The McDowell-Dreyfus Debate*. London: Routledge, 110–42.

2015. 'Merleau-Ponty's Transcendental Theory of Perception' in Sebastian Gardner and Matthew Grist (eds.), *The Transcendental Turn*. Oxford: Oxford University Press, 294–323.

Gaultier, Jules de. 1902. *Le Bovarysme, essai sur le pouvoir d'imaginer*. Paris: Société du Mercure de France.

Gelb, Adhémar, and Kurt Goldstein. 1920. 'Über den Einfluss des vollständigen Verlustes des optischen Vorstellungsvermögens auf das tactile Erkennen' in *Psychologische Analyse hirnpathologischer Fälle auf Grund von Untersuchungen Hirnverletzer*, vol. 1, ed. Adhémar Gelb and Kurt Goldstein. Leipzig: Barth, 157–250.

1924. 'Über Farbennamenamnesie'. *Psychologische Forschung*, 6(1), 127–86.

Gibson, James J. 1979. *The Ecological Approach to Visual Perception*. Boston: Houghton Mifflin.

Glendinning, Simon. 2007. *In the Name of Phenomenology*. London: Routledge.

Goldstein, Kurt. 1923. 'Über die Abhängigkeit der Bewegungen von optischen Vorgängen. Bewegungsstörungen bei Seelenblinden'. *Monatschrift für Psychiatrie und Neurologie*, 54(1), 141–94, Festschrift Liepmann.

1931. 'Über Zeigen und Greifen'. *Nervenarzt*, 4, 453–66.

Grünbaum, Anton Abraham. 1930. 'Aphasie und Motorik'. *Zeitschrift für die gesamte Neurologie und Psychiatrie*, 130(1), 385–412.

Gurwitsch, Aron. 1949. 'Gelb-Goldstein's Concept of "Concrete" and "Categorial" Attitude and the Phenomenology of Ideation'. *Philosophy and Phenomenological Research*, 10(2), 172–96.

1979. *Human Encounters in the Social World*, trans. Fred Kersten and ed. Alexandre Métraux. Pittsburgh, PA: Duquesne University Press.

Halák, Jan. 2021. 'Body Schema Dynamics in Merleau-Ponty' in Yochai Ataria, Shogo Tanaka and Shaun Gallagher (eds.), *Body Schema and Body Image: New Directions*. Oxford: Oxford University Press, 33–51.

Hammond, Michael, Jane Howarth and Russell Keat. 1991. *Understanding Phenomenology*. Oxford: Basil Blackwell.

Hass, Lawrence. 2008. *Merleau-Ponty's Philosophy*. Bloomington: Indiana University Press.

Head, Henry. 1893. 'On Disturbances of Sensation with Especial Reference to the Pain of Visceral Disease'. *Brain*, 16(1–2), 1–133.

Head, Henry and Gordon Holmes. 1912. 'Sensory Disturbances from Cerebral Lesions'. *Brain*, 34(2–3), 102–254.

Hegel, G. W. F. 1977. *Phenomenology of Spirit*, trans. A. V. Miller. Oxford: Oxford University Press.

Heidegger, Martin. 1962. *Being and Time*, trans. John Macquarrie and Edward Robinson. Oxford: Basil Blackwell.

Heinämaa, Sara. 2002. 'From Decisions to Passions: Merleau-Ponty's Interpretation of Husserl's Reduction' in Ted Toadvine and Lester Embree (eds.), *Merleau-Ponty's Reading of Husserl*. Dordrecht: Kluwer, 127–46.

Hopp, Walter. 2020. *Phenomenology: A Contemporary Introduction*. New York: Routledge.

Hull, John M. 1997. *On Sight and Insight: A Journey into the World of Blindness*, 2nd ed. London: Oneworld Publications.

Hung, Wai-Shun. 2005. 'Perception and Self-Awareness in Merleau-Ponty: The Problem of the Tacit Cogito in the *Phenomenology of Perception*'. *The New Yearbook for Phenomenology and Phenomenological Philosophy*, 5, 211–24.

Husserl, Edmund. 1960. *Cartesian Meditations*, trans. Dorion Cairns. The Hague: Nijhoff.

  1969. *Formal and Transcendental Logic*, abridged trans. Dorion Cairns. The Hague: Nijhoff.

  1970. *The Crisis of European Sciences and Transcendental Phenomenology*, trans. David Carr. Evanston, IL: Northwestern University Press.

  1973. *Experience and Judgement*, trans. James S. Churchill and Karl Ameriks and ed. Ludwig Landgrebe. Evanston, IL: Northwestern University Press.

  1981. *Husserl: Shorter Works*, trans. Quentin Lauer et al. and ed. Peter McCormick and Frederick Elliston. South Bend, IN: University of Notre Dame Press.

  1982. *Ideas Pertaining to a Pure Phenomenology and to a Phenomenological Philosophy, First Book*, trans. Fred Kersten. The Hague, Nijhoff.

  1989. *Ideas Pertaining to a Pure Phenomenology and to a Phenomenological Philosophy, Second Book*, trans. R. Rojcewicz and A. Schuwer. Dordrecht: Kluwer.

  1991. *On the Phenomenology of the Consciousness of Internal Time (1893–1917)*, trans. John Barnett Brough. Dordrecht: Kluwer.

  1997. *Thing and Space: Lectures of 1907*, trans. Richard Rojcewicz. Dordrecht: Kluwer.

  2001a. *Analyses Concerning Active and Passive Synthesis: Lectures on Transcendental Logic*, trans. Anthony J. Steinbock. Dordrecht: Kluwer.

  2001b. *Logical Investigations*, trans. J. N. Findlay and ed. Dermot Moran, 2 vols. London and New York: Routledge.

Hyland, Sheena. 2012. 'Between Health and Illness: Positive Pain and World Formation' in Lisa Folkmarson Käll (ed.), *Dimensions of Pain*. London: Routledge, 84–93.

Inkpin, Andrew. 2017. 'Was Merleau-Ponty a "Transcendental" Phenomenologist?' *Continental Philosophy Review*, 50(1), 27–47.

Jackson, Gabrielle Benette. 2018. 'Merleau-Ponty's Concept of Motor Intentionality: Unifying Two Kinds of Bodily Agency'. *European Journal of Philosophy*, 26(2), 763–79.

Jacobs, Hanne. 2014. 'Transcendental Subjectivity and the Human Being' in Sara Heinämaa, Mirja Hartimo and Timo Miettinen (eds.), *Phenomenology and the Transcendental*. London: Routledge, 87–105.

James, William. 1981. *The Principles of Psychology*. Cambridge, MA: Harvard University Press.

Jensen, Rasmus. 2009. 'Motor Intentionality and the Case of Schneider'. *Phenomenology and the Cognitive Sciences*, 8(3), 371–88.

  2013. 'Merleau-Ponty and the Transcendental Problem of Bodily Agency' in Rasmus Jensen and Dermot Moran (eds.), *The Phenomenology of Embodied Subjectivity*. Heidelberg: Springer, 43–61.

Kant, Immanuel. 1933. *Critique of Pure Reason*, 2nd ed., trans. Norman Kemp Smith. London: Macmillan.

    1938. *Opus Postumum. Kants Gesammelte Schriften*, Band 22. Berlin: Walter de Gruyter.

    1992. *Immanuel Kant: Theoretical Philosophy 1755–1770*, trans. and ed. David Walford with Ralf Meerbote. Cambridge: Cambridge University Press.

    2000. *Critique of the Power of Judgement*, ed. Paul Guyer and trans. Paul Guyer and Eric Matthews. Cambridge: Cambridge University Press.

Kee, Hayden. 2018. 'Phenomenology and Ontology of Language and Expression: Merleau-Ponty on Speaking and Spoken Speech'. *Human Studies*, 41(3), 415–35.

Kelly, Sean D. 2002. 'Merleau-Ponty on the Body'. *Ratio*, 15(4), 376–91.

Köhler, Wolfgang. 1938. 'Physical Gestalten' in Willis D. Ellis (trans. and ed.), *A Source Book of Gestalt Psychology*. New York: Harcourt, Brace and Co and Kegan Paul, Trench, Trubner and Co, 17–54.

Lachièze-Rey, Pierre. 1937. 'Utilisation possible du schématisme kantien pour une théorie de la perception'. *Études philosophiques*, 11, 30–4.

Lagneau, Jules. 1926. *Célèbres leçons*. Nimes: La Laborieuse.

Landes, Donald A. 2013. *Merleau-Ponty and the Paradoxes of Expression*. London: Bloomsbury.

Levinas, Emmanuel. 1969. *Totality and Infinity*, trans. Alphonso Lingis. Pittsburgh, PA: Duquesne University Press.

Lewis, Michael, and Tanja Staehler. 2010. *Phenomenology: An Introduction*. New York: Continuum.

Lhermitte, Jean. 1998. *L'Image de notre corps*. Paris: Éditions L'Harmattan.

Liepmann, Hugo. 1905. *Über Störungen des Handelns bei Gehirnkranken*. Berlin: Karger.

Locke, John. 1975. *An Essay Concerning Human Understanding*, ed. Peter H. Nidditch. Oxford: Oxford University Press.

Marcel, Gabriel. 1949. 'Outlines of a Phenomenology of Having' in *Being and Having*, trans. Katherine Farrar. Glasgow: MacLehose and Glasgow University Press, 154–75.

Matherne, Samantha. 2014. 'The Kantian Roots of Merleau-Ponty's Account of Pathology'. *British Journal for the History of Philosophy*, 22(1), 124–49.

    2016. 'Kantian Themes in Merleau-Ponty's Theory of Perception'. *Archiv für Geschichte der Philosophie*, 98(2), 193–230.

Merleau-Ponty, Maurice. 1963a. *The Structure of Behaviour*, trans. Alden L. Fisher. Boston, MA: The Beacon Press.

    1963b. *In Praise of Philosophy and Other Essays*, trans. John O'Neill and ed. James M. Edie and John Wild. Evanston, IL: Northwestern University Press.

    1964a. *Signs*, trans. Richard C. McCleary and ed. James M. Edie and John Wild. Evanston, IL: Northwestern University Press.

    1964b. *The Primacy of Perception and Other Essays*, trans. Arleen B. Dallery et al. and ed. James M. Edie and John Wild. Evanston, IL: Northwestern University Press.

1968. *The Visible and the Invisible, Followed by Working Notes*, trans. Alphonso Lingis and ed. Claude Lefort. Evanston, IL: Northwestern University Press.

1973. *The Prose of the World*, trans. John O'Neill and ed. Claude Lefort. Evanston, IL: Northwestern University Press.

2005. *Phénoménologie de la perception*, 2nd ed. Paris: Gallimard.

2012. *Phenomenology of Perception*, trans. Donald A. Landes. London: Routledge.

Mill, John Stewart. 1878. *An Examination of Sir William Hamilton's Philosophy*, 5th ed. London: Longmans, Green, Reader.

Milner, A. David, and Melvyn A. Goodale. 1995. *The Visual Brain in Action*. Oxford: Oxford University Press.

Milner, A. David. 2017. 'How Do the Two Visual Streams Interact with Each Other.' *Experimental Brian Research*, 235(5), 1297–308.

Montero, Barbara. 2013. 'A Dancer Reflects' in Joseph K. Schear (ed.), *Mind, Reason, and Being-In-The-World: The McDowell-Dreyfus Debate*. London: Routledge, 303–19.

Mooney, Timothy. 2011. 'Plasticity, Motor Intentionality and Concrete Movement in Merleau-Ponty'. *Continental Philosophy Review*, 44(4), 359–81.

2012. 'Review of Donald A. Landes' New Translation of Phenomenology of Perception'. *International Journal of Philosophical Studies*, 20(4), 589–94.

2017. 'Repression and Operative Unconsciousness in *Phenomenology of Perception*', in Dorothée Legrand and Dylan Trigg (eds.), *Unconsciousness Between Phenomenology and Psychoanalysis*. Dordrecht: Springer, 61–74.

2019. 'Merleau-Ponty and Developing and Coping Reflectively'. *The New Yearbook for Phenomenology and Phenomenological Philosophy*, 17, 59–76.

Moran, Dermot. 2010. 'Husserl and Merleau-Ponty on Embodied Experience', in Thomas Nenon and Philip Blosser (eds.), *Advancing Phenomenology: Essays in Honor of Lester Embree*. Dordrecht: Springer, 175–95.

Morris, Katherine J. 2012. *Starting with Merleau-Ponty*. New York: Continuum.

Mulligan, Kevin. 1995. 'Perception' in Barry Smith and David Woodruff Smith (eds.), *The Cambridge Companion to Husserl*. Cambridge: Cambridge University Press, 168–238.

Nietzsche, Friedrich. 1967. *On the Genealogy of Morals and Ecce Homo*, trans. Walter Kaufmann and R. J. Hollingdale. New York: Random House.

Overgaard, Søren. 2017. 'Other Minds Embodied'. *Continental Philosophy Review*, 50(1), 65–80.

Paillard, Jacques. 1991. 'Knowing Where and Knowing How to Get There' in Jacques Paillard (ed.), *Brain and Space*. Oxford: Oxford University Press, 461–81.

Pascal, Blaise. 1966. *Pensées*, trans. A. J. Krailsheimer. Harmondsworth: Penguin.

Peacocke, Christopher. 1986. 'Analogue Content'. *Aristotelian Society Supplementary Volume*, 60(1), 1–18.

Piaget, Jean. 1922. 'Essai sur la multiplication logique et les débuts de la pensée formelle chez l'enfant'. *Journal de Psychologie, normale et pathologique*, 19, 222–61.

Pick, Arnold. 1922. 'Störungen der Orientierung am eigenen Körper'. *Psychologische Forschung*, 1(1), 303–18.

Ramachandran, Vilayanur, and Sandra Blakeslee. 1998. *Phantoms in the Brain*. New York: William Morrow.

Ramachandran, Vilayanur, and William Hirstein. 1998. 'The Perception of Phantom Limbs'. *Brain*, 121(9), 1603–30.

Reynolds, Jack. 2019. 'Embodiment and Emergence: Navigating an Epistemic and Metaphysical Dilemma'. *Journal of Transcendental Philosophy*, 1(1), 1–25.

Reynolds, Joel Michael. 2017. 'Merleau-Ponty, World-Creating Blindness, and the Phenomenology of Non-Normate Bodies'. *Chiasmi International*, 19, 419–34.

Riddoch, George. 1941. 'Phantom Limbs and Body Shape'. *Brain*, 64(4), 197–222.

Robinet, André. 1963. *Merleau-Ponty: Sa vie, son oeuvre avec un exposé de sa philosophie*. Paris: Presses Universitaires de France.

Romdenh-Romluc, Komarine. 2007. 'Merleau-Ponty's Account of Hallucination'. *European Journal of Philosophy*, 17(1), 76–90.

2011. *Merleau-Ponty and Phenomenology of Perception*. London: Routledge.

Russell, Bertrand. 1948. *Human Knowledge: Its Scope and Limits*. London: George Allen and Unwin.

Ryle, Gilbert. 1949. *The Concept of Mind*. London: Hutchinson.

Sacks, Oliver. 1985. *The Man Who Mistook His Wife for a Hat*. New York: Summit Books.

Sartre, Jean-Paul. 1958. *Being and Nothingness*, trans. Hazel Barnes. London: Methuen.

Scarry, Elaine. 1985. *The Body in Pain: The Making and Unmaking of the World*. Oxford: Oxford University Press.

Scheler, Max. 1954. *The Nature of Sympathy*, trans. Peter Heath. London: Routledge and Kegan Paul.

1973. *Formalism in Ethics and Non-Formal Ethics of Values*, trans. Manfred Frings and Roger Funk. Evanston, IL: Northwestern University Press.

Schilder, Paul. 1923. *Das Körperschema: Ein Beitrag zur Lehre vom Bewusstsein des eigenen Körpers*. Berlin and Heidelberg: Julius Springer.

1950. *The Image and Appearance of the Human Body*. New York: International Universities Press.

Schopenhauer, Arthur. 1969. *The World as Will and Representation*, vol. 1, trans. E. F. J. Payne. New York: Dover.

Sheets-Johnstone, Maxine. 2011. *The Primacy of Movement*, 2nd ed. Amsterdam: John Benjamins.

Sherrington, Charles. 1907. 'On the Proprio-ceptive System, Especially in Its Reflex Aspect'. *Brain*, 29(4), 467–85.

Shusterman, Richard, 2005. 'The Silent, Limping Body of Philosophy' in Taylor Carman and Mark Hansen (eds.), *The Cambridge Companion to Merleau-Ponty*. Cambridge: Cambridge University Press, 151–80.

Sinclair, Mark. 2011. 'Is Habit "The Fossilised Residue of a Spiritual Activity"? Ravaisson, Bergson, Merleau-Ponty'. *Journal of the British Society for Phenomenology*, 42(1), 33–52.

Smith, A. D. 2003. *Husserl and the Cartesian Meditations*. London: Routledge.

2007. 'The Flesh of Perception' in Thomas Baldwin (ed.), *Reading Merleau-Ponty: On Phenomenology of Perception*. New York: Routledge, 1–22.

Soffer, Gail. 1999. 'The Other as Alter Ego: A Genetic Approach'. *Husserl Studies*, 15(3), 151–66.

Staehler, Tanja. 2008. 'What Is the Question to Which Husserl's *Fifth Cartesian Meditation* Is the Answer?' *Husserl Studies*, 24(2), 99–117.

Stein, Edith. 1989. *The Problem of Empathy*, 3rd ed., trans. Waltraut Stein. Washington, DC: ICS Publications.

Steinfeld, Julius E. 1927. 'Ein Beitrag zur Analyse der Sexualfunktion'. *Zeitschrift für die gesamte Neurologie und Psychiatrie*, 107(1), 172–83.

Taipale, Joona. 2014. *Phenomenology and Embodiment: Husserl and the Constitution of Subjectivity*. Evanston, IL: Northwestern University Press.

Tanaka, Shogo. 2015. 'Intercorporeality as a Theory of Social Cognition'. *Theory and Psychology*, 25(4), 455–72.

2021. 'Body Schema and Body Image in Motor Learning: Refining Merleau-Ponty's Notion of Body Schema' in Yochai Ataria, Shogo Tanaka and Shaun Gallagher (eds.), *Body Schema and Body Image: New Directions*. Oxford: Oxford University Press, 69–84.

Tiemersma, Douwe. 1982. '"Body-Image" and "Body-Schema" in the Existential Phenomenology of Merleau-Ponty'. *Journal of the British Society for Phenomenology*, 13(3), 246–55.

Toadvine, Ted. 2001. 'Phenomenological Method in Merleau-Ponty's Critique of Gurwitsch'. *Husserl Studies*, 17(3), 195–205.

Toadvine, Ted, and Lester Embree (eds.). 2002. *Merleau-Ponty's Reading of Husserl*. Dordrecht: Kluwer.

Uexküll, Jakob von. 1926. *Theoretical Biology*, trans. D. L. Mackinnon. London: Kegan Paul, Trench Trubner and Co.

2010. *A Foray into the Worlds of Animals and Humans, with a Theory of Meaning*, trans. Joseph D. O'Neill. Minneapolis: University of Minnesota Press.

Varela, Francisco, Evan Thompson and Eleanor Rosch. 2017. *The Embodied Mind: Cognitive Science and Human Experience*, rev. ed. Cambridge, MA: The MIT Press.

Waldenfels, Bernard. 1980. 'Perception and Structure in Merleau-Ponty', trans. J. Claude Evans. *Research in Phenomenology*, 10, 21–38.

2011. *Phenomenology of the Alien: Basic Concepts*, trans. Alexander Kozin and Tanja Staehler. Evanston, IL: Northwestern University Press.

Weiss, Gail. 1999. *Body Images: Embodiment as Intercorporeality*. London: Routledge.

Wertheimer, Max. 1938. 'Laws of Organization in Perceptual Forms', abridged trans., in Willis D. Ellis (trans. and ed.), *A Source Book of Gestalt Psychology*. New York: Harcourt, Brace and Co. and Kegan Paul, Trench, Trubner and Co., 71–88.

Windholz, George. 1990. 'The Second Signal System as Conceived by Pavlov and His Disciples'. *The Pavlovian Journal of Biological Science*, 25(4), 163–73.

Wittgenstein, Ludwig. 1958. *Philosophical Investigations*, trans. G. E. M. Anscombe. Oxford: Basil Blackwell.

1974. *On Certainty*, trans. Denis Paul and G. E. M. Anscombe. Oxford: Basil Blackwell.

Woelert, Peter. 2007. 'Kant's Hands, Spatial Orientation and the Copernican Turn'. *Continental Philosophy Review*, 40(2), 139–50.

Wrathall, Mark. 2005. 'Motives, Reasons and Causes' in Taylor Carman and Mark Hansen (eds.), *The Cambridge Companion to Merleau-Ponty*. Cambridge: Cambridge University Press, 111–28.

Zahavi, Dan. 2014. *Self and Others: Exploring Subjectivity, Empathy and Shame*. Oxford: Oxford University Press.

Zaner, Richard. 1964. *The Problem of Embodiment: Some Contributions to a Phenomenology of the Body*. The Hague: Nijhoff.

2003. 'Sisyphus without Knees: Exploring Self–Other Relationships through Illness and Disability'. *Literature and Medicine*, 22(2), 188–207.

Index

For EU product safety concerns, contact us at Calle de José Abascal, 56–1°, 28003 Madrid, Spain or eugpsr@cambridge.org.